# Dance Production Handbook
## or Later Is Too Late

Lois Ellfeldt /
Edwin Carnes

*University of Southern California*

NATIONAL PRESS BOOKS   850 Hansen Way / Palo Alto / California 94304

# Contents

## Performance

# Figures

# Before
# Rehearsals
# Begin

# 1

# The Decision to Produce the Dance Program

All dancers need to perform and nearly every choreographer needs to produce his dance. The dance teacher who must present a program already knows the elements of choreography but may know little of the techniques that transform choreographic ideas into a dance production. How does it all come about? This book tries to tell you just that, starting with the beginning decisions and going on through the management and technical work. It concludes with a look at the odds and ends that wind up the final performance.

Some very specific questions need to be asked before initiating any dance production. Is there choreography available? Is it worth showing to an audience? Do the dancers have sufficient skill and sensitivity to project the choreographer's intent? Is everyone in the program interested enough to work hard for a finished performance? Can you rely on the backing of administration and colleagues?

A dance production, whatever the purpose, form, or style, is the result of many people working together to objectify the intent of the choreographer. Of course, sound choreography is important, but let us admit that a good production is more than this. The imagination of the choreographer must also be directed to the design, setting, lighting, costuming, and accompanying of the dance, into rehearsals and ultimately into the finished performance. Choreography is not complete until the dance has been danced.

Whatever the occasion—a formal concert, an open house, a showing of works in progress, or an informal studio program—consider the responsibility of any performing group to its audience, and especially if there is an admission charge. If the production cannot be presented with pride wait until it can!

## LEADERSHIP

Somebody has to be boss! While the democratic process is desirable in early planning, there is no place for group discussion in later stages. There must be one person who is responsible for determining the interaction of people, events, and places, for allocating responsibilities, for making final decisions. Usually this person is the teacher; sometimes it is a choreographer or even a dancer. Whoever it is must know a great deal about dance and especially about other aspects of the production process. Ability and experience are his prime attributes. It helps if he can get along with people! In the professional theater there is a proven hierarchy of responsibility, but dancers in almost every situation, jealous of their peculiar talents, seldom fit such a pattern.

3

Illogical as it may seem, most school and community dance productions are organized and directed by teachers with little experience in the vagaries of production. These teachers readily assume the roles of producer, director, choreographer, designer, stage manager, business and publicity director and, in many cases, performer. It is not at all certain that any one of them would be willing to relinquish any of these controls, even if he had able assistance; nor is it certain that anyone could accomplish it better.

Without assistance the task is difficult. As productions become more complex it is impossible for one person to both manage and implement all details. He obviously cannot change scenery, operate lights, act as usher, and then be stage manager and performer. But he inevitably continues to oversee all of these details. There is no doubt that he needs able and responsible help. An outline of tasks and necessary aides for the person who attempts the single-handed venture is given in Figure 1-1.

Figure 1-1    Tasks and Necessary Aides of the Producer-Director-Choreographer

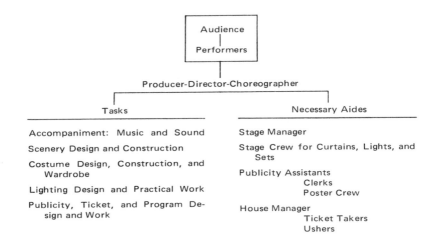

Who can say if the assets of concern, insight, and discrimination of the producer-director-etc. are not outweighed by the liabilities of undue pressure, excessive concern for choreography, and incomplete plans for publicity? The problem is to get a series of tasks done well—in time. Good leadership, by someone who really cares, will ensure that.

There are probably as many classifications and combinations of leadership as there are of productions. The problem is, of course, to ensure maximum results with the least personal conflict and fewest hours of effort.

ortunately, those who are really involved in such a venture seldom count ours or shirk responsibility. This is the secret formula—find people who really care about the end-product and who enjoy the process of bringing it into focus. Otherwise there is tension, bickering, and wasted motion. There will be tension, bickering, and wasted motion in any event, but a concern for the final product can force potential enemies to sit down calmly and re-evaluate their efforts. A typical dance production-staff relationship is shown in Figure 1-2.

Figure 1-2    A Typical Production-Staff Relationship

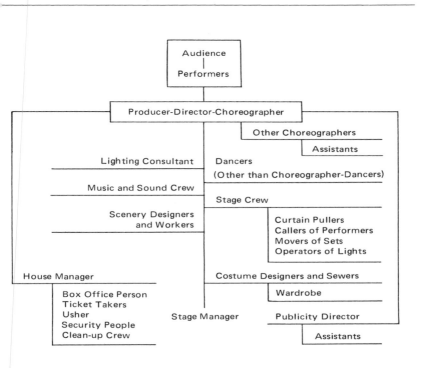

A good director must be respected by the entire staff and cast. He must have authority and, hopefully, persuasive powers. He must be willing to spend endless hours in planning and then in considering alternatives to things that will not work. He must be able to make quick decisions and to identify sources of trouble. He must have rapport with technicians, performers, designers, and choreographers. The latter will probably concern him the most. Unfortunately, many choreographers assume chaos to be a necessary companion to production. Their rehearsals are long and confused, and dress rehearsals

5

are angry. Costumes are being fitted and sewn at the last minute, in spite of schedules or designers. Choreography is not quite finished so cues cannot be set. Everyone works too hard, the dancers are nervous, the backstage staff complains. And most of the difficulty results from a failure to follow a simple schedule. It is up to the director to keep everyone in step with the schedule.

The good director knows that the process of production begins long before the first dancer reaches the rehearsal floor. And even though the creative mind of the choreographer may rebel at lists and schedules, design and construction, clarification and reclarification, he must, nevertheless, pre-plan everything that contributes to the presentation of dance to an audience. Later is too late.

One of his first and most important responsibilities is to meet with the choreographers to consider:
(1.) What choreography there is.
(2.) Who the available dancers are.
(3.) Their relationship to the director, musicians, and other consultants.
(4.) The focus of the event, such as a demonstration, folk festival, or formal concert; possible content, relationship, and sequence of program material.
(5.) Possible performance space.
(6.) Estimates of time needed before production; discussion of particular needs.

It is especially helpful if choreographers prepare written accounts of their material at this time, in as much detail as possible. An example is given in Figure 1-3.

Now is the time for planning, seeking information, making commitments, and designing and building, all of which determine the success or failure of the entire project. There are certain things to do, and they should be done early. One list at the beginning can prevent a disaster at the end.

## PURPOSE OF THE PRESENTATION

While there may be many reasons for presenting a dance production, one will certainly be paramount. Is the aim to present a formal dance concert as an art product? Is it to display works in progress, present dances or dancers to an invited audience, celebrate a certain festive occasion, exhibit technical skills, educate an audience by lecture-demonstration, dazzle an audience with colorful costumes and movement tricks, provide a ballet for an opera, or just give the dancers a chance to perform? Proceeding without knowing this is like trying to answer a question that has never been asked. While your purpose may be influenced by available choreography, dancer skills, and type of facilities, until the real reason for presenting the production is apparent, subsequent plans cannot be made on any rational basis.

One insidious problem faced by many dance teachers is the implied necessity for "putting on a show" regardless of available performance material or ability. This is not fair to anyone, for at best it takes a rare coordination of effort and talent to bring about the magic of a good production.

**Figure 1-3    Choreographer's Preliminary Description of Dances Available for Program**

---

1. Title:

   To be chosen.

   Accompaniment:

   Two members of the Dance Club are developing a tape of freeway sounds for the accompaniment.

   Number of dancers:

   Seven to nine, probably.

   Visualization:

   A dance that covers a lot of space; fast in tempo and with an exciting rhythmic structure. Several movement themes are introduced by the entire group, and then smaller groups perform variations of these. The dance could either begin the program or come after an intermission.

   Length:

   The present length is six minutes, but the dance probably will be ten to twelve minutes when all the group interactions are complete.

   Tentative costumes:

   Beige tights and spaghetti-strap leotards; mid-calf full white skirts; pipestem hairpieces; full-face color make-up.

   Tentative staging:

   No stage-level sets because of the space coverage of the dancers. The dance may call for liquid colors with an overhead projector.

2. Title:

   Dance for Two and Nine (tentative).

   Accompaniment:

   To be chosen.

   Number of dancers:

   Six boys, three girls.

   Visualization:

   Unusual shapes in space, unreal, almost surrealistic, nothing quite "as it should be."

   Length:

   To be determined.

   Tentative costumes:

   Long-sleeved leotards, enveloping capes, fluttering pieces for attaching to heads and shoulders.

   Tentative staging:

   Suspended mobiles; angled door-frame downstage right; three movable screens, higher than the dancers.

3. Title:

   Free-Falling.

   Accompaniment:

   To be chosen.

   Number of dancers:

   Three or five boys or girls.

   Visualization:

   Manipulation of the movement experience of both giving into and resisting gravity. No particular theme has been developed yet.

   Length:

   To be determined.

   Tentative costumes:

   To be determined.

   Tentative staging:

   A series of cylindrical and angular shapes. Will try air-filled plastic bags.

Figure 1-4     Preliminary Plan for Studio Showing of Student Dances

1. **Title:** An opening dance (as yet untitled)

   **Choreographer:** Bonnie A.

   **Accompaniment:** Piano and guitar score, being composed by J. S.

   **Number of dancers:** Seven girls, five boys.

   **Visualization:** Bright, exciting, sharp contrasts, full and broad.

   **Length:** Approximately five minutes.

   **Tentative costumes:** White leotards and tights; black and brown half skirts for girls, boleros for boys.

   **Tentative staging:** Clear stage, lights warm and full; possible entrance from the audience.

2. **Title:** A Tail Is to Sit On

   **Choreographer:** Susan L.

   **Accompaniment:** Choreographer's tape of animal sounds.

   **Number of dancers:** Three girls, three boys.

   **Visualization:** Bright, surprising, satirical, funny.

   **Length:** Approximately four minutes.

   **Tentative costumes:** Brown tights and leotards with green and blue lengths of jersey that drape around each dancer.

   **Tentative staging:** Two-foot risers upstage left, two ramps leading downstage right. Will try overhead projection of abstract trees and a jungle-gym.

3. **Title:** Designs through space (as yet untitled)

   **Choreographer:** Marilyn V.

   **Accompaniment:** Flute and percussion, composed and performed by Sam S.

   **Number of dancers:** Seven girls.

   **Visualization:** Dim, misty, dissolving, like oil paint on water.

   **Length:** Eight minutes, plus.

   **Tentative costumes:** Assorted-color leotards and tights; will attempt tie-dying and spatter-spray.

   **Tentative staging:** Vertical lines suspended from ceiling to floor downstage (ropes or heavy string); diagonal lines from left to right upstage; area lighting; possible projections.

4. **Title:** The Trouble with Hats

   **Choreographer:** Eleanor M.

   **Accompaniment:** Taped voice sounds and dancers' voices.

   **Number of dancers:** Five girls, one boy.

   **Length:** Twelve minutes, plus or minus.

   **Visualization:** Marked contrasts, "tongue-in-cheek," extremes of exaggeration followed by understatement, area lights.

   **Tentative costumes:** Princess-style long gowns for the girls; leotard, tights, and frock coat for the boy; assortment of fancy hats; irrelevant props such as ski pole, coffee pot, ball of twine, egg beater, cluster of balloons, large paper flower, small high-pitched bell, etc.

   **Tentative staging:** Series of 5 1/2, 1 1/2, and 1-foot risers across upstage; four high, narrow screens downstage left.

   Intermission

5. Title:                  Farenheit 006

   Choreographer:          Judy E.

   Accompaniment:          Experimenting with gongs, metronomes, and wood-blocks.

   Length:                 Three to four minutes.

   Number of dancers:      Three girls.

   Visualization:          Moody, "as if under water," many shadows and blurred outlines; nothing bright or clear.

   Tentative costumes:     Black overdress, open to hips on each side; bright orange tights; striped wraparound short skirts; headpiece made of pipe cleaners.

   Tentative staging:      One heavy rope attached upstage right, looping toward downstage left (should be secure enough to resist one dancer's bodyweight); will try overhead projection of revolving roll with fused gelatin bits.

6. Title:                  Robe of Shadow

   Choreographer:          Suzi I.

   Accompaniment:          Taped selections from recorded Noh accompaniment (authentic).

   Length:                 Thirteen minutes, plus.

   Number of dancers:      Eight girls, three boys.

   Visualization:          Formal, serene-to-tragic, one section bright and gay; contrasting deep night, dusk, dawn, and midday qualities. Need intense light upstage left.

   Tentative costumes:     Adaptations from ancient Japanese Noh, earth colors with bright bits, brocades and heavy garments. Masks.

   Tentative staging:      Adapted from Noh stage with pine tree and torii gate; one scene change to shrine set.

7. Title:                  Closing dance (as yet untitled)

   Choreographer:          Don B.

   Accompaniment:          Taped sounds of street, airport, freeway, harbor.

   Length:                 Six to seven minutes.

   Number of dancers:      Six girls, six boys.

   Visualization:          Bright, gay; run-chase-catch and abstract love scenes; a scrambled square dance, a game of hopscotch, and a mock wedding ceremony; accenting the unusual and surprising changes in life. All warm and hopeful.

   Tentative costumes:     Lavender sleeveless leotards with loose-knit tights in orange for the girls; gray tights and loose-knit tops in lavender and black for the boys. Exaggerated "Kathakali make-up" in shades of green to brown with sparkle-dust on hair and eyelids.

   Tentative staging:      Suspended roll-scrim mid-stage; three free-form papier-mâché sets from up to downstage left. May have to change costume color for lighting.

Alternate dances already choreographed and ready for rehearsal:

Three-Part Time:     Eight minutes; three dancers; Lynne E., choreographer

Baroque Piece:       Four minutes; four dancers; Dennies B., choreographer

Monologue:           Two minutes; one dancer; Paulette S., choreographer

Now I Remember...:   Three minutes; six dancers; Jill P., choreographer

9

1. Subject:                Space study with small units of basic technique, in one place and moving through space, with no narration.

Choreographer:       Teacher.

Accompaniment:      Musical improvisation or selected recording.

Number of dancers:   Six.

Visualization:       To project the apparent ease, range of action, and control of the dancers; to indicate something of a dancer's potential for in-place and through-space action.

Length:             Four minutes.

Tentative costumes:  Class costumes.

2. Subject:                The development of technical skill and group sensitivity; small group demonstration of the same basic techniques used in first section; whole group moving as narrator discusses the interrelationship among dancers as they move in space.

Choreographer:       Teacher, assisted by students.

Accompaniment:      Same as above.

Number of dancers:   Same as above.

Length:             Eight minutes (including three for narration alone).

Tentative costume for narrator:
                        Teaching costume.

3. Subject:                The potentials for design in movement; small groups demonstrating a study in space-and-shape relationships in more complex patterns (developed from the first section).

Choreographer:       Teacher, assisted by Diana G.

Accompaniment:      Taped sounds with percussion accompaniment by members of the group.

Number of dancers:   Eight.

Visualization:       Clarify space around the dancers as well as the path they take; clean-cut direction and level changes; crisp action with obvious design.

Length:             Seven minutes, plus.

Tentative costumes:  Class costumes with small accessories.

Tentative staging:   Screens, poles, open frames, elastic bands, lengths of plastic.

4. Subject:                Discussing improvisation in movement; dancers demonstrate with a series of preplanned improvisations. Suggestions from the audience for some "on the spot" improvisations.

Choreographers:      Students.

Accompaniment:      Piano improvisation.

Length:             Seven minutes.

Tentative costumes:  Student improvisation with assorted pieces of material and props.

Tentative staging:   Student improvisation with screens, boxes, and free-form papier-mâché structures.

5. Subject:                The choreographic process as it parallels composition in music, painting, and poetry. Discussion of selection, organization, and forming of movement. One of the

improvisations from part 4 is chosen and the group members identify it and perform movements based on it, as follows:

(a) Statement of the theme by one of the dancers.
(b) Restatement by the entire group.
(c) Individual contrasting patterns.
(d) Two variations on the original theme by each of the dancers.
(e) A manipulation of the original theme, contrasts and variations using different relationships.

|  |  |
|---|---|
| Accompaniment: | Improvised by pianist or guitarist. |
| Number of dancers: | Three to five. |
| Tentative costumes: | Same as above. |

6. Subject: Short dance-study with obvious thematic development. The narrator identifies movement themes as the dancers perform; examines and discusses simple sequential form with a simultaneous demonstration by the dancers; and asks for choreographer's comment on his intent and his plans for further development. (The group may repeat the whole study with lights, costume change, accompaniment, sets, and dancer-projection as a finished performance.)

|  |  |
|---|---|
| Choreographer: | Jean Ellen H. |
| Accompaniment: | Student composed or selected. |
| Number of dancers: | Four or five. |
| Length: | Three to four minutes. |
| Tentative costumes: | Contrasting-color leotards and tights. |
| Tentative staging: | Determine available lights, need two 3-foot by 6-foot flats or screens. |

7. Subject: Presentation of a finished dance, with full staging and costuming. After one performance, the narrator points out the major movement themes and makes some criticism of the dance (choreography, performance, and production), and asks the choreographer to explain his intent, his visualization; then asks for comments from the audience. The dancers then repeat the dance without any more interruptions.

|  |  |
|---|---|
| Choreographer: | Alice D. |
| Accompaniment: | Taped flute and autoharp score composed by Alice D. |
| Number of dancers: | Five girls. |
| Visualization: | Accent on as free and open a space as possible in the upstage area, uncluttered; as many specific areas identified as possible; soft to bright light. |
| Length: | Eight minutes. |
| Tentative costumes: | White-jersey, long-sleeved leotards and tights with diaphanous skirts of three darker and two lighter shades of gray, full-circle. |
| Tentative staging: | One broad black line and two narrow red ones (rolls of plastic rope) suspended from overhead upstage right, falling in a series of swirls out over the stage. |

8. Dancers and narrator come back on stage for informal questions and comments from the audience. Be prepared to answer questions and to demonstrate for clarification.

## CONTENT OF THE PROGRAM

The nature of the dances to be produced is the key to the entire process. This determines the kind of program, where it will be done, what the production needs are and, indeed, whether or not you can even attempt it.
Is there some unifying idea or series of happenings? Is the available choreography worth developing, rehearsing, and framing for production and finally, worth showing to an audience? Nothing should be allowed just to happen. The choices made at the beginning determine everything to follow.

Does the content have variety and contrast? Or do all of the solos bunch up in one section and the heavy dramatic dances follow one after the other? Remember that the order of the program can always be changed when the dancers are assigned to performance roles. If a dancer appears in two successive dances the director will ask: Can he make a costume change quickly enough to avoid a long stage wait? Will he be able to go on immediately with no rest? If dancers are in short supply they will go on anyway, but it is certainly worth considering. Will there be time enough to change scenery and lights or to prepare special effects? Try to think of all possible problems that might confront you, and then be ready for some others.

Screen the information from the first meeting of choreographers and all of the written dance proposals and draw up tentative plans for the program. Then have another meeting of choreographers and other available personnel to assess production possibilities. Should there be changes, new choreography, or reconsideration of the whole event? Consider such specific problems as the following:

(1.) Tone and balance of program content.
(2.) Plans for auditions and selection of dancers and assistants.
(3.) Tentative, but more direct than before, estimates of production needs (accompaniment, scenery, costume, rehearsals, lighting).
(4.) Possible performance dates.
(5.) Recommendations and discussion of consultants and assistants.
(6.) Consideration of the tentative plan for the production. (See Figures 1-4 and 1-5.)

After this meeting go home and think about some of the problems of costuming, scenery, lighting, budget, and publicity. Are you still willing to keep going?

## CHOREOGRAPHERS, PERFORMERS, WORKERS

The availability of sensitive and able choreographers, performers, and workers is of vital importance in determining if the planned program can be a full-scale theatrical production, a less formal studio production, or a simplified class-like presentation. Despite a great desire to produce a dance performance, no amount of wishing and imagining will ever take the place of creative effort, technical skill, performance ability, and rehearsal. Are people capable of the task before them? Are they dependable, involved, and sensitive? Are they willing to rehearse the dance and also work on other aspects of the production? Beware of student enthusiasm. All too often it is only temporary. Be sure that everyone is willing to work and not just anxious to perform.

Since there is seldom time or energy enough to assure every dancer's technical virtuosity and projection for really outstanding performance, the choreographer and director must decide at what point choreographic changes must be made in order to fit the dancer's abilities. Certainly everyone agrees that the performers must be sure of their own action as well as of their relationship to other dancers before the real intent of the dance may show through. Are you willing to change the choreography to benefit the entire production? You may have to.

It is up to the choreographer to determine the cast for his dance, though this can certainly be decided by choreographer and director, or even by the choreographer and performers. In many cases auditions are helpful in choosing dancers. One typical plan for such an audition is suggested in Figure 1-6.

The director must find or attract assistants for all of the numerous tasks that precede a dance production. Sometimes certain departments of a school may be helpful: the art department for program and poster design; home economics for costume sewing; English or journalism for publicity copy; business for clerical and budgetary aides; drama for helpers with lights and scenery; Girls' League for ushers.

Sometimes requests for volunteers are run in school or community papers, announcements are made, or needs are posted on a bulletin board. Since there is seldom remuneration for such work it will almost always involve people who have an interest in dance. The more helpful workers are those who are excited about dance and feel this may offer a chance to operate in terms of their major interest. For example, photography enthusiasts and graphic artists enjoy experimenting with action pictures and sketches as a challenge to their talents; those interested in costume design and construction solve different kinds of problems; technical crews from the drama department find new opportunities for improving their sensitivity to performers. Musicians and composers can really explore their imaginations and media and often surprise you with interesting scores and exciting performances.

Preliminary contact and early follow-up of volunteers is vital. If they know of plans, and are given enough time, you may be surprised! When they begin to feel that they are really needed for the success of the event, you will have dedicated helpers.

In the early stages of production it seems obvious that you will need many assistants but later, when they begin to duplicate each other's efforts, you may find yourself worrying about what they are up to. Forget it. If you have even a few people who have minimum skills but a maximum sense of

13

responsibility, you are fortunate. Just remember there is only one boss and he sets the rules for what is to be done by whom.

Figure 1-6    Audition for Dancers

Auditions for dancers with good movement skills, rhythmic sensitivity, and interest in production will be held in the dance studio, Room 43, in the Physical Education Building on Wednesday, October 21 and Friday, October 23 from 3:30 to 4:30 in the afternoon.

Come in practice clothes, ready to move. You will be led in walks, runs, jumps, leaps, turns, and falls as well as simple movement phrases and short themes from some of the dances being choreographed for the May Dance Program.

Sign up on the bulletin board opposite the dance studio, not later than the day before the audition time you can come.

Choreographer Renee Peters needs 3 girls, 2 boys (boys need no experience).

Choreographer Susan Marshall needs 6 boys and 2 girls (all should have had some experience in dance).

Choreographer Charles Byson needs 3 solo dancers, male or female. One needs classical ballet experience.

---

SIGN-UP FOR DANCER'S AUDITION ON WEDNESDAY, OCTOBER 21

| Name | Class | Address | Telephone | Dance Experience |
|------|-------|---------|-----------|------------------|

---

Please see the bulletin board opposite the dance studio for posted results of the auditions. THE DANCE CONCERT WILL BE PRESENTED IN THE SCHOOL AUDITORIUM ON MAY 7 AND 8. Rehearsal dates are posted on the bulletin board in the dance studio. Please check ALL dates before you indicate your acceptance of this responsibility.

## PERFORMANCE SPACE

Where will the dancers perform? This is one of the specific questions that must be answered now. Obviously the availability of facilities will influence any decision, but some programs are well adapted to an outside field or playground, others to a studio setting. A gymnasium, studio, or armory, even an arena space marked off on a playground or field, can be effective if reasonable entrances can be devised and suitable lighting provided. Generally the less complete dances, the studies, the works in progress, lecture demonstrations, and experimental works are better suited to less theatrical settings, though some can be presented informally on a stage. Certainly the traditional proscenium stage, where lights, curtains, wings, and staging equipment are readily available, is still the easiest place to present the formal concert.

The problem with most studio, gymnasium, or outdoor productions is the poor view of ground-level performance. The use of risers or bleachers will help. Corner or circular seating can also improve the perspective. (See Figure 1-7.) These unusual formations may be disturbing to the choreographers, who usually prefer dancers on one side and audience on the other. But consider the relative values in terms of comfortable accommodation of spectators within the space to be used.

Figure 1-7   Three Simple Seating Plans for a Rectangular Space

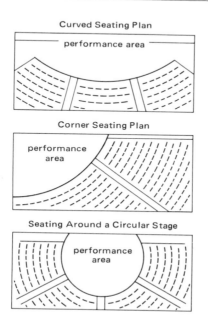

Curved Seating Plan

performance area

Corner Seating Plan

performance area

Seating Around a Circular Stage

performance area

Chairs or benches should be placed evenly and there should be generou
space between each row of chairs. Access aisles to the entrance of the facilit
should be set up no farther apart than every twelve seats. Make a call to th
local fire department inspector to ensure compliance with regulations.

Examine the surface of the performance area for irregularities, broke
boards, splinters, buried rocks, or other hazards for dancers. Take carefu
measurements and make a diagram of the exact performance area so tha
equivalent space may be marked off in the rehearsal studio. Indicate on you
diagram entrances and exits, access to dressing rooms, toilets, drinking fou
tains, and storage areas. Performance space can seldom be altered so it
important that all dancers become familiar with the exact space available t
them. Choreographers must design the action for this space.

## The Studio

Typically the studio is a large room with a flat floor and windows in the wal
For rehearsals it is usually adequate; for performance it leaves much to b
desired.

Of prime importance is enough room—for the audience, the dancers, an
the dance. And here you must be realistic. If you intend the performance t
be no more than a display of classwork, unadorned, then you can line som
chairs against the wall and proclaim them audience seating and say that th
spectators will not be bothered by dancers running back and forth to mak
entrances or to change costumes. But if you want something more, sta
planning far ahead.

Carefully survey the floor space. First, determine how much room th
dance requires. Second, decide how much space is required for entrances an
exits and crossovers behind the dance area. This has to be separate spac
unless you are willing to jam everything together. Third, consider space f
instrumentalists or a piano, table for a record and tape machine, or whatev
is to be used. Fourth, think of where the light-stands must be placed,
light-stands are used. Additionally, you may worry about the distance tha
the lights require if they are to be spread enough to cover the dancers. Fift
where is storage space for scenery, costumes, and props?

The audience also requires its space, and it always needs more than yo
think. Don't guess! Line up some chairs to find out and be sure to inclu
aisle-space. Now, ask yourself—can the number of paying customers be seate
that your budget demands? Can they see the dancers? Will they be distracte
by latecomers entering through a door at the back or side of the performanc
area? Will they be adequately comfortable? Does the setup appear decentl
professional, or are you using a collection of mismatched chairs arranged i
ragged rows? Even a nonpaying audience deserves consideration, a payin
audience much more!

For a semitheatrical arrangement—that is, with the dancers at one end c e room and the audience at the other—certain technical problems will arise. ome kind of concealment for entrances and crossovers is needed. Often ee-standing screens will be adequate and at the same time they may serve as cenery. In an arena setup the concern is not with concealment but with roviding places for the dancers to enter and leave. Even here, a little thought out the bare surrounding walls—some colored lights or drapery—will en-ance the picture. Circular staging is exciting for dance, and it is certainly orth a try. But consider the cost and work involved. It may be more than ou expect.

Proper lighting depends upon control. Since artificial lighting and day-ght do not mix well all windows should be covered. And, of course, too any things turned on at once cause the electrical system to break down. A ssion with an electrician, or someone who knows about circuit capacity and urrent requirements, will prevent later panic and disappointment. Of course, ou can always plug in a bunch of lights until a fuse blows and find out for ourself! And then, where will all of those lights and cables be placed?

Every year thousands of performances are given in studios (see Appendix ). Planning and imagination can invest them with an interest and excite-ent that make the dancers' work worthwhile.

## he Theater

heaters are strange and terrible places. Most of them are designed by archi-cts who have never been backstage, equipped by purchasing agents expert nly in classroom supplies, and run by people who don't know why dancers eed all that time to set up their lights and run around in rehearsal.

If you are very, very lucky the theater will be a beautiful plant, spot-ssly clean, superbly equipped, a joy to work in—and the stage manager will e pleasant. More likely, the theater will be too big or too small, the stage will e dirty and nothing like a studio, the lighting will be inadequate, the scenic cilities limited, the dressing rooms disgraceful, and the stage manager surly. ut there it is, so you will have to accept it.

Don't take the negative attitude of the typical stage manager to heart. irst, he has been around a long time, has probably seen dance productions efore, and regards them as nothing particularly special, only another event n the schedule. You, of course, consider your production vitally impor-nt—at least you had better or it won't be very exciting. Understand his oint of view, because he might not consider yours, and the relationship will e fairly smooth and the cooperation at least adequate. This is particularly ue where a custodian or other nontheatrical person is in charge of the stage.

Another reason for the stage manager to appear uninterested and even rly in his attitude toward your grand affair is that you give him reason to oubt that you know anything about production. He cares little for your first ositions and contractions—these are part of the choreography, not produc-

17

tion—but he does care about the physical conversion of your performance from rehearsal on, for an audience. If you start out asking for things like "speckled lights during the pliés" or a "follow spot that can cover two dancers on both sides of the stage" or "an underwater cavern that dissolves at the touch of the little mermaid" or "six feet more dancing space over the orchestra pit," he will probably nod his head affirmatively and then forget the whole business.

Know as much as you can about production. Remember that there is difference between the artistic point of view—that of the choreographer and designer, and the practical—that of the stage technicians. Fantasy easily created by imagination is subject to hard reality in the theater; and reality always wins the battle here. For his own protection the stage manager may discourage you completely. He, after all, is more limited than you. On the other hand, if your requests are within the capability of the theater and crew and will really add to the performance—a very delicate point sometimes—the stage manager will usually do his best to see that you get what you want.

Now is the time to talk over what you want and what you may get instead. Look at the stage first. Is it as big as you had imagined? Walk across it, do a series of leaps from one side to the other, from back to front. Is it still big enough for the action you planned? Or do you have to alter the size and shape of the dance to fit?

Is there sufficient wing space? Can your dancers make entrances and exits as needed? Even Nijinski needed some free space in the wings from which to take off in a leap onstage; your dancers need no less. If you have large group they need more space, especially if the whole group must enter from one place. And it is hard for a dancer to make an exit leap or run into the wings if he bangs into a concrete wall before his foot touches the floor. Since that wall is going to be there at the time of performance, it should be marked off for rehearsal also, preferably with a heavy bench or other solid reminder.

Perhaps the program calls for a small dance downstage in front of the main curtain while a large set is rigged behind. Pull the main curtain and again determine just how much space you have. Don't just look at it, *try it*. Nothing impresses you more than the recollection of the small steps and restricted movements you were forced to make.

If the theater uses legs, borders and a cyclorama, ask the stage manager to lower everything so that you see the exact setup, *as it will be*. Sometimes there will be a reason for him to refuse; perhaps the things are standing in the wrong place or there is something already on stage that will interfere. Ask him to at least show you, on the floor, where the legs will hang and where the traveller curtain will cross. This is an expected request and will usually be granted.

Become more specific now and ask for the measurements of the stage *with the legs and curtains in place*. Make a diagram for yourself. (See Figure 1-8.) You should carry a tape measure to determine any particular spaces that

Figure 1-8    Diagram of Stage Space

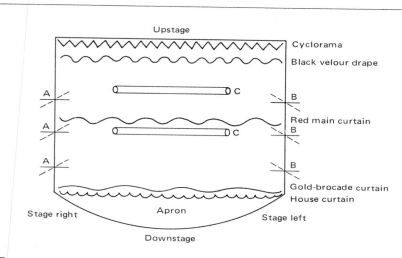

Upstage

Cyclorama

Black velour drape

Red main curtain

Gold-brocade curtain
House curtain

Stage right          Apron          Stage left

Downstage

Entrances and exits through
A — Stage-right legs
B — Stage-left legs
C — Overhead battens

Size of stage: 37-foot opening X 27 feet deep.
Light board and curtain—stage right.
Try audio-equipment upstage left.

might affect the dance, such as wing space, distance from one place to another, and relationship to curtain line. Be very specific in your measurements and diagram for this is the most useful information you will have when you return to the rehearsal studio. Measure, evaluate, and plan *now*.

As long as you are concerned with space, investigate the dressing rooms. Unfortunately, in too many theaters the dressing rooms seem to be afterthoughts. Occasionally they are adequate and not a haphazardly curtained space at the end of the auditorium-cafeteria-gymnasium, and you may even have mirrors and lights. Or, when the rooms are too small, too warm, too cold, with or without running water, with or without privacy, you may decide that the dancers will come already costumed and made-up.

With space on and off stage reviewed, turn next to consideration of what your program requires in the way of scenery and lighting. This is also the time to explore who builds scenery, operates lights, and carries out technical assignments. This varies with the production and the theater; sometimes the responsibility is assumed by the dance department, sometimes by the theater staff. Sometimes the theater personnel will do the whole job and you merely provide the dances and the designs for lights and staging. Usually, however, the choreographer designs and constructs scenery and costumes, and makes important decisions about lighting equipment. If the theater is a commercial one, ask about union rules and charges. Get all the details now.

Your ideas about scenery and lighting may seem odd to the stage manager, but this is to be expected. Go ahead and express them anyway, but try to know something in advance and be specific—don't ask for "three lights like the ones we had at the college last year," or "a kind of a thing that looks like the ocean rolled over it."

Although this is not the time to be specific about your needs, since your choreography is not yet complete, it is the time to discuss some of the basic problems you may encounter in carrying out your visual scheme. Suppose, in your version of *Sleeping Beauty*, you want a castle to emerge from a tangle of brush, or you long for a jungle-gym to be constructed out over the audience. Some theaters can do an acceptable illusion with projected scenery and scrims; others do not have such facilities or equipment. The stage manager who might be able to handle it will probably tell you the trouble you may get into, the space requirements, the time necessary, and the expense incurred. You may change your ideas; indeed, it is remarkable how often you *will* change your plans in order to fit the circumstances.

Again, and this is a problem that recurs with amazing frequency, the dance, as visualized, encompasses two widely separated dancers moving through darkness, lighted only by follow spots. Does the theater own two follow spots? The list goes on. Forever it is *want* versus *get*.

Anything specific that is *absolutely required* in your plan should be discussed. That famous "speckled light" that dancers ask for so often *can* be achieved as well as all sorts of odd effects. But this does take advance planning and perhaps some compromise. For one group to have a speckled light, another may have to do without the murky green light that slowly changes to a ghostly blue!

## Other Places

You may be asked to perform on the field between halves of a football game, or on a rickety platform set up in the park for a folk festival, or on the cold and solid concrete rotunda of a museum, or in a hospital ward, or the boxing ring of the athletic club, or the deck of a Navy ship. Before considering such a request make sure that your material is appropriate to the occasion and can be performed under these circumstances.

For the moment dismiss the production values of lighting and scenery and make a realistic appraisal of your chance for success. If you can't do a creditable performance, offer your apologies and forget it. If you think you can do it, go ahead, but plan the performance for the conditions and don't hope for a last-minute miracle. And remember the audience. A group of sailors will hoot at a sensitive little ballet about a tender snowflake falling in love with the handsome prince. A football crowd will not concentrate on a premiere dancer pirouetting her solo path through an inch of mud. A museum audience will raise eyebrows at a honky-tonk spectacle.

Don't automatically turn down an invitation to perform at a hospital or army camp; the audiences are eager for entertainment; just remember that this audience wants excitement. If the material is too removed from television and Broadway standards it may fall flat.

The real secret of any away-from-home performance is to plan for the worst. Costumes (usually more than leotards and tights) can dress up a production and successfully carry it through the absence of lights or set. Try to be realistic in appraisal of facilities, of help, transportation, and everything you can think of. Figure 1-9 will remind you of important details to be checked.

**Figure 1-9    Check List for Details of Away-from-Home Performances**

---

Place _____

Date _____    Time _____

Kind of Audience _____

Contact _____

Transportation _____

Parking (location, permit) _____

Sketch of stage (performance space) _____

Dressing facilities _____

Lights available _____

Publicity _____

Security _____

## CHOOSING A PERFORMANCE DATE

The facility chosen, the dancers selected, and the choreographies to be used are all so interrelated that it is impossible to indicate any priority. Decisions about all must be made and each will necessarily affect the others.

The choice of performance date depends on (1) preparation time required for dancers and production elements, (2) availability of the dancers, (3) availability of space for rehearsals and performance, and (4) a resolution of conflicts among these factors.

## Preparation Time

Consider how long it will take to complete the choreography and bring the dancers to the point of dress rehearsal. Whenever possible, choose the longest time available for preparation. If the dancers are not ready you will push them anyway, and always regret not having more time. For an informal presentation this is probably not too serious.

Scenery, costumes, and lighting do not just appear, nor can you arbitrarily push them on stage with instructions to "come alive." And obviously a complex production requires more time than a simple one. But how much more? Of course, there is no answer to that; as usual, "it depends." It depends upon how soon the designs are started, how soon the work begins, how the workers participate, how many hours each gives to the project, and how many changes are made by the choreographer. In any case it will probably take longer than expected. All you can do is make an educated guess, based preferably on past work experience in the theater or at a sewing machine or before a typewriter writing a publicity story.

## Availability of Dancers

Availability of dancers for rehearsals—regular, technical, and dress rehearsals—as well as for performance dates, must be determined early and clarified for all concerned. If some consideration is given to previous commitments of dancers, technicians, and crew as the schedule is being developed, all concerned will feel a greater sense of responsibility. In any event no one should ever be absent from any rehearsal because he didn't know of it. A well-planned schedule includes verification of the availability of *all* personnel. Post schedules and be sure that changes or subsequent corrections are noted on all copies.

## Availability of Space

Whatever performance space is chosen, arrangements must be made to ensure good performance dates and ample rehearsal time. Hopefully the choreographers control studio space and can set any date, but if the studio is shared it is necessary to check the master schedule. A theater is ordinarily a shared facility and is usually booked far ahead. Verified notice, sometimes a year in advance, must be secured. See Figure 1-10 for a sample form.

The eventual compromise on dates may not be to your liking. Check then on what else is available. Is there time for preliminary rehearsal, technical set-up, and dress rehearsal? If not, a performance date is of little value. In a school situation, a meeting of all those who plan to use the facility usually occurs months before the fall term begins. Certainly an argument in

April saves a disaster in January. And don't let the music or the drama department schedule a concert between your dress rehearsal and performance date. Dress rehearsals and performance times must be consecutive, or you redo the lighting and reset the scenery and move costumes in and out.

**Figure 1-10    Verified Record of Performance Area and Time Schedule for Use**

George Washington High School Auditorium available for dance performance May 5, 7, and 12. Rehearsals on the stage every Monday, Wednesday, and Friday from 3:00-6:00, starting the second week in April. Additional rehearsal time from 6:00-11:00 April 28 and 29; technical rehearsal April 30; dress rehearsal from 6:00-11:00 on May 2 and 4.

Signed _____

Date _____

Verification of campus security _____

The facilities available:

1. 35 x 46-ft. stage area with standard lighting equipment, curtains, cyclorama, legs, and auxiliary equipment as previously determined.

2. Two 15 x 16-ft. stage-level dressing rooms on each side of the stage, with storage space, hanging area for costumes, running water, toilets and wash basins; no mirrors, poor lighting, drafty.

3. One 25 x 35-ft. dressing room in the basement, no toilet or wash basin. Broken mirrors, poor lighting, drafty and dirty.

4. Auditorium seating for 500.

5. Bulletin boards and wall cabinets at entrance to the auditorium for posters and pictures.

## Conflicts

Very careful consideration should be given to the inevitable conflicts of holiday dates and other special events. Unless you are a part of the entertainment, forget Christmas week, Thanksgiving, New Year's Eve, and vacation periods. In schools, overlook an open date on the weekend of the Big Game or during examination period. There is no point in dancing to an empty house.

Consider the number of vacations during the preparatory period before production. Not all dancers are equally available during these times. Assistants, technical crew, designers, musicians, and even the custodian who will open the doors must be considered when resolving the conflicts.

Are there any remodeling plans for the studio or theater? Sometimes there is a crew who finally gets around to rewiring the electrical outlets at this awkward time. Be sure to ask questions—perhaps you will be told, and then again perhaps no one really knows when work will start on long-held plans. Be ready to follow up on every rumor. It is better to cope with rumor than with the reality of such an interference with a performance date.

## VISUALIZATION OF THE PRODUCTION

Several important questions have now been answered. One more must be considered, for upon the answer, or series of answers, depends the budget, design, and construction. What will the dance look like on the stage?

No one needs to encourage a choreographer to close his eyes and envision the final performance of his dance. This he does well! The performance space is always "spacious and ideal," the scenery "tasteful and exciting," the lighting "gloriously provocative and smooth," the dancers "inspired," and the whole production "well meshed and without a hitch." This is the vision. But no amount of envisioning will ensure its happening. The choreographer must face the circumstances of reality even as he anticipates the illusion he seeks to project.

Begin with the physical space. If you have designed a splendid dance, surpassing Petipa's grandest offering to the Czar, only to discover that the stage is not large enough for all the dancers, you tend to curse the architect, never your own failure to investigate, measure, and rechoreograph. How many times does a rehearsal come to an abrupt stop because the dancers who should appear at center stage can't find an entrance through a tightly stretched cyclorama? Surprising as it may seem, choreographers often disregard the physical limitations of their performance space. But the concrete and wood remain fixed, imposing all of their spatial limitations. The choreographer must determine what *is*, not just what he wants. And if he can manage to cope with the realities of the performance space early in the choreographic process, problems of adjustment will be minimized.

Consider the setting for the dance. Does it require more than spartan simplicity? Have you really thought about it, or do you use black draperies because they are there, and it is easier than thinking about scenery? A Fourth-of-July celebration might seem bare without flags, bunting, and colorful costumes, just as an abstract dance might resolve into a confusing spectacle if enveloped in lush scenery.

Unfortunately, many choreographers are so concerned with enough space for moving that they think *only* of open space. Even a casual consideration of this point of view suggests a possible reason for its prevalence. Choreographers are too busy manipulating movement to seriously examine the potential for shape, color, and contrast of symbol in the setting for the dance action.

And what is the mood in which the dance takes place? Both setting and lighting will depend upon this decision. On a stage, under varying lighting, placement, color, and use, the same dance can seem gay or nostalgic, exciting or bland. Picture a girl walking down a street. Suppose the sun is out, warm and bright; the effect is usually pleasant and relaxed. Then bring her back at night; a shaft of red light spills out, the only light visible on the dark street; the girl passes through the red light; then the light wavers as if someone else had passed through the beam. What has changed? The girl is the same, she makes the same movements, the street is the same; but the lighting has changed and with it the mood.

Try to see beyond the immediate action of the dance and the interrelationships among the dancers; beyond the shapes of the dancer's bodies and the shapes of space between and around them. Visualize the *over-all* mood that you wish to establish, the impact you seek.

Space, background, and mood—these are three conditions that determine the appearance of the finished production. All present problems. They determine the stage picture; the choreographer chooses what that picture will be. Until these decisions are made the designers wait, the builders wait, the costumer waits, the lighting crew waits, everybody waits.

# Before Moving into the Performance Area

# 2

# Management

or most choreographers and dancers the details of making a budget, planing for expenditures, keeping records, organizing schedules, preparing otices, and keeping track of things to be done are uninteresting aspects of he whole affair. They are happy to foster the stereotype that the creative rtist is a poor businessman, usually unable to balance his own checkbook. ut this is the "artist" first to howl when there is no money for the chareuse satin for a costume, or when someone else is on stage when he is finally eady to rehearse.

There should be a business manager, or at least a reliable assistant for the ance teacher who will probably manage the business details of the producon. There must be order to the initiation, development, and final staging of he event; there must be a plan for a budget and careful directions and checks n keeping track of expenditures and maintaining records. While this may be dious it is not particularly difficult. The allocating of time, space, and effort the real challenge and can become a hair-raising adventure, demanding the ombined skills of a child psychologist, a minister of the gospel, and a sea iptain of the clipper days. But this is the magic that makes the parts evolve ito a whole.

Making schedules, issuing notices, posting bulletins and keeping them irrent, as well as controlling interrelationships between events and people, e most important. This is the only assurance that the hours of work on the art of all concerned will result in a final production in which shared responbility becomes shared success.

## ETTING UP A BUDGET

o matter how simple the performance there are bound to be some expenses, it is necessary to consider raising and controlling funds to meet them. Once rvices have been rendered and facilities and equipment used it is embarssing if bills cannot be paid. So first assess all possible sources of income, cluding audience admission charge or donation as well as previously budted income available for production. Then prepare a breakdown of anticiited income and expenses that will serve as a basis for planning. (See Figure 1.) This can also be made available for administrative consideration of quests for money or for the establishment of a requisition number.

There are many ways to estimate costs and the closer you can come to ality, the better. First, itemize, in order of importance, every potential pense you can think of. It is helpful to refer to reports of similar events to

Figure 2-1    Budget Proposal

Dance Program to be presented May 5, 7, and 12. Tickets suggested at $1.00 for adults and 50¢ for children and students. Performers will be chosen from classes and the Dance Club.

| Estimated Expenses | | Estimated Income | |
|---|---|---|---|
| Costumes | $ 65.00 | Ticket sales, with | |
| Scenery, sets, props | $ 25.00 | expected attendance | |
| Publicity | $ 30.00 | of 150 for each of | |
| Programs | $ 27.00 | three performances | $275.00 |
| Stage crew | $ 25.00 | Production budget | $100.00 |
| Lighting crew | $ 30.00 | PTA donations | $ 36.00 |
| Records, tapes, accompani- | | Student drives | $ 22.00 |
| ment costs | $ 30.00 | Previous income | |
| Equipment rental | $ 65.00 | available | $ 88.00 |
| Gels, frames, bulbs, etc. | $ 20.00 | | |
| Refreshments for cast and | | | Total $521.00 |
| crew party | $ 20.00 | | |
| Miscellaneous | $ 50.00 | | |
| | Total $387.00 | | |

_____ Director

_____ Student
                         Assistant

_____ Director of
                         Ticket Sales

see what has been done previously. Attempt to determine costs. For a costume, calculate the yardage, the number and kinds of trimming, the accessories. Scenery requires lumber, paint, and nails. How much of each? All items can be broken down into individual parts. The cost for each totals into the cost for the whole.

Next identify for each item two or three possible sources. Confer with a purchasing agent or business-office representative who is sensitive to your needs and budgetary status. It is possible that arrangements can be made for discounts—be sure to inquire. For finding sources look in the yellow pages of local telephone directories, search through special theatrical catalogs and directories, inquire of production groups in your area, and check with university, college, high school, community center, and professional drama and dance groups.

Then telephone, write, or visit these sources and discuss your needs, verify costs, inquire about discounts, check availability of material, and determine the best way of making orders. Don't be satisfied with the first response

with any single source. Call again and continue inquiring at other places
d then compare your results.

When you identify expenses for the production be sure to consider:

1.) The fee for performance and rehearsal space and custodial services.
2.) Payment to the technical crew for rehearsals and performance.
3.) Accompaniment expenses: recordings, tapes, scores, performance fees,
piano tuning.
4.) Expenses for lighting and sound equipment and materials for both
rehearsals and performance (rental or purchase).
5.) Publicity costs: duplicating, paper and envelopes, postage, posters-
fliers-banners, paints and brushes, etc.
6.) Program and ticket costs: assistants to sell and take tickets.
7.) Set and prop materials, equipment, and construction.
8.) Costume design and construction, make-up, first-aid materials.
9.) Special-effects equipment and materials.
10.) Cartage, clean-up, and storage.
11.) Refreshments, cast and crew party.
12.) Miscellaneous expenses: and there are always more than you anticipate.

In estimating income consider:

1.) Ticket sales, on basis of cost and attendance.
2.) Regular budget allocation.
3.) Previous income still available.
4.) Aid from student drives and funds.
5.) Income from sustaining groups such as clubs, PTA, etc.

## EXPENDITURES

The bills and expenses for any aspect of the production should be covered by
available cash or by requisition. Requisitions are a more reliable method of
keeping track of expenses but they are also more complicated because of the
many small items purchased from numerous sources. Another solution is to
have funds available through a business manager, who collects receipts for
items and later submits them to the director with a final report. It cannot be
emphasized too often that an accurate final accounting is not only possible
but even desirable. The rule is: all expenses and potential purchases must be
okayed by you, the director; and if people have no receipt, they get no money!

In general:

The fewer people handling money, the better.

Keep a complete record of *all* purchases.

Keep an equally accurate record of all funds yet available.

Establish priorities for all expenses. For example:

1. Rental of performance and rehearsal area.

31

2. Music and costume expenses.
3. Fee for technical crews.

Also establish priorities for payment of bills. This would supposedly be controlled by initial plans for expenses.

Anticipate unscheduled expenses.

Decide what to do about the money that is left after all expenses have been paid.

## How to Establish a Requisition Number

(1.) A requisition is a special, numbered office form that serves as a contract between some sponsoring business office and a vendor. It is a promise to pay when evidence of materials received is given. It is usually prepared in duplicate or even in triplicate and serves as an order blank.

(2.) The procedure for setting up a special budget and requisition number is relatively simple but it will vary in different situations. Advice from the comptroller, business office, or administration is needed, of course, in each case.

(3.) It is always necessary to present a budget proposal for any such request. Additionally, it is important to identify an authorized signer of all the forms.

## How to Buy by Requisition

(1.) Contact the vendor and make sure of his acceptance of your particular requisition form.

(2.) Verify the availability, condition, and price of the materials.

(3.) Complete the requisition form according to the established procedure. It is then the equivalent of a check or cash.

## How to Buy by Check

Find out the policy for establishing a checking account. The authorized signers then draw checks and keep accounts according to practices set. It is the better part of wisdom to have only *one* authorized signer. (Unless there is a substantial sum available it is not usually worthwhile to establish a checking account for dance concert expenditures.)

## How to Buy by Cash

(1.) Establish a policy for submitting requests for proposed purchases. If the request is in accord with the plan then cash may be made available as soon as verified estimate or complete receipts are presented. Insist that purchases be made only with your consent or that of the business manager.

(2.) See to it that itemized receipts bearing the name of the store and date of purchase are submitted.

(3.) It is an additional safeguard if the name of the person who made the purchase is attached to the receipt.

The inevitable final accounting is usually prepared in duplicate. One copy is for your file, for future use both as a record of the production and as a guide to actual, instead of estimated, expense and income. The other copy is sent to the business office or to whoever provided the money. The final report, including the income-expense breakdown and a complete and neatly organized set of receipts or requisition forms, should be finished as soon after the production as possible.

## GENERAL BUSINESS DETAILS

Cooperation is the essential ingredient for a successful production. Since duplication of effort is frustrating to everyone, make sure each person knows clearly his role and responsibility. Obviously there are many ways to achieve this—just be sure that you have found the one that suits you.

Any director will need assistance with such generalized business details as: detecting production needs and potential solutions; fostering community spirit, from choreographer to usher; setting up and publicizing schedules and notices; dealing with budget and expenditures; cooperating with the publicity committee on programs, tickets, fliers, mailing lists, production pictures, etc.; organizing necessary reports; maintaining production records; and learning house management and security procedures, as well as janitorial, custodial, and clean-up action.

## RECORDS

File in an easily accessible place any information dealing with the production, including dated copies of the okays for the event, both time and place; a listing of the facilities and equipment available; budget proposals and clearances; a copy of the current mailing list; preliminary and subsequent publicity plans; listings and correspondence regarding assistance, suggestions, and recommendations; progress reports and final reports; designs and plans for construction of sets, costumes, scenery, props; committee membership and sequential records of all meetings; consecutive bills, receipts, or records of all production expenses; copies of *all* rehearsal schedules; a complete record of attendance numbers and income; correspondence with parents; and all recommendations for future events. This serves as a record to consult for the next production and to use for verification of payment of expenses. Figures 2-2 through 2-5 are examples of such records.

Figure 2-2    Administrative Approval of Proposed Dance Production

```
Proposed dance production:_____

Where:_____

When:_____

Who:_____

Sponsored by:_____

Proposed price of tickets:_____


        Tentative Expenses              Tentative Income
        _____               _____


                            Directed by_____

                            Assisted by_____

                            Tentative OK_____

                                        Title_____

                            Final OK_____

                                        Title_____
```

Figure 2-3    Detailed Specifications by Choreographer X

| Title: | Fanfare (tentative) |
|---|---|
| Accompaniment: | To be composed by Arthur Bonelli. |
| Number of dancers: | Eight, plus a trio of children. |
| Length: | Eight minutes (tentative). |
| Costumes: | Yellow and white leotards and tights. |
| Staging: | An opening dance. Curtains open on a preset stage, and dancers enter upstage left. There are three 2-foot risers and a fitted ramp entering upstage left. Orange swatches of net are suspended and draped from an upstage overhead pipe. Lights are warm and bright. |

Figure 2-4     Letter to Parent

The dance students at _____ are planning a
series of dance programs at the school on _____
and _____ from _____ to _____ . Your
son/daughter has been selected as a member of the cast and we hope
that you will consider this a valuable experience for him/her to
join the rest of the students in this venture.

The production is being directed by _____ and
will include some student choreography. _____ and
assistants _____ and _____ , all
regular teachers at the school, will make every effort to make this
an educational experience as well as an esthetically satisfying one.
Complete arrangements have been made for student comfort and security.
The enclosed rehearsal schedule is for you to keep so that you may
verify times and events.

We will depend upon your son/daughter to attend rehearsals
faithfully so that our production will be as polished and complete
as possible. Please feel free to telephone or stop by the principal's office if you have questions or comments. You are welcome to
attend any of the final rehearsals, and we look forward to seeing
you at one of the final performances. Will you kindly indicate your
willingness to have your son/daughter participate in this program by
signing the enclosed Parent Consent Form?

Sincerely yours,

_____ Director

_____ Principal

Enclosures:

1.  Complete rehearsal schedule
2.  Parent Consent Form

Figure 2-5     Parent Consent Form

I approve of my son's/daughter's participation in the High

School Dance Production to be presented at the High School Audi-

torium on _____ , with rehearsals as indicated

on the schedule sent to me.

Name of dancer(s) _____

_____

Parent or guardian _____

Address and telephone number _____

_____

Figure 2-6    Master Schedule

Administrative approval of
    production . . . . . . . . . . . . . . . . . . . . . . . . (12-6 months)

Preliminary meeting of director, choreographers,
    dancers, musicians  . . . . . . . . . . . . . . . . . . . (12-6 months)

Preliminary decision on program material . . . . . . . . . . . (12-4 months)

Auditions and final casting of dancers . . . . . . . . . . . . . (10-4 months)
    Mark off rehearsal space according to performance area

Tentative rehearsal schedule . . . . . . . . . . . . . . . . . . (10-4 months)
    Survey suitability of dates, revise if necessary

Detailed plans for choreographer  . . . . . . . . . . . . . . . . (6-4 months)

Investigation of performance area . . . . . . . . . . . . . . . (12-4 months)
    Survey facilities and equipment, anticipate needs

Budget all estimated costs . . . . . . . . . . . . . . . . . . . (12-4 months)
    Prepare estimated income-expense form;
    determine cost of tickets

Determine production staff:
    Director  . . . . . . . . . . . . . . . . . . . . . . . . (12-6 months)
    Choreographers . . . . . . . . . . . . . . . . . . . . . (12-6 months)
    Composers-accompanists . . . . . . . . . . . . . . . . . (12-4 months)
    Designers for costumes and sets  . . . . . . . . . . . . . (6-4 months)
    Designers for program and posters . . . . . . . . . . . . . (3 months)
    Lighting design . . . . . . . . . . . . . . . . . . . . . . (3 months)
    Publicity director . . . . . . . . . . . . . . . . . . . . . (6-3 months)
    Stage manager . . . . . . . . . . . . . . . . . . . . . . (2 months)
        Technical crew, stage crew, lighting crew . . . . . . . (1 month)
    House manager and ushers  . . . . . . . . . . . . . . . . (1 month)

Plan procedure for needed equipment and materials  . . . . . . . (6-2 months)
    Sound equipment, lighting accessories, sets, props,
    and paraphernalia for final production

First coordinating meeting of production staff  . . . . . . . . . (12-1 month)
    Delegate responsibilities, anticipate progress reports

Initiate publicity plans  . . . . . . . . . . . . . . . . . . . . (6-3 months)
    Process mailing list, plan for posters, fliers,
    notices, news stories, photographs; contact critics,
    prepare list of complimentary tickets

Rehearsal of all dances for production staff . . . . . . . . . . . (2-1 month)

Final rehearsal schedule  . . . . . . . . . . . . . . . . . . . . (1 month)
    Arrange for technical and dress rehearsals

Anticipate ticket and program arrangements  . . . . . . . . . . . (2 months)
    Contact ticket sellers and takers; give head usher
    list of emergency telephone numbers—police, fire,
    ambulance, extra ushers, clean-up crew; order tickets;
    compile copy for programs, check spelling of names

Complete details of post-production:
    Move equipment and materials to storage
    Return borrowed or rented paraphernalia
    Pay all bills
    Prepare financial statement and final report
    Write "thank you" letters

## SCHEDULES

It is suggested that a series of schedules be made in order to plan and direct the sequential development of the production. After major decisions have been made about the what, where, and when, it is then possible to plan how the event will be brought into being. Figures 2-6 through 2-9 are examples of these schedules. Please note that the numbers in parentheses suggest first, the recommended, and second, the minimum, time before the production date for getting started. Other schedules will be found within appropriate chapters.

## NOTICES

Don't ever take your participants for granted—make all notices to them as interesting and concise as possible. It is often helpful to make a particular kind of information always appear in a particular form, shape, or color; for example, all notices for the dancers might be on bright yellow cardboard with black poster paint, notices for the costume committee could be on rectangular sheets of bright blue poster board, and notices from the stage manager always on circles of white and black. Post them in the same place and before

Figure 2-7    Choreographer's Schedule

Dances completely choreographed, ready for rehearsal  . . . . . . (10-4 months)

Casting of performers complete, ready for rehearsal . . . . . . . . (10-4 months)

Separate meetings with music and costume designers  . . . . . . . .(6-4 months)
      Be prepared to show dance themes

Planning meeting with director  . . . . . . . . . . . . . . . . . . . .(6-4 months)
      Preliminary ideas about set-prop-scenery, lighting,
      costumes, staging, accompaniment

First coordinating meeting with production staff  . . . . . . . . . (12-1 month)
      Be  prepared to show dance themes and discuss
      production needs.

Complete performance rehearsal schedule . . . . . . . . . . . . . . .(3 months)

First complete rehearsal with accompaniment, sets,
      and costumes . . . . . . . . . . . . . . . . . . . . . . . . . . . .(5 weeks)

Submit final list of dancers' names, complete
      credits (music, scenery, costume, lighting, etc.),
      program notes, and full titles . . . . . . . . . . . . . . . . . .(3-2 months)

Second coordinating meeting with production staff . . . . . . . . . (6-1 month)

Rehearsal of dancers in the performance area . . . . . . . . . . . . . (4-1 week)

First dress rehearsal in performance area  . . . . . . . . . . . . . . (2-1 week)

Second dress rehearsal in performance area  . . . . . . . . . . . . . . (1 week)

Technical and dress rehearsal of all concerned . . . . . . . . . . . (as scheduled)

Figure 2-8    Stage Manager's Schedule

---

Check to be sure performance space measurements
   are marked in rehearsal area  . . . . . . . . . . . . . . . . . (4-2 months)

Recruit stage crew  . . . . . . . . . . . . . . . . . . . . . . . . . (4-1 month)

Compile addresses and telephone numbers of cast and crew  . . . . . (4-1 month)

Assemble prompting book to include sequence of dances,
   staging details, scenery changes, entrances, exits, cues,
   curtain calls, arrangements for cues from choreographers   . . .(4-2 weeks)

Coordinating meeting with production staff . . . . . . . . . . . . .(4-2 weeks)

Assignment of dressing rooms and fast-change areas . . . . . . . . . (1 month)

Incorporate all details of sound, lighting, scenery,
   costume, and props into prompting book  . . . . . . . . . . (2-1 week)

Clarify all details of staging at final rehearsals

Figure 2-9    Tentative Rehearsal Schedule for May Dance Concert

---

Monday and Wednesday, 3:15-5:00. . . . . . .starts after Christmas recess

Add Friday same time. . . . . . . . . . . . . . . . . . . . . . . .third week in March

These Monday-Wednesday-Friday rehearsals move on stage the second
   week in April.  Same time.

Friday, April 28, 6:30-10:00. . . . . . . . . . . . . . . .technical rehearsal

Saturday, April 29, 6:30-11:00. . . . . . . . . . . . . .first dress rehearsal

Tuesday, May 2, 6:30-10:00. . . . . . . . . . . . . . . . .final runthrough

Thursday, May 4, 6:30-11:00. . . . . . . . . . . . . . . .final dress rehearsal

Please Note:  Small group rehearsals will be scheduled at extra
              times.  Please watch for notices on the bulletin
              board.

a specified time each day (say 2 P.M.). Above all, these notices should be removed from sight when they are no longer correct or relevant. The same ingenuity and imagination should be displayed here as in all other phases of the production.

Figure 2-10 shows four sample notices.

Figure 2-10    Sample Notices

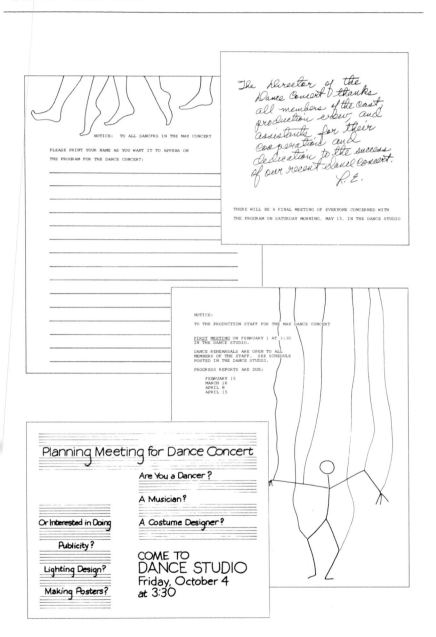

NOTICE:    TO ALL DANCERS IN THE MAY CONCERT

PLEASE PRINT YOUR NAME AS YOU WANT IT TO APPEAR ON
THE PROGRAM FOR THE DANCE CONCERT:

The Director of the
Dance Concert thanks
all members of the cast,
production crew, and
assistants for their
cooperation and
dedication to the success
of our recent dance concert.
L.E.

THERE WILL BE A FINAL MEETING OF EVERYONE CONCERNED WITH
THE PROGRAM ON SATURDAY MORNING, MAY 15, IN THE DANCE STUDIO

NOTICE:

TO THE PRODUCTION STAFF FOR THE MAY DANCE CONCERT

FIRST MEETING ON FEBRUARY 1 AT 3:30
IN THE DANCE STUDIO.

DANCE REHEARSALS ARE OPEN TO ALL
MEMBERS OF THE STAFF.  SEE SCHEDULE
POSTED IN THE DANCE STUDIO.

PROGRESS REPORTS ARE DUE:

    FEBRUARY 15
    MARCH 16
    APRIL 8
    APRIL 15

Planning Meeting for Dance Concert

Are You a Dancer ?

A Musician?

Or Interested in Doing

A Costume Designer?

Publicity ?

Lighting Design?

COME TO
DANCE STUDIO
Friday, October 4
at 3:30

Making Posters?

# 3

# Accompaniment: Sound and Music*

Usually, "accompaniment" implies a close relationship between one thing and another. In dance, the musical accompaniment often fits the dance closely in form or style or rhythm or mood or combinations of these. Sometimes, however, the sound chosen to accompany a dance has little or no relationship to the choreography, and hence we will use the term "dance accompaniment" to mean any sound that is provided by the composer or selected by the choreographer to be heard in conjunction with the dance.

There are as many ways to accompany dance as there are ways to choreograph it. In all of them, the views of the composer and the intentions of the choreographer will be the basis of choice.

There is the sound that exists as a result of the dancer's action—his feet against the floor, his breathing, and the slap of his hands against his body as he moves. These may be called the sounds of "internal accompaniment"; they have been extended in the characteristic heel beats and finger snaps of the Flamenco dancer, the ringing ankle bells and finger cymbals of the Indian dancer, and the shouts, hand claps, and foot stamps of the folk dancer. In contrast are the sounds of "external accompaniment," sounds provided by someone or something other than the dancers.

When the accompaniment is closely related to the movement it acquires something of the dynamics of internal accompaniment. When there is no relationship between accompaniment and dance, when the sound is merely simultaneous with the movement, it seems to exist for some purpose other than to augment the dance. It appears not only external but also irrelevant. Somewhere between these two extremes is the usual accompaniment for dance, chosen by the choreographer or musician-consultant.

Traditionally, music has been closely allied with dance, sometimes by design, often by tradition, and, too many times, by accident. But there is a wider source for dance accompaniment than that of formal music!

## BASES FOR CHOICE

Sounds made by the dancer range from voice and breath sounds, body slaps, hand claps, and foot stamps to those sounds made by manipulating a variety of gongs, cymbals, drums, and other portable instruments and sound-makers. External accompaniment can be provided by single, small, or large groups of

---

*Thanks to Ted Courtenay, teacher and music consultant-accompanist for dance at the University of Southern California, for many of the ideas included in this chapter.

drummers, instrumentalists, or musicians—even a full orchestra. Any "live" music is exciting for both audience and dancers, but it takes time, rehearsal, and planning. Recorded sounds on tape or record, either commercial or homemade, provide a number of advantages for both rehearsal and production. But this too takes imagination, skill, patience, and above all, planning.

How the choreographer chooses the sound accompaniment to be used in any production is a long and complicated procedure, parallel in many respects to the choreographic process. It cannot be discussed in any detail in one chapter, especially a chapter dealing with production techniques. However, it may be appropriate to identify some of the common practices.

There are many who insist that a musical score is necessary before any choreography begins: music first and then everything else fitted to it. Others are equally sure that sound can be developed only after the choreography is complete, in order to assure an intact movement form. This implies either composing a special sound accompaniment that is based upon the dance form or, almost impossible task, finding a completed score that fits. In some cases the music and dance are formed simultaneously, in which case the choreographer and composer work together in coordinating the two arts.

Spectacular and entertaining dance forms are often accompanied by brilliant and provocative popular tunes, the folk dance by folk melodies, jazz dance by jazz music, and the classical ballet with the classical music associated with it. Accompaniment for modern dance production ranges from full orchestration of traditional music to Moog synthesizer experimentations; from the dancer's internal accompaniment to solo singer with guitar; from harp or French horn to recorded string quartet; from piano composition to random sounds by chance.

Some choreographers are satisfied with whatever is available, some say "I just can't find anything." Somebody else might ask: "Did you try?" The world is filled with sounds waiting for anyone willing to reach out; sound is inescapable, at home, on the street, in the country, in the studio. Music, sound, words—they are all waiting.

Music is probably the easiest and most conventional accompaniment for dance. You can either use music that is already written, or you can find a composer to write it for you. In both cases it will help if you have some ideas about what kind of sound, style, and form is appropriate for your dance. This is easier said than done. Much of the already written music is complete in itself while some music was written expressly for dance (always some *other* dance than yours).

Music is chosen for such reasons as: it helps to establish a mood or setting, the tempo and rhythm are consistent with the dance, the style and form seem right, it is of appropriate length, or, very simply, the choreographer *likes* it. Many times the choreographer will choose the music first and then develop the dance to fit. In this case he must realize that the form of the dance is secondary to the form of the music. If, however, the form of the dance is really important, then the form of the music must be made to fit the

41

form of the dance. Here is the classic dilemma. Seldom will a previously written musical score fit the dance without some change in one or the other. It is for this reason that many choreographers prefer to have music written for their dance. But able composers, sensitive to the problems of dancers and choreographers, are hard to find. Consider the length of time necessary to formulate the music after the choreography has been completed!

It is sometimes useful for choreographers to keep a list of composers who have written in a style, form, or manner that interests them. Any list of titles or taped selections will be of great value. Written music, especially for the piano, can be useful. Obviously it would be necessary to have long sessions with an accompanist or to have tapes or records of the same music available.

Working with a composer is a complicated adventure. If the task is to develop music that is somehow inevitable to the dance then the composer must see the dance many times. He must know the general tone of the work, the rhythms, phrasing, and interrelationships. He must observe the dancers in rehearsal and even try some of the movement himself so that he may be more sensitive to some of the problems of tempo and dynamics. He must talk with the choreographer about the intent, and especially he must know how to visualize the final performance. Ideas, clarification of themes, and lists of the counts of the dance should be supplied by the choreographer. Then, given the full cooperation of the dancers, the composer may come up with just the right accompaniment.

Less conventional forms of accompaniment for dance include selected or even random sounds, which can be organized and played or taped; patterned sounds from string, wind, brass, or percussion instruments; human, animal, or bird sounds; sounds from electronic or mechanical sources; and a host of manipulated sounds resulting from such experimentations with a tape machine as dubbing several sounds at one time, recording a tape played in reverse, and varying the tempo, volume, or tone.

## Listening to Music

Hearing music at concerts, on radio, or on television can be valuable to the choreographer looking for ideas for dance accompaniment. But most listening is casual. Pretty sounds flow and the ear accepts all of them, or may not even hear some of them. For the ordinary listener that is enough; for the choreographer it is not. He must become an active listener, alert and attentive to the sound, rhythm, and melody; he must take note of differentiations of style, technique, and form. Purposeful listening requires participation. Almost any music can conjure up some kind of an idea, recall a movement phrase, even fit something you are working on right now. But a few phrases of sound that fit do not necessarily mean that the whole thing is suitable.

Provide yourself with a notebook and when you hear something that nterests you, note the title, opus number, composer's name, instrumental combination, and any other information given by the announcer. Write down your impressions of mood and rhythm, even your visualization of action, setting, or lighting. Identify, in descriptive words, all of the important characteristics that you find. (See Figure 3-1.) It is surprising how soon you will

Figure 3-1    Sample Notes on Possible Music for Dance*

---

SÁPARA from Nigeria and CUECA from Chile, two easy folk dances for couples. Recordings of authentic music; directions for the dances are included in brochure. HI NEIGHBOR III, 1960, U.S. Committee for UNICEF, United Nations, New York, N.Y.

COURT DANCES OF MEDIEVAL FRANCE from Arbeau's ORCHESOGRA-PHY. Short and authentic music for preclassic dances from branles to galliardes. Ancient instruments such as krummhorn, recorder, tabor, harpsichord. Would be good for a suite of authentic court dances or a period piece. See especially Side I, Band I: Pavane, BELLE QUI TIENS MA VIE. Turnabout TV 4008 (TV 34008 Stereo)

BECHET AND BLUES is a complete album of blues with famous musicians performing. See BECHET'S CREOLE BLUES with Bechet on clarinet, with orchestra. An interesting quality with unstereotyped melody. Obvious rhythm and transitions. Side A, No. 6, Scepter Records SRM537 A-B

IMPROVISATIONS ON HINDU RAGAS. Strange rhythms, melodies, and moods played on tabla, with hand sounds and altered Western instruments. Side A CC 612-3. Ruth White's MUSIC FOR CONTEMPORARY DANCE, Vol. 1 CC612. Rhythms Production

Béla Bartók, BARTÓK PLAYS BARTÓK, Side 2 IMPROVISATIONS: Opus 20, No. 1, simple, stately, and slow; Opus 20, No. 6, playful and rhythmically mixed. Piano. Remington R199-94

Stefan Wolpe's CHAMBER PIECE NO. 1. A severe and dissonant serial piece, elegantly constructed and strictly "unemotional." Almost impossible to come up with any "it sounds like"; rather, it sounds only like itself! Excellent as background for large group abstraction. Nonesuch H71220

Karlheinz Stockhausen's HYMNEN is the result of a strange manipulation of several national anthems in combination with electronic sounds. Rhythms and harmonies interact; hard to find and identify a fixed rhythm. Good springboard for social satire. Music would overpower anything else; it might need considerable volume change. Interesting idea for a composer to try. Deutsche Grammophon 139421/2

TROIS GYMNOPÉDIES by Erik Satie are all slow, and all sound unhappy and grave. Curious archaic quality; strange and haunting melodies. Clear rhythm and form. Piano. Angel 35442

STRUCTURES FOR SOUND, a collection of electronic sounds featured by the New York Museum of Modern Art. (BAM, Éditions de la Boîte a Musique, Paris, distributed by Record and Tape Sales, New York, N.Y.) Daniel Ouzounoff's VALSE is a strange little waltz, melodically and rhythmically true but with a fresh electronic flavor. Jacques Lasry's SPONTANEITÉ, an almost primeval sound, pure, stark, and elegant, with fascinating progressions. Seems slow and sustained, almost sticky-flowing—an auditory experience. Impressionistic or even surrealistic.

*Always check the copyright.

develop a reservoir of source materials. In this way you will be listening with a dancer's view and will become aware of things that you never noticed before.

In some areas a monthly magazine containing radio schedules is available at newsstands or by subscription. Some stations provide their own monthly schedules; all will answer a request for information about programming.

## Other Sounds

Many times music does not solve the dancer's special problem. Other kinds of sounds may be needed—perhaps words or some unusual sound. There is an ever-increasing range of natural and distorted sounds in our world. Many of these have been captured and made available on records and tapes. There are sounds of a throbbing heart and the roar of a jet plane, the noise of a saw and the bleep of a porpoise. While any of these may provide the stimulus for accompaniment, it is even more exciting when the choreographer himself takes a tape recorder to the source of some sound that interests him. It is well worth your while to acquire the technical skill for recording and playing back.

Some of the city sounds that have been used by choreographers are from freeway, racetrack, machine shop, traffic on a busy street, footsteps on a quiet street, a boiling tea kettle, a dripping faucet, muffled conversation, sounds from radio or television, a telephone or door bell, angry voices, a baby's cry, the hum of a formal reception, or children's voices on a playground or in a classroom. There are few sounds that do not lend themselves to a choreographer's use. The magic lies in the choice and in the organization.

Sounds from the country are equally versatile and interesting. The following have been used by choreographers as a basis for further development of accompaniment for dances: bird, animal, insect, and fish sounds; raindrops on a metal roof; the roar of surf and roll of thunder; winds whistling across a mountain meadow; the magnified crack of lightning; the rumble of a rock slide.

A dancer makes many sounds without being aware of them. He can easily pattern and accentuate these, as well as many others, so that instead of being spontaneous they become a planned accompaniment. For example, a patterned phrase might be made up of combined foot stamps and shuffles; of hand claps and body slaps; of whistles and finger snaps; of hissings and tongue clickings or other such sounds.

Poetry as well as other verbal materials can be used for different effects. The following have been used by choreographers: Wallace Stevens' *Thirteen Ways of Looking at a Blackbird;* selections from Walt Whitman's *Leaves of Grass* or the works of Federico Garcia Lorca; sonnets of Shakespeare and bits from *Mother Goose;* readings from Emily Post's *Etiquette,* the Motor Vehicle Code, and the telephone directory; snatches of radio or television broadcasts;

istorted telephone conversations; selections from political speeches; texts om sermons; bits from editorials and missing-in-action reports. Sometimes ie dancer (or others), speaking or chanting words while moving (or even hen not moving), can provide vivid and exciting accompaniment. Of course, is difficult for a dancer to move and speak simultaneously, but the neces- .ry diaphragmatic control can be acquired.

The degree to which any of these more unusual sounds may be appropri- e as accompaniment is a problem for the choreographer. It is up to him to :termine the composition of sounds, or he must delegate the responsibility ir such a decision to a composer. But here again, as with costuming and tting, no one is as sensitive to the unique problems and possibilities of teraction as the choreographer—or, to be more precise, the choreographer ho is imaginative and has the time to explore such possibilities. Unfortu- itely, he is so often overcome by all of his other responsibilities that he mply takes the easiest course and uses a readily available and often stereo- ped arrangement of sounds that does little else for the dance than provide :company ing sound.

## OURCES

iere is no readily available source for dance accompaniment unless you can : satisfied with the current recordings and tapes that are in good supply at e corner drug store. These might be right for some dances; you may as well ok at them. But the chances are that you will spend considerable time ciding what kind of accompaniment you need and want. And then you will end twice as long again in finding it. You may be looking for a record, sheet usic, an orchestral score; or perhaps you need a portable tape recorder or a und system. You may be looking for an imaginative composer, a soprano, a utist, or a jazz drummer. More likely you are looking for something, *any- ing*, that in some way fits both the idea and the form of your dance. What really needed is imagination and the incentive to look beyond the obvious.

## ecords and Tapes

usic scores and able performers are luxuries that few choreographers can ford for more than a few productions. Records and tapes are more easily ailable, but without knowledge and experience one must spend considerable ne just looking for something to listen to! The obvious place is, of course, e record shop, but the average one has little more to offer than the standard assics of the concert field and music in the popular idiom.

Those who have access to the large record shops in big cities will fare tter. Here there is a greater selection from all kinds of music, but the oreographer will still be limited almost entirely to the standard repertory.

45

While this music may be appropriate for some dance productions it is often unsuitable for contemporary styles. There are exceptions, of course, but unless the choreographer is knowledgeable about musical forms and period styles his search among the standard works will be unrewarding.

An important source for listening is the public and school library. Almost everywhere libraries are building impressive collections of recorded material of all kinds. Some of the larger libraries have vast stores of listening material—so much that one must spend time learning catalog classifications. Recordings are usually classified as classical, popular, opera, vocal, jazz, drama, spoken word, history, appreciation, and shows. Some libraries have listening rooms and if you use them you often save time in choosing what you want to check out. And don't forget the librarians. They can be very helpful, but don't expect them to understand a dancer's needs.

There are a number of record clubs that operate much as a book club and advertise regularly in popular magazines. Some require that you purchase a specified number of records each year, others have a membership fee but no specified purchases. Before joining any be sure that you read the fine print in the information brochure so that you know exactly how the club operates. Beware of the club that advertises *unlimited* choice. They more often offer a choice of only standard works. However, there are a few clubs that do offer anything printed in the *Schwann Catalog,* and often at discount prices. You might consider the advantage of such a club, especially if you do not have access to a large discount record store.

One of the most valuable sources for recorded music is the *Schwann Catalog,* which is usually obtainable at record stores. This is a monthly publication listing all records recently issued in all categories and on all labels. A store can order anything listed and will probably be able to deliver it to you. Schwann also publishes a supplementary catalog for international pop and folk and children's records.

There are several magazines available at newsstands that give assorted kinds of information about music. *Hi Fidelity* and *Stereo Review,* for example, include a broad scope of information about records, the recording business, new trends and developments as well as reviews of music and recordings. Additionally, there is information about electronic equipment, tape recorders, amplifiers, and sound systems. *Dance Magazine* carries notices and advertisements of special music for dance, some designed for technique, some for studies and dances. *The Saturday Review* and *Harper's,* among many others, periodically carry listings and reviews of records and tapes. Make an effort to find these references and keep informed about what is happening in the fast-changing world of sound.

Many cities have specialty shops like The Children's Music Center in Los Angeles and The Dance Mart in New York City that cater to dancers and dance teachers. These shops supply such specialized areas as folk, ballet, children's, jazz, and modern dance. They often have music, books, periodi-

ls, costumes, and instruments and will usually send catalogs on request. The
tter shops may have a good selection of music for the choreographer to
nsider, including albums made especially for dance.

ve Music

ierever you are, especially if you are in a school, it may be possible to find
sic students who are interested and able to perform or compose for you.
t remember, they are just learning and probably not as adept or flexible as
professional, nor do they always have enough time. If you have a large
dget you may be able to pay union scale for your musicians. Remember
it rehearsal time is expensive and be cautious about changes in choreo-
iphy that seem necessary. Of course, if you are paying professional musi-
ns you will get professional cooperation and dedication. Commissioning a
sical score from a professional composer can also be expensive. Just be
e that the production is worth it.

Sometimes a choir, orchestra, or small ensemble in a school or commun-
will be interested in playing for you. Be sure that you plan well in advance
d, hopefully, choose your own music and staging. Too often it comes to be
ompromise of "If you will perform with us we will develop a dance to fit
music you want to use." Is it really worth it in this case?

A more workable alternative is to seek out solo, duo, or trio instrumen-
ists to play something that approximates your choice of accompaniment.
metimes a simple folk melody on a guitar, a plaintive flute sound, or a
orus of children's voices can be appropriate.

Experimentation with prepared piano, percussion, brass, and toy instru-
nts and noise makers can initiate a refreshingly different accompaniment.
her improvised or formally patterned, it may be just the right thing. Dan-
s often perform very well to such accompaniment, especially when they
derstand the rhythm and dynamics of the work.

The larger and more sophisticated the group of accompanists, the more
nplicated are all the details of rehearsal and production. The effectiveness
y compensate, but unfortunately the choreographer, with all of his other
ncerns, seldom has the courage to try this. He too often abandons live
sic for records and tape, but if plans are made far enough in advance, if
nsideration is given all participants, and if schedules are prepared months
ore important dates, successful coordination can be achieved.

If you do plan for live music, decide before the choreography is com-
ted where the musicians are going to be. Are they on stage or in an
chestra pit or in the auditorium? Is there any room for them at all? Can
u provide what they need? A piano in the studio is not a piano in the
ater, and unless arrangements are made in advance for moving, placement,
l tuning, your piano or other instrument may not be ready for the perfor-
nce. Be realistic in your appraisal and your plans or you will be in trouble.

47

## RECORDING TECHNIQUES

For most purposes, a standard tape recording will suffice—just set up the recorder, place the microphone, and turn on the switches; for special effects you will need special techniques.

### Standard Recording: Record to Tape

A choreographer needs to know how to transfer from record to tape. There are two ways to do this. The easiest is to place a microphone about a foot away from the speaker through which the music will be playing, switch to "record," start the record, turn up the tape recorder's volume control, and wait until the end of the music. The other way, which is the best way if you have the equipment, is to connect the phonograph cartridge directly to the tape recorder. If you have a separate record player and amplifier, take the cord that comes from the player and plug it into the microphone input of the recorder. It helps to have earphones for the recorder if you want to hear.

A few cautions must be observed. First, use a good record. Scratches, clicks, and poor sounds will be amplified in the process of recording, and any defects will be more noticeable in an auditorium than in a small room. The purchase of a new record is a worthwhile investment. Second, use a good hi-fi system and recorder. Bad equipment means bad sound. Third, the music should be played at a fairly loud level, or the tape may be too quiet to hear during the dance. Whenever the microphone level is turned up too much the recording will be distorted or contain too much hum. Fourth, the recording level light or meter should not exceed the limits set for that particular re corder. If there are no instructions available, the general rule is that a light should flash only occasionally, and a meter should seldom cross the line into the area marked in red or otherwise indicated as an overload of sound. Fifth, make tests. Listen to the sound and make certain that the music is loud enough but not distorted. Change volume readings and microphone placement if you have to. Discard bad records and tapes. Make enough tests to satisfy yourself that the tape is good enough to play for an audience. Sixth, resist the temptation to change the volume while recording unless you like music that fades in and out. Once a test has been approved for loudness and clarity, the controls should be left alone, except when there is some reason to increase or decrease volume at a particular point. While you are at it you may as well make a duplicate tape by playing the first tape on one recorder and dubbing a second on another. Keep the first tape for performance. The duplicate can be used for rehearsal.

### Standard Recording: Live Music or Sound to Tape

Commercial recordings are made with one microphone or with dozens, from

istant point and from nearby. As you can see, there is no best way. If there is
rule, it is simply to set up the microphone and record. Listen and then
ecide. As general as that may be, that is the only answer.

Ordinarily, a piano sound is recorded with a single mike placed about a
ot and a half above the strings and nearer the high octaves than the bass. A
nall group can use a single mike about six feet away. A large group requires
single mike far enough away to pick up the total sound instead of individual
ctions. Use two microphones if one doesn't sound right; add others if you
ant to emphasize one instrument.

Stereo requires sound from at least two directions. The microphones
ive to be separated. Listen until you are satisfied with the sound. The room
ou record in may need some blankets hung around the walls to cut down
ome of the hollow-sounding effect of the usual untreated room, or you may
ive to move the microphones close to the group. As always, try it.

## pecial Recording Techniques

ou may want a sound that is not commercially available. With a tape re-
order, imagination, and a little experimentation, the possibilities for interest-
ig and unusual sounds are unlimited. You may be surprised at what you can
roduce with the commonest of materials. For percussive sounds try clap-
ing, slapping, tapping, hitting various objects such as clay flower pots, ordi-
iry drinking glasses, or tea cups; shaking or rattling a plastic box of bobby-
ins or a can of little stones; scraping two blocks of wood covered with sand
iper; or pulling a stick across a venetian blind. For more sustained sounds
ie bells, gongs, cymbals, or piano with pedal. Explore the possibilities of
eech sounds, then hiss, hum, murmur, and blow. Get two or three people
gether and experiment with some of these techniques—the results can be
ite effective.

Try recording and playing the tape backwards, not at fast rewind speed
it at regular speed. Try recording at one speed and playing back at a differ-
it one. Hold the tape as you record and slow it or bounce it with your
igers. Your material can be music or sound effects or even people sounds—
hatever can pass through a microphone. You may not get anything worth-
hile, but again you might. Try it.

With two recorders you can add sound to sound, provided that one of
e recorders is capable of running in the "record" position without erasing
e tape. Most recorders do erase, so you have to find one that does not. Play
tape on one machine and record on the other. Rewind the tape to the
irting position and add another layer of music, speech, or sound. Some
mmercial recordings may have a dozen overlays to create the effects you
ar—the single singer becomes a trio, the one guitar expands to ten, the pop
oup is interrupted by crowds and the sounds of war.

Record a sound on one tape, another sound on another, and other

49

sounds on other tapes. You can play them back through individual machine all at once or one at a time, fade them in and out, or make the sound con from different locations on the stage or in the auditorium. The pattern a volume of sound could add interest to any dance and might be especial useful in a total theater experience.

Splicing and Leaders

Splicing simply means making firm connections between loose ends of ta The fewer splices necessary, the better chances you have for clarity a continuity. While it is said that well-spliced junctions will be stronger than unspliced series, they do come apart sometimes. Some people have succe with a simple taping of the ends, but unless you have a lot of experience i best to get a special splicing device from your record or audio store a carefully follow the directions. There is nothing more nerve-wracking than have a splice separate in the midst of a performance.

Leaders to each sound sequence—that is, enough empty tape to give y a running start before the sound starts—are a must. These leaders should titled, timed, and carefully rehearsed. It is also advisable to write on t leader the reading for volume and tone control of the machine to be use Always be sure that leaders for rehearsal and performance tapes are identic

## REPRODUCTION OF THE RECORDED SOUND

Each detail of sound coverage, volume, and timing must be planned. The things change for different auditoriums and stages, so rehearsal is as imp tant for this as it is for the dancers.

The best arrangement for loudspeakers is to have one or two in front the curtain and one or two backstage. The front speakers can be set to volume level that is comfortable for the audience, the backstage speake providing enough sound for the moving dancers. When there is only o speaker it should be placed backstage center, near the back wall. The sou will carry to the audience, even through a curtain. A single speaker, or ev two speakers, in front of the curtain would have to be turned up loud enou for the dancers to hear, and that volume of sound would probably be exc sive for the audience.

For stereo operation, the same arrangement is suggested: in front of t curtain and backstage as the preferred arrangement, backstage placement there is only one pair of stereo speakers. Try to keep the wires tight agains wall and to keep them together with a tape or string so that they will not loosely in the path of a moving foot, or stretch across air at neck lev Remember that the dancers have priority.

Test the volume levels. Play the tape and move around on the stage a the auditorium, down front, in the middle, at the sides, and in the back. he audience wants to hear; it does not want to eavesdrop on a distant sound, either does it want to suffer an ear-splitting riot. For each tape section, the olume should be set and a reading marked down on the tape leader and in ie cue script. Pencil and paper do not forget. Later changes will probably be .ade as people listen during rehearsals.

For a large auditorium the tape recorder's amplifier will probably not be owerful enough to reproduce the sound at a comfortable listening level. It ill then have to be played through another, more powerful amplifier. Ask ound until you can find someone who can tell you what kind of equipment needed, or even if something is already available. You will need someone ith special knowledge to plug your tape recorder output into an amplifier ith such a high-level input. Larger loudspeakers will probably be needed ith the more powerful amplifier because the small ones will be damaged if ie sound is too loud.

Does the music start before the curtain opens, as it opens, or after it is ened? What comes first: sound or lights or movement? Does the sound ntinue, without any stopping of the tape? If it stops, where does it stop, id what is the cue to start it again? Sometimes a timed space is left and the ent tape continues to run for the entire length of the break. This is fine if it rehearsed, but in case of some human or mechanical failure, it may not nchronize as the sound comes on again! The more variables there are, the eater the possibility of disaster. When the dance is finished, does the sound ntinue? Does the sound finish and the dance continue? What is the relation-ip to the lights and other sequences? All of these questions must be con-dered, planned, rehearsed, and written down. How you finally use your tape determined by the interaction of all these events.

It is helpful if the sound technician has a sequentially numbered cue eet, starting with number one and continuing through the entire event. This necessary to run the show, just as it is necessary to have a carefully edited pe so that there is no unnecessary threading and re-threading of the ma-ine between sections. The cue sheet should be available for the stage man-er so that he understands the running order. Never leave this until the :hnical rehearsal! (See Figure 10-1, a sample cue sheet.)

## VE MUSIC

usicians need space and light. Hopefully the placement has been decided— ry realistically—during the choreographic phase, or there will be a stage led with people and instruments. Since there will be problems enough with e music, playing position should be settled before moving into the perfor- unce area. The soloist or the band or the orchestra can be on stage or off, pending upon the dance and the amount of available room. If they are on ge, they and their equipment should be portable enough to set up and clear in a reasonable amount of time, unless you like long, suspenseful, stage wait

Light is needed to read music. Where does it come from? Sometim
stage lights can work, provided they do not need to be dimmed or switch
off at awkward times. Stand lights can be used, provided that you have mu
stands and lights. What happens during a blackout?

A piano is a big, heavy instrument. To get it where you want it may c
money for movers. It usually has to be tuned and that means arrangemer
for the tuners to move in, usually when a rehearsal is scheduled.

Orchestra pits are made to hide musicians. If you want to hide yours a
do not have a pit, use screens. Can everybody see what needs to be see
Probably not, unless you have planned ahead to solve the problem.

Rehearsals are necessary. They take time, more than you may imagir
They have to be scheduled for starting time and finish time. If only one o
of four dances uses musicians, what happens when the players are late
want to keep playing past the allotted time? You'd better know the answ
and make it clear to everybody. Schedules cause troubles; breaking the
causes more.

Finally, find a place for everybody when they are not playing for t
dance. Otherwise they will be hanging around dressing rooms in the middle
a quick change, or warming up noisily in the only entrance. Did you prom
to pay them?

## HINTS AND CAUTIONS

The most all-pervasive advice is: plan carefully, experiment as much as y
can, design the sound carefully, and rehearse every detail with all the tech
cians and dancers concerned. Be sure that *everyone* knows what to do,
what sequence, and on their own initiative.

### About the Recording Machine

Practice operating the recording machine so that it doesn't make a "blur
when starting and stopping. Some machines make more noticeable soun
than others when the tape is stopped, but this can be avoided. Try using t
"hold" lever temporarily so as to avoid the sound. When starting the machir
first turn down the volume, then quickly turn it up to the predetermir
level. Reverse this action when stopping: first turn the volume down and
and then stop the machine.

The volume of the accompaniment is often too great for an audien
When the treble tone-control is set too high it tends to amplify every imp
fection in the recording, every minor scratch. It also cuts down on good to
quality.

What if the tape recorder fails to operate? Perhaps it isn't the machir maybe it's the electrical current, a pulled plug, or some human error. But in such an emergency you don't have time to search for causes. You can save your nerves by having a stand-by recorder handy and ready. On most machines the two tape reels can be lifted out without rewinding and placed on the other machine. If the tape is properly spliced, with leaders for each section, it will be easy to find the place and start again. Every precaution should be taken when so much effort has been made in the complex preparation of such a production.

## About the Recording Tape

Put as much of your accompaniment as possible on one tape, or, more important, put selected portions on one tape—for example, everything before the first intermission. Be sure that everything is properly spliced and has clear leaders between each section. This is better than having separate tapes that have to be run off, re-wound, and changed during performance. It is also advisable to have a splicer, or splicing materials, available. Be sure that you have small scissors, a knife, and a dependable flashlight. Better be safe than sorry later.

Don't forget to have at least two tapes on hand for the performance. This could be the rehearsal tape and, hopefully, a duplicate, as well as the performance tape. Obviously these should be exact copies in every detail. If you ever experience a mishap to your tape you will never again need be reminded of this. Many unsuspected and unusual things can and do happen under the stress of performance.

## About Copyright

The Copyright Statute of the United States offers protection for creators of drama, literature, music, and, to a limited degree, dance. Copyright regulations do not permit the use of music, literature, or dramatic works in public performance without special permission or payment of royalty fees. In the past, certain exceptions were permitted for educational institutions or purposes, especially when the performance was nonprofit. At the present time many of these copyright laws, especially those dealing with education, are being reconsidered by a Congressional committee. For this reason there is some confusion in that area that deals with education.

Generally there are the following categories to consider: first, "public domain," in which music published before copyright statutes or music whose copyright has expired is available to everyone interested; second, "common-law copyright," by which the law offers automatic protection for any recorded form of expression, provided the work is neither published nor registered for copyright; third, "statutory copyright," which is received from the

Copyright Office in Washington, D.C., upon completion of requirements of the registration regulations.

Anyone concerned with music for dance production should become acquainted with these regulations. He should also be aware of the registration of some notated dances. Especially with reference to music the copyright statute protects creativity by: first, granting control to any composer over *what* is performed with his music (thus you must secure the composer's permission, either personally or from his agent or publisher); second, protecting the arranger of any music, even music that is in the public domain; third, protecting performance rights which, in music, are of two types: the small, incidental public performance that can be licensed by ASCAP (American Society of Composers, Authors and Publishers); and the grand, stage rights which must be negotiated with the copyright owner or with his representative.

An Important Check List

(1.) Check the music that you want to use. Is it protected by statutory copyright? If it is it will display a copyright notice, and, in the United States, will bear the date of registration. The maximum time of protection is 56 years.

(2.) If you wish to use an unpublished manuscript, check to see if it has been registered in Washington, D.C.; if not, it comes under common-law copyright and is protected as long as it is both unregistered and unpublished. Get clearance from the composer, or from the publisher, who may hold it unpublished, for rental.

(3.) Very often permission to use music does not involve the payment of a fee. In any case the fee is not excessive, especially for educational or community purposes.

(4.) If you are in doubt regarding any music and its copyright status, contact the publishers or the Copyright Office in Washington, D.C.

(5.) Remember that arrangers of music, even music in the public domain, are still protected by copyright.

(6.) Do not use music until you have had clearance from the holder of the copyright. Don't take a chance.

(7.) Consider the possible royalty payment in your original budget proposal. Remember, even if there is no fee, you must still have clearance for use.

(8.) When writing to a composer or a publisher for permission to use some work, be sure to include such information as:

Name of the composer and the title of the music you wish to use. (Complete score or some part? What part? Are you using the music as it was originally written? What changes do you wish to make?)

Name and address of the performance group.

Names of: director, conductor, choreographer, stage and costume designers, business manager.

Name and address of the performance area. Its maximum and average seating capacity.

Price you will charge for a ticket, exclusive of tax.

Maximum and average box office gross.

Dates of performance. (Any broadcasts or telecasts?)

9.) If you are using commercial tapes or records, either for rehearsal or for performance, you must have clearance from the recording company and/or the musicians through their union.

**Figure 3-2     Schedule for Accompaniment**

---

Preliminary meetings with choreographers . . . . . . . . . . . . (12-5 months)

Thematic materials ready for consideration . . . . . . . . . . . (10-6 months)

First copy of the accompaniment . . . . . . . . . . . . . . . . . (8-5 months)

Final accompaniment ready for rehearsals, with
    rehearsal tape . . . . . . . . . . . . . . . . . . . . . . . . . (6-4 months)

Accompaniment as it will be performed for production . . . . . . . (4-1 month)

## Final Word

It is vitally important to plan ahead, especially with reference to clearance for the use of copyrighted material. When rehearsal time approaches, it is too late to worry about whether you will be able to use the music that you have chosen. (See Figure 3-2 for an accompaniment schedule.) It will be helpful for you to consult your librarian for the most current information on this important issue.

# 4

# Scene Design

A primitive ritual requires a dancer and a circle of earth; a sophisticated dance requires a dancer and a circle of floor. Why bother to provide anything else? For most of its history dance has existed without scenery or special lighting, and there is no reason why it cannot continue to flourish so. Yet, in response to a desire felt by both artists and audience, the decorated background appeared, sometimes in such splendor that it overwhelmed the dancers.

Design represents an attitude toward creative material. It provides answers to two basic questions: What does the audience see? What does the choreographer or designer want the audience to see? These are two separate questions; all too often the answer to the first does not correspond to that of the second. Suppose that you have planned a quiet, nostalgic solo—perhaps a single girl winds slowly across the stage to the accompaniment of a Debussy quartet. But the lights burn brightly and the cyclorama glares as white as a desert sky at noon. What happens? The dance and dancer remain the same, as does the music; but the evocation of quiet nostalgia vanishes from the stage. The choreographer visualized one effect; the audience saw another. What went wrong? The choreographer forgot that dance is more than movement; it is a picture seen on a stage. Design provides the right picture.

Design begins with the choreographic idea, continues through a formulation of the means to express that idea, and ends in a program to convert the idea into physical representation. The choreographer controls the first aspect of the process and can determine the second and third, as needed; if he avoids this commitment, as all too many do, then the designer makes an arbitrary choice right or wrong. When the choreographer is also the designer the decisions are still there to be made, preferably long before dress rehearsal slips into its unyielding spot on the schedule.

## THE CHOREOGRAPHIC IDEA

The beginning designer should concentrate on the more practical aspects of the task before him, since the theory of design can become confusing and the philosophy of dance rather esoteric. However, both are interesting and of concern to the dedicated designer, and sometimes both are determining factors in the production, although the results are more apparent to an occasional critic than to the general audience.

Stripped of subtlety and variation the theatrical purpose of choreography is generally one of six:
(1.) To display movement

(2.) To tell a story
(3.) To create a mood
(4.) To convey a message
(5.) To overwhelm an audience through spectacle
(6.) To formulate a movement experience

Each category is broad and often overlaps another, and the design for each may be simple or complex, of any style from baroque to pop-art; but from one of the six springs the design concept, the beginning of the answer to the question: What does the audience see on the stage?

## Displaying Movement

The dance teacher demonstrates the fundamentals of classic ballet; the folk group romps through a reel; the bright-eyed soloist flashes along in a vaudeville tap routine; youngsters imitate painted Indians; a disciplined quartet forms abstract patterns. These are all dances whose primary purpose is to display movement. Often they form the core of the program, and often they lack visual interest.

It is simple enough to place the soloists or groups on the stage, turn on the lights, and expect the movement to carry the dancers along to success. But then you begin to wonder if those dancers would look best against a black background or a red one, or perhaps a blue cyclorama or a painted backdrop. And are the lights bright or dim? Should the soloist be bathed in the golden glow of a follow spot? Is the amount of stage space used spacious or confining?

If your imagination is working as well as it should be, the act of presenting an interesting picture begins to involve more than dancer and movement. You may even begin to think about adding a potted palm and a vaudeville signboard for the tap dancer, or a series of pictures projected on the back wall for the demonstration of classic techniques. A fiddler and a caller might be just the thing for the folk dancers, a teepee for the little Indians, or shafts of crystal plastic dangling overhead for the abstract group, along with a platform placed in the center of the stage to force a disruption of movement. Or you may decide, for budgetary or aesthetic reasons, that a neutral background is adequate. At least think about the possibilities.

## Telling a Story

The story-telling ballet requires some kind of scenic assistance to set the place of the story and to establish the general atmosphere. Giselle without her graveyard is an odd girl flitting around for no particular reason; the Sylphides deprived of their misty forest and moonlight are just girls involved in a vaudeville routine. The audience wants to know where these people are. Even

57

in a low-budget production they deserve more than a mere program listing of "graveyard" or "forest glade bathed in moonlight."

In the old days theaters provided stock sets, which were a collection of drops and flats suitable for almost any play to come along the circuit. When the script called for "prison" or "millionaire's mansion" the stage carpenter pulled out the required numbers and that was it. Later, when writers and designers wanted their settings to reveal character or to illustrate psychological factors, stock sets lost much of their usefulness. Yet they still appear. Some choreographers, if they think about scenery at all, will ask for a "fairy-tale castle" or a "river-bank," without bothering to specify whether it is a Disney castle or a Piranesi castle, a Rembrandt river bank or one photographed by the county flood-control engineer. A story-telling ballet usually requires some kind of differentiation of place.

## Creating a Mood

The primary intent of any art form is the evocation of emotional response. Story-telling accomplishes one kind of response, direct explanation another, and abstraction yet another. A more subtle response than any of these, and more individual, arises from a confrontation with a theatrical statement of atmosphere. One person sits enthralled, caught up in secret thoughts of his own, as two dancers bound together by silken streamers slowly wind toward a softly swaying fall of white chiffon; another stirs restlessly and mutters about all the foolishness. One spectator blends his experience and dreams into the half-lighted world of Arthurian legend; another rattles his program and wonders when the scrim will lift and the fog dissipate so that he can see the pretty girl better.

Mood is a tricky thing in the theater, but it is often an indispensable companion of dance. Oberon and Titania floating through their midsummer forest exist in moonlight and mystery; the killing and terror of *The Miraculous Mandarin* are not events of clean streets and daylight; the torment of the man falling from Heaven into Hell is no normal newspaper picture; the old woman dreaming of the sunlit past lives the nearly forgotten days of childhood in dreamlike filtered sunshine. Give the devil-driven man a stage filled with the old lady's soft sunshine and the dance takes on a different meaning, or perhaps no meaning at all.

The audience is always willing to help create the illusion. Their minds complete the suggestion offered on the stage. If the suggestion is adequate—and it may be little more than a swirl of fog or a shaft of brilliant red light—the audience accepts a meaning in terms of its own experience. The problem arises when the audience's version of the meaning conveyed does not correspond to that desired by the choreographer. The choreographer and designer can only offer their version of what constitutes the clues to the supposed atmosphere. The clues are often clichés: the shadowed horror castle, the old-fashioned front porch with its swing and Kate Greenaway frocks, the symbolic giant, the beating heart, the strange spires and rocks, the desert sunset. Clichés are useful because they offer a shortcut to understanding; only the stubborn refuse them.

A collection of pictures cut from magazines or the memories of movies and television provides a source of atmospheric ideas. Some of them are easily converted to theatrical conditions for your dance.

## Conveying a Message

There are always a few people who wish to convey messages through dance. The best way to do this is to display a sign that proclaims that message for all to understand. That is not as bald a statement as it might sound. After all, a theory of design has grown around the writings and practice of Bertolt Brecht, whose concept of the play as a teaching device has influenced a considerable part of modern theater. He advocated the use of lettered signs, perhaps because he realized that even though he could rely on actors to make long and repeated references to the message, the audience preferred to follow the story and neglect the propaganda.

If you want to show youth in revolt, or evil in the ghetto, or declining public morality, or whatever is of current interest, you can provide some of the meaning in the dance, and perhaps even more in a printed program. The scenery can help, but probably not as much as a good title and a short description blackening the pages of the program.

And remember—only one message per dance, and make it clear through title, choreography, and background.

## Overwhelming an Audience through Spectacle

Back in the first decades of this century artists proclaimed that the only purpose of the theatrical experience was an intoxication of the senses. Sight and sound were supposed to be combined in such a way that no individual could resist the magic of the theatrical producer. The Dadaists and Surrealists sought to impose that idea on their audiences. Presently the rock and roll concerts attempt to do the same: assault the senses, submerge the intellect, release primitive emotions so long hidden in the mind, discover for a brief time the true self buried behind the facade of civilization, live again the primal urges of mankind before huts displaced caves. Or so go some of the theories. And if you are interested in theories, along with a fine collection of tips for theatrical production, read Antonin Artaud, the madman of the avant-garde. Read the descriptions of the Dada and Surrealist oddities of the nineteen tens and twenties and the reviews of pop-art happenings. Study rock concerts, with all their loudness and psychedelic lighting; see underground movies. These are all reminders that theatrical production does not have to be routine and sedate.

If you intend to overwhelm an audience with noise, light, and movement the idea has to come at the very first stage of choreography, because the design is part of the dance and the dance is part of the design. They cannot be separated. In this sort of thing imagination is the king, boldness the queen, and all the forces that the theater can muster are the army. But remember one point—many audiences will not accept such an assault on their senses, especially if they have assembled to watch the children float through the garden with Peter Pan. However, there are times when you might try it.

### Forming a Movement Experience

If the movement sequence exists for its own sake—for the pure kinetic experience—then all scene design must serve to enhance the movement, relate to shapes and spaces and either complement or contrast with the event. As in no other category, here the designer must be particularly aware of dynamic and spatial aspects of the dance. Whether the resulting design intrudes upon the dancer's space as, for example, with three-dimensional forms within the space of the performance area, or extends out from the dancer, with projections from his body, it is closely woven within the dancer's action.

### THE DESIGN APPROACH

After the controlling idea of the dance has been established the problem becomes that of devising a visual accompaniment. Again the basic question is asked: What is the audience supposed to see?

Before the designer begins to draw pretty pictures there are more decisions to be made.

Assuming that some kind of setting is necessary the designer chooses a general category as the basis for beginning work. Simplifying the choices of approach results in a list of five general ways of considering the design:

(1.) Neutral background
(2.) Decorative scenery
(3.) Descriptive scenery
(4.) Atmospheric scenery
(5.) Active background

### Neutral Background

No particular features of pattern or shape distract the eye from its focus on the dancers. The soft black glow of velvet curtains surrounds the dancers, isolating them from time and space; the audience's imagination ranges, seeing hat it will, either the dancers themselves or the place of a private dream.

In practice, the neutral background, especially that provided by a set of black velvet drapes, is the most useful single setting available to the choreographer, providing at once an uncluttered background free of unwanted connotations and a relatively easy way out of the entire design problem. The variations that can be worked on a drape set increase the effectiveness of curtains so much that what is sometimes considered a simple, makeshift substitute for scenery can provide an excellent setting for an entire dance program. If the choreographer is caught in that all too familiar trap of the one-person production then some kind of generalized background may become a necessity. On the other hand, using this kind of background may just be a substitute for imagination and work.

Still neutral, though more insistent in its forward thrust, is the cyclorama, that theatrical version of the sky. Color here is a necessity, since otherwise the cyc will look like the big white sheet that it is. Daylight blue is not a requirement. Think of the difference between a vast expanse of yellow and one of red, or the faint glow of a pearly pink dawn and the flat statement of midday blue. A soloist can survive a cyc if the color is muted or if the dancer is seen in silhouette, but it is probably wiser to save the cyc for a group dance. If the cyc cannot be stretched tight enough to remove the wrinkles, then you may be better off to forget it. Wrinkles are very distracting.

In addition to the black-drape set and cyclorama there are other combinations of bare, uncluttered walls, such as might be found in a studio, and drape sets of other colors, which might be found in the theater or could be sewn together by the dancers in their odd moments of freedom. Although a gymnasium or cafeteria wall is sometimes the only available background, a little surface cover can easily be arranged to set off the dancers from the plebian surroundings. To help in keeping attention focused on the performance, use black, since other colors will eventually clash with costumes and will remind the audience of the presence of that colored cloth after more than one dance has been presented. Dark grays, blues, greens, and browns can be used, but black is always safe. Velour is the first choice; it is sturdy and its soft finish does not reflect light. Velvet and velveteen come next. Duvetyn is cheap and often adequate.

Then there are always screens. A few folding screens of fair size should be in the scenic stock of any studio. Material can be draped over them, a miscellany of things pinned to them, and when covered with black or neutral material they can solve some of the problems of blocking off exits or steam pipes or work tables.

For many reasons a background of black drapes will be the first choice for many productions; a cyclorama may be next, if it can be properly stretched and lighted; and screens may offer a satisfactory alternative. Add a little color from the lights, a little variety in arrangement or draping, and many of the design problems are easily solved.

But do you like the idea of a neutral background for your dance?

Decorative Scenery

Decorative scenery is just what the name implies. It makes no pretense to being much more than a picture to look at. Sometimes it may bear a resem blance to the suggested place or atmosphere of the dance and then may b compared to the stock sets so often seen on television variety shows—th garden, the beach, the ranch house. The line between decoration and state ment of location can become blurred. As with all scenery there is no singl form to characterize it. There may be painted drops, a few strips of flowing china silk, a light pattern projected on the cyc, a mobile twisting in the air, few ribbons wound across the stage. Its purpose is to provide a little color an visual interest, and occasionally to inspire the spectator's imagination.

If you have the time and talent you can paint a backdrop rivalling any o the extravaganzas displayed by the Ballet Russe in its days of glory. After all those spectaculars were merely painted canvas hung from battens, and there i no reason why you cannot have something similar, if you choose. A decora tive drop may be just what is needed when the dancehall girls perform in th Tombstone saloon. Vaudeville acts please the customers in front of an adver tising curtain, Hawaiians sway along before the garish palm tree and blu ocean, and the Diaghileff ballet comes to the stage again wrapped in a Baks flourish of color.

Flowing silks and ribbons are quite interesting when dancers move around and through them. Seldom do they convey a meaning of their own although they can suggest one, but they look nice, either above the stage or ir the path of the action.

If you are lucky enough to find a crystal chandelier or a Tiffany lamp you can make that standard black-drape set sparkle. Hang a mobile and watch the reflections and shadows play across the dancers. Fly that comic cardboard airplane or swing that glittering harvest moon. There are so many decorative ideas waiting to be used.

Pure decoration can be overwhelming in its impact. If you look through some of the ballet designs of the early twentieth-century you may wonder if the audience ever saw the dancer against the clutter of the background. Contemporary dance production is usually simpler, but there is no reason to be too simple.

Descriptive Scenery

To make sense to an audience, which sees the story but hears no words, a dance may need a background establishing the place of the action. Although a program title listing *Swan Lake* may serve to indicate that the cyclorama is supposed to represent that fabled lake in the haunted wood, the audience will be happier if they can see something vaguely resembling water and trees. So i you plan a story-telling ballet you should think about a story-telling back ground, whether you obtain one or not. The usual solution is a painted drop, ometimes with side wings added, or a few cutout pieces of scenery, or pictures projected on the cyc or on a screen.

Even without having a story to tell, the choreographer may wish to set the scene in a specific place. The story of a backstage rehearsal can use the actual stage stripped of its concealing drapes; poles and the edge of a cardboard house become a corral for the dramatic piece about a sundown gun duel; a chandelier and a couple of columns transform the stage into a ballroom.

## Atmospheric Scenery

Atmosphere is a very indefinite term. Theatrical usage generally confines the meaning to a suggestion of mystery or nostalgia, to the unusual or highly dramatic. The setting usually ends up as a kind of misty hint of an ancient castle where doomed lovers wander through dark corridors, or as a threatening foreboding of evil in a vampire-haunted crypt, or as a smoke-filled gambling den on the China coast. Even if you can never explain atmosphere, you know what is means, and you can vaguely visualize all that mist and gloom. Gauze, a fog machine, and judicious lighting can do wonders.

## Active Background

The mad scientist's laboratory bubbles and flashes, a volcano flames, a computer grinds out yards of paper, giant chess figures crush the villain, a tower crumbles to the ground, birds fly at the audience, unknown things spin crazily. What does all this have to do with dance? The answer may be: absolutely nothing. Again, it might be an interesting production idea.

The main problem with any kind of unusual production technique is the unpredictable response of the audience, which sometimes rewards all this display of splendid anarchy with laughter or, in extreme cases of displeasure, a noisy departure from the theater. The trick is to start early in the season with a few sample effects to prepare an audience for the unusual and then to spring the full spectacle for the year's finale. Unless you are very brave, or foolhardy, or just determined, don't toss this kind of thing into the middle of a Tchaikovsky festival.

The idea of an active background is not as radical as you might think. Some of the early religious festivals were in temples where statues of gods spoke and moved and sometimes claimed their human sacrifices. Renaissance ballets featured chariots flying across the sky and mountains opening to reveal magic caves. English pantomime prided itself on the transformation scenes in which a forest might whirl into a fairy-tale city. The Dadaists confused audiences with a little bit of everything, including semistaged riots. Pop-art people thought up "happenings." Protestors of today attempt to fuse performer, production, and audience into a single entity.

Certainly there is a difference between the single appearance of a theatr cal machine such as a Renaissance cloud and the mass confusion of a sem organized "happening" in which the gimmicks of production overwhelm th dance movement, but there is a place for both, if the choreographer ca justify any kind of scenery that does something more than stand patientl behind the dancers.

It could be worth a passing thought. Start thinking early though, fo dance and production are inseparable.

DESIGN PROCEDURES

Now the work begins (see Figure 4-1). Some people draw pictures, some pla with ground plans, some try to tell a puzzled builder what they want. Pei sonal preference dictates the method. One way to create a design is perhaps a good as another, especially if you are not primarily a designer.

Figure 4-1     Scenery-Set Schedule

Check all available materials and facilities . . . . . . . . . . . . . (4-3 months)

Preliminary meeting with director and choreographer . . . . . . . (6-4 months)

Anticipate construction needs, loans, rentals  . . . . . . . . . . . (4-3 months)

Complete drawings and designs  . . . . . . . . . . . . . . . . . (4-2 months)

Attend as many dancers' rehearsals as possible  . . . . . . . . . (4-2 months)

Begin construction  . . . . . . . . . . . . . . . . . . . . . . . (3-2 months)

Deliver sets, props to rehearsal area  . . . . . . . . . . . . . . . (8-4 weeks)

All scenery, sets, props ready for performance area . . . . . . . . (5-4 weeks)

Attend rehearsals to see dancers and sets interacting  . . . . . . . (8-4 weeks)

Attend all final rehearsals to check

Begin with a description of the intended visual effect. Then write dow on paper what elements the stage picture should contain to bring about thi visual effect. This includes possible backgrounds, scenic units, curtains, an cycs—anything that may appear on the stage. If you have decided on a chore ographic idea and the kind of design that fits the presentation then most o the imagining has already been done. Now is the time to collect and refine th products of imagination.

Next, draw the ground plan, which is nothing more than a drawing o everything that touches the floor or hangs above it. At the outset you wil make rough sketches of several plans, deciding on the best position for plat forms and screens. The final plan will be measured to scale or provided with written measurements to fit the stage. Of course, if you intend to use onl black legs and curtains or the open stage backed by the cyc, the ground pla is a simple affair.

Then come sketches of what the scenery may look like. Often these will
be rather vague, little more than doodling, until the right one comes along. If
you are artistic and want to do the work, you can paint an illustration of the
setting as it will appear, or even make a model. If you are a choreographer
trying to finish a dance on schedule then forget the art work, because these
nice paintings are really done to impress producers or directors. The time
needed to draw and paint such a display piece can usually be spent in more
valuable ways. But the designer, if someone other than the choreographer,
should go all the way.

Finally, assuming that somebody else will build and paint the scenery,
the designer provides *elevations*, which are clear drawings giving information
about sizes, special construction, and painting. Avoid them if you don't need
them.

So, with numerous picture books nearby to provide suggestions for scenery, you are ready to become a designer. For the moment forget about crew,
technical difficulty, program order, and budget, expect for the obvious limita-
tion of million-dollar scenery on a ten-dollar budget. Allow your imagination
and pencil to roam; the adjustment with reality comes later.

## Some Sample Productions

The following examples are generalized versions of what a designer might
provide for the choreographer's approval and then, with a few additions, to a
technical crew.

1. *An abstract dance in a neutral background of blacks*

*Title:* Variations on a Theme

*Type:* Abstract ballet for six dancers

*Music:* Arensky, "Variations on a Theme of Tchaikovsky"

*Description:* Six dancers dressed in red and white perform a classic abstraction on a bright stage. The background is black legs and a black traveller.
There are no changes in lighting or setup.

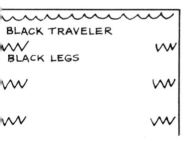

Ground Plan

The purpose of the ground plan
in this instance is to provide a guide
for the stage manager and the light
crew. The stage manager needs a reminder of what curtains are to be
dropped in place, and the light crew
wants to know if the curtains are open
or closed. Since the arrangement of
the blacks will be standard, measurements may be omitted.

2. *A solo against the cyclorama*
*Title: The Girl with the Flaxen Hair*
*Type:* A quiet solo
*Music:* Debussy, "The Girl with the Flaxen Hair"
*Description:* A man plays the Debussy piece on a piano near downstage left. A dim light surrounds him. After a few bars of music the cyc begins to glow soft pink. Outlined against the cyc is a girl slowly moving in quiet circles. As the stage lights brighten somewhat we see a young girl, blonde, and dressed in an 1890 spring frock. The mood is quiet, dreamlike, as though the girl is a memory faintly recalled by the pianist. During the last measures of the music the stage lights fade and the girl returns to the place near the cyc where we first saw her. The cyc light fades and only the pianist can be seen. A few seconds after the music ends all stage lights dim out.

## Ground Plan

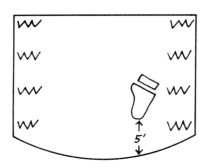

Notice the size and placement of the piano. A piano takes more room than people think, so measure. Since the placement is seldom critical the position can be adjusted later.

Sketches may be forgotten, except for a nice presentation. The cyc color will be determined after experimentation with gelatin colors.

3. *A lecture-demonstration using decorative projections*
Projected scenery is not as complicated as often supposed. For dance production many of the objections are not applicable anyway, so go ahead with the slide projector or the overhead classroom projector. Photograph a painting you like to make a slide or pour analine dye onto a square of celluloid and allow it to dry to make a plate for the overhead projector. Sometimes a shadow will appear on the cyc or a pattern on the dancer. If it really matters, change the position of projector or dancer, or forget the whole idea. For lecture-demonstrations the technique is useful enough to make the attempt.

An explanation of the creation and use of projections can wait until a later chapter on the practical work of scenery. For now it is enough to realize that the theater wall or a studio screen offers an excellent opportunity for a dramatic slide show or even movies.
*Title: Lecture-demonstration*
*Music:* Miscellaneous

*Description:* The commentator stands downstage left, just behind the main curtain. The curtain opens and the light dims up on the lectern. The lecturer introduces the program and then comments on the first dance. On her cue, the lectern light dims, the first projection dims up on the cyc, and the dance lights dim up. When the dance ends the lights dim, the projection fades, and the lectern light comes up again for the next introduction. The entire series of dances is done in the same way.

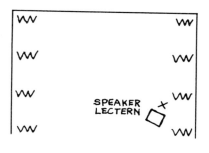

Ground Plan

Dance 1. *Medieval.* Four minutes. Music: from *Play of Daniel.* Six dancers in a cathedral in a dramatic pantomime. Projection: Jan Van Eyck "The Virgin and the Canon Van Der Peale." (Robert Genaille: *From Van Eyck to Brueghel,* p. 29.) 35 mm. slide. (Note that the source of the picture to be projected is given so that whoever prepares the slide will not have to search the files. Possibly a sketch of the picture may be provided, or even a photographic copy.)

Dance 2. *Seventeenth Century French Court Ballet.* Six minutes. Music: Lully or Couperin, not decided yet. Eleven dancers in a re-creation of a ballet presented to the courtiers of Louis XIV. Projection: "Ballet Design." (Drama Department Scenery File, picture 17-F-24.) 35 mm. slide.

Dance 3. *Patterns.* Four minutes. Music: Original electronic. Contemporary dance, very fast, with strong movements. Projection: Ransburg advertisement, *Fortune,* October 1968, p. 239. 35 mm. slide.

Dance 4. *Astrology* (an excerpt). Five minutes. Music: Lambert, "Horoscope." A short excerpt from a longer ballet. This section represents the two sides of Gemini, the quiet and the bold. Projection: choreographer's original, 8-by-10 dye painting on acetate for the overhead projector.

Dance 5. *Lolo and Bobo, the Go-Go Dancers.* Four minutes. Music: Excerpts from various Beatles records. A comedy presentation of rock and roll exhibition dancing, all very lively and noisy in a semipsychedelic atmosphere. Projections: a small-scale light show using 35 mm. slide projectors and overhead projectors, as well as a 16 mm. motion picture projector. The slides are to be supplied by the choreographer. The color patterns used in the overhead projectors will be created by the dance instructor with the help of a former student. The 16 mm. film is a compilation of odds and ends from the cinema department, comprising pieces from old Laurel and Hardy movies and lengths of whatever is handily spliced together. Projections are shown on the cyc and on the dancers.

(For this one presentation three kinds of projectors are used: a 35 mm. slide projector, an overhead classroom projector, and a 16 mm. motion picture projector. Pictures come from a variety of sources: art books, a school department file, a magazine advertisement, an original painting on acetate or glass, studio-created psychedelia, and short lengths of motion picture film. For a few dollars the designer can present an exciting and visually interesting production. It is worth trying.)

4. *A folk dance in a decorative setting*

The fourth piece of choreography in the program might be an American folk dance. Suppose the choreographer decides to complicate the scenery just a little bit.

Before deciding on the ground plan and stage picture you will consider several alternatives. The dance will be an adaptation of traditional dances from the Tennessee mountains. What does that bring to mind?

Perhaps you visualize the entire stage filled by a lively group of costumed mountain people. Behind them, a view of the mountains. Or maybe a giant sampler. So you sketch possible backdrops.

Mountains                                    Giant Sampler

For some reason you discard these ideas. Draped gingham combined with props could be a better choice, or possibly patriotic bunting hung above the stage.

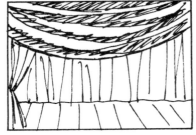

Draped Gingham                                   Bunting

Perhaps you can round up a real fiddler and banjo player. What can you do with them? Why not turn the set into a kind of mountaineer's barn? The musicians play for the dance. The people gather around. That means a platform or the musicians cannot be seen. A bare platform? Decorated, of course. Why not use both the platform and its banner and a painted backdrop? The

Sketch 1

Sketch 2

scenery budget may allow for the expense. But the director says, "Money is short." Which is more important—the backdrop or the platform? The platform wins, and besides there should already be one in the studio that can be draped with some costume material, and a banner behind it needs only about a dollar's worth of muslin. Against the back wall, just to break the emptiness, you can add a cardboard cutout of a fence and a big Indian-summer moon.

Now that you have decided on the platform and its decorations, and that hanging moon and a cardboard haystack, where do they all go? The ground plan specifies the position.

Should the platform be in the center? Or would the side be better? Since the music is accompaniment to the dance, the side position is probably better.

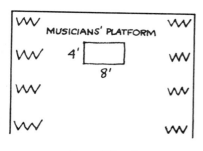

Ground Plan 1

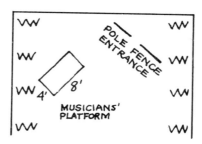

Ground Plan 2

Now the decisions have been made, and everything is gathered into the presentation.

*Title:* Smoky Mountain Jubilee

*Music:* Traditional mountain fiddle tunes, played by fiddler and banjoist.

*Description:* A crowd of gaily costumed mountain people gather in a barn for a grand Saturday-night dance. The fiddler and banjo player are on the platform all ready to go. One of the mountain men steps up onto the platform, raises his arms, and announces: "Let her go!" The fiddler and banjo player strike up the music. The crowd rushes into the dance. Contesting couples and fours spin around the floor, urged on by their friends. After the winners are chosen everybody gathers for a grand fast round.

Bunting is draped across the front and sides of the platform. On a banner strung behind the platform the words SMOKY MOUNTAIN JUBILEE are spelled in red block letters. The cardboard moon and stars hang in front of a dark blue cyc. A cardboard cutout of a haystack provides a piece of background.

Ground Plan            Sketch

### Ground Plan

Be sure to measure the platform size. It should be some standard size, if possible, or whatever is already available. If back legs are used to mask the wings remember to include them in the ground plan; they cut the amount of stage space.

### Sketch

Using pastels, watercolor, or whatever is easiest, the designer should try the colors he thinks would look best. It is easier to change now than it will be after the scenery is painted.

### Elevations

The final part of the design presentation includes the *elevations.* These are flat drawings of anything to be built or painted. Ordinarily they are drawn to scale; most commonly, 1/4-inch or 1/2-inch equals one foot. If the construction is simple, or if the designer prefers, measurements may be given instead of drawn to scale.

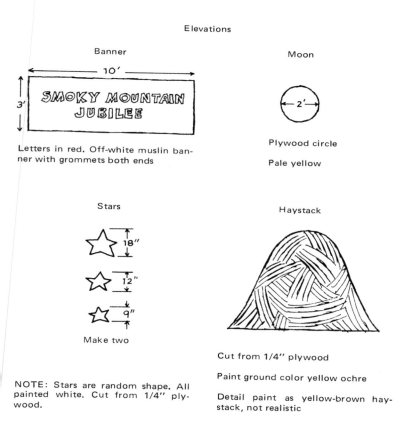

Elevations

Banner

10′

3′

SMOKY MOUNTAIN JUBILEE

Letters in red. Off-white muslin banner with grommets both ends

Moon

2′

Plywood circle

Pale yellow

Stars

18″

12″

9″

Make two

NOTE: Stars are random shape. All painted white. Cut from 1/4″ plywood.

Haystack

Cut from 1/4″ plywood

Paint ground color yellow ochre

Detail paint as yellow-brown haystack, not realistic

5. *An Indian ceremonial in a descriptive setting*

The choreographer visualizes the dance of a medicine man in a moonlit Indian camp. Drummers sit around a fire; the medicine man performs a ceremony to cure the chief's malady. The choreographer wants a fire and some kind of representation of an Indian camp.

*Title: Indian Medicine Dance*

*Music:* Indian music and chants

*Description:* Moonlight glows on the Montana plains camp of the Indians. Drummers sit around the fire, slowly drumming a ceremonial call to the spirit of healing. In a teepee the medicine man waits. The cry of a nightbird is

71

heard. The medicine man leaves the teepee and the dance begins. Others join him. At the climax a masked figure rushes from the teepee. The dance ends.

Required are a teepee of actual or near-actual size, a fire, and scenic units representing the Montana plains.

Sketch 1

Sketch 2

The tent upstage center

Fire (China-silk and fan) surrounded by rocks.

Mountain projection.

Teepee UL

Fire DR

Projected mountains—ground row

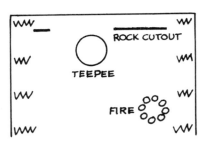

Ground Plan 1

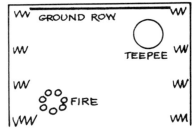

Ground Plan 2

The teepee and the fire need a definite amount of space. The second plan will be chosen because of its balance.


## DESIGN COMPROMISE

Unfortunately, design ideas meet theatrical reality. The question is always: How much compromise? The answer is: As much as necessary, but only after

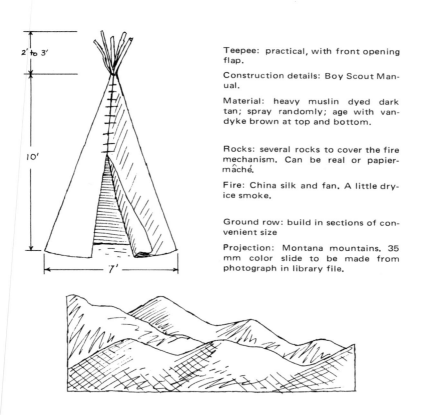

Teepee: practical, with front opening flap.

Construction details: Boy Scout Manual.

Material: heavy muslin dyed dark tan; spray randomly; age with vandyke brown at top and bottom.

Rocks: several rocks to cover the fire mechanism. Can be real or papier-mâché.

Fire: China silk and fan. A little dry-ice smoke.

Ground row: build in sections of convenient size

Projection: Montana mountains. 35 mm color slide to be made from photograph in library file.

trying to bring the original concept to the stage. If the budget is five dollars, the designer offers a five-dollar production, however much that may conflict with his ideas. But five dollars can buy a lot of ribbon and some interesting gels for the lights, even if it cannot pay for platforms and merry-go-rounds. The design problem requires a combination of artistry and improvisation and business management. It is no more frustrating than choreographing a classic ballet with a collection of beginners, stray athletes, and girls who can practice only one hour a week.

Think a lot, try hard, and you can do the job.

# 5

# Costumes

A whole book could be devoted to the design and construction of dance costumes; our goal in this chapter is to help the choreographer answer the question: How do you choose a dance costume? And, as with every other phase of production, there are many answers, each reflecting the imagination, experience, and concern of the one who makes the decisions. A few suggestions for make-up are offered at the end of the chapter.

The process of designing, choosing fabric, fitting, and constructing—all links between the idea and the costume—will be successful only if there is a sensitive and skilled blending of all these elements. Sometimes the process is accomplished by one person; sometimes many are involved. Unfortunately, it is often the dance teacher who is also the choreographer, the performer, the designer, and the seamstress. A formidable task! Maybe it is for this reason that so many dancers seem satisfied with simple leotard and tights.

Each costume is a fresh solution to some different problem. If sparse or simple costume is used by design, then it is logical; but if it is used simply because no one had the time or inclination to bother with anything else, then it is illogical. Whoever designs the costume must select the line, form, shape, color, texture, and pattern. Then he, or someone he delegates, must search out the fabric, measure the dancers, fit the material, and cut, sew, and make adjustments in the garment. The idea must be transformed into a wearable costume.

## PREPLANNING

As with every other part of the production process, a plan is necessary. Time, effort, and money can be saved, unnecessary pressures relieved, and rehearsal time in costume assured if advance preparation and organization of details is done carefully. Responsibilities must be delegated and a schedule set up.

Assemble all of the available production facts.

For example, you need to know:

> Program content, production date, time of technical and dress rehearsals, availability of technical assistance, facilities to be used.
>
> Names of choreographers, with a schedule of all rehearsals. Time scheduled for meeting with choreographers.
>
> Names of dancers, with time scheduled for careful measurements
>
> Current rehearsal schedule, to observe dance and conduct fittings for each dancer.
>
> Names of all assistants with times they are available for specialized work.

While much work can be delegated, it is not until the costumes are designed and the patterns are ready that intensive labor begins. If assistants are resourceful and dependable they can be helpful in many ways—searching out and purchasing fabric, preshrinking and dyeing, cutting and sewing, and making final adjustments. With reliable help the designer need only prepare and duplicate very specific directions and a copy of the original costume sketch. It is strongly recommended that only one person do the measuring and fitting—and preferably this person will have experience and skill.

A responsible wardrobe crew can be a great help. Their responsibilities will include: making sure that the costumes get to the correct dressing rooms for preliminary viewing and for technical and dress rehearsals, as well as for the performance; checking costumes in and out; laundering, repairing, and pressing; being ready for emergencies during performance; assisting dancers to dress; planning and discussing all costume changes *prior* to technical rehearsal; and, very important, taking notes of costume difficulties apparent at any rehearsal.

Give yourself a chance with your production. Slow down, think about what needs to be done, and who will do it. Make some decisions about when the process starts, how it progresses, and when it should be finished. Make some schedules and post reminders. An eye-catching bulletin board with notices of major *current* issues will help. It is never too soon to start this kind of planning.

Figure 5-1 is an example of a schedule for the costume designer.

**Figure 5-1    Costume Schedule**

Attend rehearsals to see movement themes and anticipate
    needs of dancers as well as discover design of the dance   . . . (6-2 months)

Check available costumes and materials. Investigate loans
    and rentals . . . . . . . . . . . . . . . . . . . . . . . . . . . . . (6-2 months)

Preliminary discussion of the dance with the choreographer;
    begin recording design possibilities . . . . . . . . . . . . . (6-2 months)

Complete measurement chart for each dancer . . . . . . . . . . . (5-2 months)

Submit preliminary costume designs, sketches; discuss
    with the choreographer and business manager . . . . . . . (5-2 months)

Submit final costume design . . . . . . . . . . . . . . . . . . . . (4-2 months)

Procure or develop pattern, adapt to varying sizes.
    Estimate yardage; prepare fabric by preshrinking,
    dyeing, or special treatment . . . . . . . . . . . . . . . . (3-2 months)

Cut fabric, delegate sewing . . . . . . . . . . . . . . . . . . . (3-2 months)

Dress parade and final fittings . . . . . . . . . . . . . . . . . . (2 months)

Complete accessory make-up plans . . . . . . . . . . . . . . . . (2-1 month)

Costumes ready for rehearsal . . . . . . . . . . . . . . . . . . . (2-1 month)

Select wardrobe crew and check out procedure . . . . . . . . . . (1 month)

Solve costume problems at all remaining rehearsals

## PURPOSE OF THE COSTUME

The dance costume, like other clothing, is more than a covering for the body (a dancer hardly needs it to keep warm, though it may be a protection in falls or body rolls). Essentially, the costume makes up a part of the dancer's most intimate environment. It may enhance or disguise body conformation, it may emphasize something of the static or dynamic posture, it may augment or contrast components of the movement pattern. It may be an obvious adjunct to the dance or it may be unobtrusive, unnoticed. With all of the elements of shape, line, color, quality, texture, and decoration, there are many effects to be achieved. While some of these may seem obvious it is usually the more imaginative, and sometimes even the accidental, that are most exciting. The successful dance costume has parallel values to good lighting, scenery, accompaniment, and staging. In addition, the costume directly affects the projection of the performer. It becomes a part of his person and helps to transform him from a dancer rehearsing in a practice place in practice clothes to a dancer performing in a theatrical setting.

## A WAY TO START

If you believe that the costume for a dance is characteristic of that one dance—that it is the way it is because the dance is the way it is—then you must do more than come up with a nice costume. The designer must capture the essence of the dance in order to design the costume that is inevitable for that dance.

And so it is important to see the dance—indeed, it is important to see the dance many times. It takes time and sensitivity to discover meaningful relationships between a dancer's movement and the garment he will wear. It is helpful to understand something of the choreographer's intent, something of the performer's problems, and anything else you can find to help identify the emphasis and tone of the piece. The designer must be willing to explore and experiment. It takes courage and imagination to come up with something fresh. It is easier to duplicate some costume that was all right last time, or to perpetuate some cliché. The designer must be imaginative and bold; the seamstress must be careful and follow directions.

### See the Dance

Look at the dance and let the first impact come from the whole action. Then as you see it again try to be aware of the movement design, the floor patterning, the moving and still shapes, the interaction of performers and space. Pick out two or three important things that you noticed happening to the space as possible motifs for decoration or pattern, such as dominant straight or curved lines for the silhouette of the costume.

Become sensitive to the dynamics of the dancers, the changes, the repetitions and variations in energy flow. Is the quality of the movement smooth, sharp, or variable? Does the action seem to hang in space or does it hurtle to the floor in a big splash? What about the intensity of the movement? Is it strong, fragile, or even dotted with changes in force? What are your chief reactions in terms of the over-all energy output and impact? What occurs to you in terms of fabric, line, color? Do you see the movement of the costume as contrasting the action of large body swings; do you favor a clinging knit or would multicolored layers of sheer fabric enhance the action?

What is the basic rhythm of the dance? Is it complicated and variable or is it regular and even monotonous? Is there a mounting syncopation or unexpected bursts of excitement? Does it progress at a slow and plodding rate or is it swift and anxious? Maybe there are changes in pace. Try to be aware of the uses of time—including the manipulations of *when* movement occurs. You may wish to try a regular and simply accented fabric design, or perhaps a huge geometric decoration to emphasize a complicated movement rhythm. The rhythm may call for a repeated line of identical dots or an irregular edging of shredded burlap moving with unexpected jabbing. Why not try something new?

Look at the dance again. Are there dominant figures or patterns? Is there solo or group action, or maybe both? Are there recurring and apparently important shapes and spaces? Do the relationships remain the same or is there an intermingling of both shape and space? Is there extraordinary focus on certain places or figures, even on certain parts of figures? Do some of the dancers seem to need a greater range of movement for their action? Do some movements blend or contrast markedly with others? Where are the dancers going? How do they get there? Does anything occur that you might use as a springboard for design?

Discover the important aspects of the space-energy-time complex. Make simple sketches of floor paths, space relationships, outstanding features of the observed dance design. Write down key phrases or words that occur to you when you see the dance. Sometimes these reactions will seem disconnected after several viewings but there is something valid about first responses. In any event, it is useful to have some record. Figure 5-2 is an example of the designer's preliminary reaction to a dance, including sketches of movement.

The designer's preliminary reaction to the dance will lead to preliminary statements about the costumes, such as the following: "In spite of the strong and frightening contrasts it is the primary spiral, in ever smaller curves, that is the vital statement. Let's try full-circle skirts with snap fasteners to hold in the fullness during the secondary theme; maybe a slipover tunic to restrain the sweeping line. Try a beige wrap-around bodice with a rust-spattered orange skirt. Use warm lights contrasting with blue-greens. Experiment with a heavy rayon crepe or even a lightweight drapery material for the skirt; wool jersey for the bodice; restraining tunic of large mesh fabric, like fishnet. May need a skirt lining at the bottom for weight and occasional color accent."

Figure 5-2    Designer's Preliminary Reaction

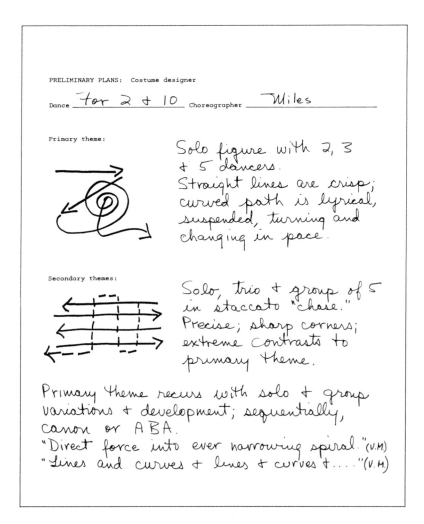

PRELIMINARY PLANS:  Costume designer

Dance ___for 2 + 10___ Choreographer ___Miles___

Primary theme:

Solo figure with 2, 3
+ 5 dancers.
Straight lines are crisp;
curved path is lyrical,
suspended, turning and
changing in pace.

Secondary themes:

Solo, trio + group of 5
in staccato "chase."
Precise; sharp corners;
extreme contrasts to
primary theme.

Primary theme recurs with solo + group
variations + development; sequentially,
canon or ABA.
"Direct force into ever narrowing spiral." (V.M.)
"Lines and curves + lines + curves +...." (V.H.)

Discuss the Choreographer's Intent

The designer should see the dance first and then talk with the choreographer,
for few choreographers can be really objective about their work. They tend to
find meanings and symbols within their dance that are not apparent to others.

If the designer has had an unbiased view he will be more likely to react to the dance and not to the choreographer.

The choreographer is the originator; he designed the action and is finally responsible for what the costume shall be. The designer must understand the mood, quality, and intent as the choreographer sees it. He must know what ideas of line, shape, texture, or color occurred during the choreography. Ask the choreographer to describe anything of special relevance. Have him pinpoint in a phrase or a word what the dance has to "say." The following is a sample of a choreographer's response:

Dance _____ Choreographer _____

Original intent:

The dance is to project two extremes of design, dynamics, mood, and dramatic implication.

The A theme presents a spiraling excitment on seeing all sides of something at the same time; in one word, "spinningness."

The B theme implies a kind of security in following a computerized map, with no chance of getting lost, or even of seeing anything beyond this perfectly logical pattern. *This* is the way!

Ideas during choreography:

From the beginning the straight lines and curves were a part of the explorations. Not until the dancers started turning did the spiral develop. Finally this narrowing funnel seemed symbolic of escape from the geometric repetition of the straight-line pattern.

I visualized the curving theme as costumed in hot and brilliant colors, the costume for the line patterns as cold, brittle, and inhuman. This will obviously have to be accomplished with lights because there is no time for costume change.

The shapes and spaces in the linear theme were almost duplicates of each other but later manipulation made it clear that such a mirroring was not necessary, the quality of the movement was sufficient as an almost overpowering statement of routine or sameness."

Unusual directive from the choreographer:

I am too close to this dance for any objective ideas on costuming. Why don't you try several things and let me see them. I would be interested in what a sensitive and unbiased observer will see.

Examine with the choreographer the tendency to allow preconceived ideas—favorite colors, draperies, or shapes—to affect supposedly objective opinions. While the final costume design is important and exciting to the designer, it is even more so to the choreographer. Here is a vital aid for projection of his ideas. He *must* be concerned with both planning and result, but it is hard for him to be objective.

## Experiment and Explore

One way to learn more about costuming dance is to become a consciously careful observer. Any costume can be examined for its shape, line, decoration, and over-all pattern. It is particularly important to see costumes and garments on dancers, to conjecture why certain things were done, and, more important, to visualize some things you would like to try. Sometimes when the designer does the movement of the dance himself, he better understands the performer's peculiar problems.

Whenever you see a dance costume, examine all facets of its design. What would happen if you changed that horizontal decoration into an expanding spiral? How would a splash of chartreuse accent that uninteresting orange drapery? What would result if those black tights and leotard were bleached and then spattered with three shades of green? How about ripping, slashing, unraveling, or shredding the fabric? Can we disguise that uninteresting leotard sleeve and neckline? We might even cover the dancer with plastic wrapping!

Duplicate outlined pictures of dance figures and get a soft pencil, an eraser, and sheets of tracing paper (see Figure 5-3). Superimpose the tracing paper over the predrawn model and sketch different shapes, lines, decorations, extensions, or additions as costume ideas. Fortunately you can erase mistakes or uninteresting solutions and start all over again. When you have found something interesting you can color with pencils or felt-tip pens. It is surprising how many exciting revelations emerge from such easy doodling.

## Recognize Your Limitations

Enthusiasm is wonderful but it is no substitute for experience and skill. The person who has never fitted a bodice will make mistakes. If he has never arranged a pattern on a narrow width of material, adapted a skirt size, dyed fabric, or used a sewing machine he will be inefficient and wasteful of material. But he may seek help from someone who knows how to do these things; he may read directions, ask questions, use common sense, and learn.

## ELEMENTS FOR MANIPULATION

The dance costume may enhance, disguise, change, or even extend the natural silhouette. It may augment the movement or serve as a direct contrast to it, limit the dancer or sometimes completely envelope him. Costume design may reiterate the shape, design, accent, space, or mood of the dance or it may have a subtle relationship that is not readily apparent.

## Appearance of the Costume

Since dance costumes are obviously to be worn by dancers they will bear

Figure 5-3    Dance Figures

Figure 5-3, continued

82

some resemblance to the dancer's body. But even so, the costume will have its own structural elements. Sometimes it is helpful to imagine the garment as standing erect, and then moving of its own power. When it later houses a dancer's body it will be just that much more dynamic.

There is the outer shape, the outline of the costume, with horizontal, vertical, diagonal, or curved accents of drapery, texture, or decoration of the material. The shape may be natural or distorted; human, animal, or neutral; realistic or abstract. It may be of a particular time and place or it may be an illusionary or surrealistic statement. The costume may be heavy and resistant to the dancer's action or it may float as a thing apart. The whole costume, or parts of it, may move in unexpected ways, simply because of the quality of the material.

The surface of the fabric may be changed by adding pattern, texture, or color—usually all three. This may be done with paint, dye, or bonding material. Whatever patterns are added should be large and distinct rather than the small and detailed ones since these are lost in a moving garment. The designs for decoration may be curved or linear, free-form or geometric, all-covering or carefully placed, symmetrical or asymmetrical, drab or colorful; they are more often simple than complex. Design resulting from applied color is perhaps the most exciting of all, but it needs most careful consideration.

Sometimes there is contrast between the dance action and the costume design. For example, a costume motif of large and small figure-eights might be interesting contrast for dancers moving in triangular shapes of interacting threes. A garment of stretch knit fabric with zigzag lines painted front and back might be covered with draped bits of chiffon hanging at irregular lengths from the shoulder and waist. Or, instead of contrast, there is emphasis: a curving action might be emphasized by full-circle skirts and swirling capes, a straight-line path with an A-line skirt topped with a boxed tunic.

There are many possible extensions or additions to the costume and to the dancer's form. There are even props that can be carried, dragged, or attached. These and many other ideas will occur to imaginative designers as they begin to explore the possibilities.

The Fabric

Material may emphasize the movement of the dancer or it may stiffly resist the action. It may jut out in perky angles of organdy, it may float like china-silk, or it may hang in deep folds of heavy rayon crepe. Any fabric that hangs free of the dancer's body will flow, but it is the more sheer and lightweight fabric that moves faster and easier. Anything that is weighted at the bottom (dressmaker's weights, chains, or cords) will move in more stately fashion. Heavy material usually hangs and moves well even when gathered close in one place and hanging free in another. The longer the costume, the heavier and more full it is, the more it will drape and hang in folds—and the more elegant its action when the dancer moves.

It might be interesting to try some of the following: Layer several widths of thick material together for heavy and massive effects; sheer fabric, even in layers, always seems delicate. The use of extremes from sheer to heavy-layered materials offers interesting contrasts. Try long, heavy, and flowing fabrics for sustained and unaccented action. For sharp and accented movement try shredded or hanging pieces; sometimes the stiff and angular fabrics with their own independent movement are worth considering.

The texture of materials ranges from dull and rough to hard and shiny; from a wide-open mesh net to a nonporous plastic finish. For most theatrical use, dull and rough surfaces are superior to hard and shiny surfaces, which reflect strongly under stage lights. But then, you may want this shimmering reflection. Exciting new synthetics are available, many of which are particularly suitable for costumes. Some of these are fragile, flammable, and difficult to work with; be sure that you understand all of the possible disadvantages.

Spatter or paint added to the surface of the fabric also changes its texture, as does layering, bonding, or adhering material, appliqué, or other such techniques. The illusion of dimension or uneven surface can also be attained by highlighting with shadow and color. Because a costume is under lights and moving, this is usually the most dramatic.

Remember that inexpensive materials are easily transformed by paint or dye. It is not the rare brocade that will appear more elegant under stage lights; rather it is the heavy canvas painted with rich colors that will surpass the real thing. Cotton flannel often looks like velvet and cotton crepe like an expensive silken cloth, when dyed or painted.

It is only when you begin to experiment and explore that you realize that stereotyped concepts of fabric texture and quality do not apply to imaginative costumes. It may be necessary to force yourself to try unusual or unlikely combinations. Try to discover what new fabrics are available. Be sure you look at inexpensive as well as expensive material. It is the drape, texture, and potential for color additive that is important.

Look in department stores, special fabric shops, and wholesale as well as retail yardage outlets. Theatrical costume houses will usually send samples on request. The following lists indicate something of the range of possibility:

*Heavy hanging and draping materials*

| | |
|---|---|
| Burlap | Monk's cloth |
| Canvas | Muslin |
| Corduroy | Plush |
| Crepe | Quilting |
| Drapery fabric | Sailcloth |
| Drill | Satin |
| Duvetyn | Terry cloth |
| Flannel | Velour |
| Moleskin | Velvet and velveteen |

*Lightweight and flowing materials*

| | |
|---|---|
| Challis | Gossamer |
| Chiffon | Lawn |
| China-silk | Ninon |
| Crepe | Nylon, sheer |
| Feathers | Pongee |
| Gauze | Ribbon |
| Georgette | Shredded fabric |

*Flexible and conforming materials*

| | |
|---|---|
| Elastic | Rubber bands |
| Elasticized fabric | Stretch nylon |
| Jersey | Tricot |

*Wide-mesh materials*

| | |
|---|---|
| Curtain material | Lace |
| Fish net | Marquisette |
| Hand knits, on | Mosquito netting |
| large needles | Penelope canvas |
| Hill-holder | Screening |
| Java canvas | Theatrical gauze |

*Stiff and angular materials*

| | | |
|---|---|---|
| Aluminum foil | Lamé | Papier-Mâché |
| Buckram | Leather | Plastic |
| Cans and cartons | Layered materials | Plastic utensils |
| Cardboard | Macaroni | Poker chips |
| Carpeting | Magnetic tape | Saran wrap |
| Cotton wadding | or film | Scouring pads |
| Chain | Metal | Sponge |
| Crash | Moire silk | Synthetic flowers, |
| Crepe paper | Mousseline | fruit |
| Crinoline | Nylon net | Taffeta |
| Denim | Oilcloth | Tarlatan |
| Dotted Swiss | Organdy | Tulle |
| Felt | Organza | Twill |
| Foam | Paper bags | Veiling |
| Hopsacking | Paper clips | Voile |
| Hoops | Paper plates | Wire |

*Transparent materials*

| | |
|---|---|
| Cellophane | Plastic bags, |
| Fine nettings | tarpaulins |

*Materials with lustrous texture*

| | |
|---|---|
| Calico | Glazed silk |
| Cambric | Metallic cloth |
| Chintz | Sateen |
| Coated fabric | Satin |
| Damask | Sharkskin |
| Fiberglas | Velvet |

## Color

Color should never be used simply because it is pretty but only as it has some relevance to the dance. While the work may have dramatic content, and you may be suceptible to time-honored implications of green for envy and white for purity, such directives are rigid and superficial. Depend rather upon the relationship of color to shapes, figures, designs, and spaces. Here intuition and experimentation must come into action.

Reds, yellows, and their related colors are called "warm" and are said to be soft, vibrant, advancing toward the perceiver. They usually make objects appear larger. Greens, blues, and their related colors are called "cool" and seem to recede back into themselves. They tend to decrease size. Most choreographers have immediate response to the implied warmness or coolness of their dance. This may be a clue.

Remember that any color will reflect its complement upon any other color that it contacts and such diffusion, especially with many colors, is apt to be disturbing. Obviously great care should be exercised in selecting colors. Even more attention should be given to the interaction of color as the performers move.

The colors to be used for the costume depend primarily upon the dance. But the color and design of the background, the nature of the scenery and the lighting equipment, must also be considered. Dull, warm colors in the background tend to unify any colors used against them, cool colors to separate them. Fortunately there is no standard recipe for color combinations. The universal adage is: "Don't just plan the colors, try them."

Many dances are best costumed in one color. Sometimes one color is used to isolate one dancer, in which case it should not be used elsewhere. Generally, contrasts are best on accessories, extensions, or props. An interesting variation is to have one dominating color with different shades or blends for the costumes of other performers—for example, blue shading to purple with lavender or rose accents; gray-green to olive-green to chartreuse; shades of orange, rust, beige, and brown; or, white to shades of gray and into black, or gray into shades of purple.

Related colors such as yellow and green, green and blue, or red and yellow are interesting together. If more than one color is to be tried it is best to use uneven proportions and to unify colors with black, or some neutral shade. Resist the temptation to use a commonplace color like fire-engine red search rather for a more unusual shade of red.

While many light values seem weak, the very dark ones are depressing. The very bright seem gaudy, the dull are drab. Great contrast in values is exciting but too much seems to lack central control or unity. A pure intensity of color seems primitive and in large areas assaults the senses of the audience. Usually, save the very intense colors for small accents; the smaller they are the brighter they can be. To reduce the intensity of any color add a neutral gray, white, or black.

Remember that the color of the material that you choose in daylight will never be the same under stage lights. Experimentation with varying colors of gelatin is a must, *before* making final fabric selections. Check on a color chart for a clearer understanding of color opposites and complements, and then look at these colors under lights. Different fabrics of apparently the same color will appear different under lights because of a particular dye, texture and thread. It is simple enough to find fabric colors that are "right," but the color they will be under the lights is another problem.

The following are examples of solutions to costume design for student choreographed dances. Some of them were carefully developed and seemed inevitable; others were obviously "off the top of the head" and were only partial solutions to the problem. Some remarks were by designers, some by choreographers.

> Let's hang a lot of half-inch streamers from a collar at the throat so as to transform a practice leotard into a more exotic costume. Could we use water-base paint for designs on the tights?

> In this dance, where the performer is obsessed with her hands, I will accent with a burst of pleats near the wrist and repeat the same thing at the hip line.

> I want to experiment with a headpiece of multicolored pipestem cleaners, curled, twisted and intertwined in the dancer's hair in order to call attention to the dancer's head and to the space above her head. Don't know about the rest yet.

> I drew a heavy cord (maybe it was a rope) through the wide hem of a full skirt of heavy crepe. Now it hangs in heavy folds, and when the dancer moves, the costume sweeps into the earth, pulling on the rest of the costume. It draws the figure down too. It seems just right!

> Will spiral a shining strip of metallic plastic around the torso, arms, and one leg of a white leotard. When I did this last week there was a forgotten trail of the plastic stuff and it seemed so good that I want it as a kind of dangling tail-appendage.

> I will choose from a skirt lined with strips of contrasting colors, multicolored underskirts, or hemline stripes on the outside. I want

to exaggerate the curves of turning as well as the changing sweep of the wide base.

I will try horizontal stripes around the costume, or maybe strips of colored tape attached to the leotard. Somewhere on a skirt, apron, or cape I want a contrasting color in vertical pleats.

At the last rehearsal I draped some brown and white checked cotton crepe diagonally around one of the dancers dressed in beige leotard and tights. If I can make this secure it is just the effect I want. Maybe I will have to sew the crepe on at each performance.

In spite of experience and admonitions there are still designers, choreographers, and dancers who seem unable to believe that the muddy colored costume they see on stage is the same lovely pale green stuff they chose at the fabric shop. This is what happens. Did you take the time to try the fabric in the lights before you got it?

The following are some sample remarks by designers who felt their choice of fabric and color was successful:

Against a black curtain the lead dancer is in dull orange with tan decoration; other dancers in the group are in shades of rust with accents in dull brown; lights warm.

With a blue cyclorama as background, a trio of dancers in blue-purple skirt with rose-coral bodice, red-purple bodice and skirt with powder-blue pleated sleeves and *godet,* and hyacinth skirt topped with blue and rose bodice; lights pink and lavender.

Against a black curtain the dancers wore bright yellow tights with white cotton jersey tunics. Bright blue cellophane was rolled and fastened onto a band around the arm holes.

For a preclassic bourée, a costume suggested by Betty Joiner was most successful. There was a purple cyclorama background and an interesting semicircular riser with two vertical pillars on stage left. The dance costume had blue cords over the shoulder supporting a dull green tunic of cotton crepe. The midcalf skirt, a one-half circle of heavy bias brown muslin, was fastened at the waist and open high at the back, like an apron. The skirt was decorated with a curving stripe of robin's-egg-blue sateen. The lights were warm and bright.

A group dance with satirical overtones was staged in front of a black curtain. The costumes were in two shades of blue with gray leotards. Knee-length skirts of heavy and stiff taffeta had occasional buckram supports to hold the skirt out from the dancer's body. Yellow skirts with the blue leotards; burnt-orange with the gray. Stripes of pink and black criss-crossed the skirts. Each dancer carried a large bow of yellow, orange, and gray ribbons. This was one of the dances that needed "speckled" lighting!

RESOURCES FOR THE COSTUMER

While each costume develops out of the dance as choreographed and per
formed it is always helpful for the designer to become aware of helpful source
material. There are many books, articles, pamphlets, and studies to be sur
veyed. There are special materials on costume including design, construction
and history or period. While little is written on dance costume as such, a grea
deal is written on theatrical costume and there is much valuable comment in
books on design, color, textiles (fabrics), sewing, dyeing, patterns, and fash
ion or dress design. There are special collections and references in libraries
and museums that will increase the designer's understanding as well as acti
vate his imagination. Attendance at dance concerts, observation of dancers in
class and rehearsal, and examination of photographs and movies of the dance
are all helpful.

Collections

To keep track of your ideas, provide yourself with notebooks, appropriate
folders, envelopes, boxes, or bags. Once you begin to look for things you wil
be surprised at all there is. But unless you are willing to spend many hour
going through all of the collected treasures, develop a catalogue system early
This may finally prove more complicated than the initial collecting, for it i
sometimes hard to know just what category is appropriate. But any system i
better than none! Keep a pad of tracing paper handy so that you can recor
and/or duplicate parts or entire sketches, patterns, shapes, designs, draperies
decorations, full costumes, accessories, or props.

Collect your own swatches of fabric from the widest possible range
Identify each and organize the swatches into packets: for example, stiff an
angular materials like taffeta, tarlatan, or organdy; shining and firm texture
like satin, rayon, or oilcloth; stretch and clings like knit, jerseys, or elasticize
fabrics. In spite of changing features of almost all fabrics, this will be useful a
a reference. And it is always possible to keep your collection current with jus
a little effort each time you see or hear of something new about fabrics.

Make a collection of color samples, with as wide a range of shade an
intensity as possible. Your sources may be paint stores; stage-light gelati
books; fabric or paper; cutouts of color from magazine illustrations; chip
prepared with colored ink, pencil, felt-tip pens, water color, ink, acrylic; dy
and yarn charts; and anything else with color. Identify each color accordin
to charts or expert opinion. Such a readily available source of color referenc
is invaluable to the designer.

Using the model-sketch technique suggested earlier, transfer the finishe
design to a heavier paper for a more permanent record of the costume sketch
There are many variations on the superimposed tracing paper technique. Yo
can prepare a series of skirt variations from full to straight, short to long

sleeves that are tight to billowing and pleated, and of varying lengths; variations on the drape of the bodice; additions of cape, collar, apron, overskirt; and many other pieces sketched on bits of tracing paper for manipulation on the predrawn figure. These too should all be categorized according to some system and the pieces kept in separate envelopes.

Collect useful patterns, especially for a simple bodice, skirts—full circle, three-quarter, one-half, and straight-line, basic pants, cape, bolero, tunic, and even a princess-line dress. Adapting these patterns to larger and smaller sizes as well as changing line and drapery requires specific instruction—it is not as simple as it would seem.

As an aid in choosing costume colors it is helpful to duplicate something of the performance situation. Take a large piece of paper, the color of the background of the performance area, and spread it on a flat surface. Using your prepared color samples to represent each dancer, manipulate each across the paper according to the floor pattern and groupings of the dance. In this way you can see the color relationships and be more sure of the interaction before you purchase your fabric.

## The Pattern

When the costume design has been completed the next task is to determine the pattern for measuring and cutting the selected fabric. There are several ways to do this, each with characteristic advantages and difficulties.

Preliminary to choosing any pattern or draping any material are the measurements of the dancers who will wear the costumes. Individual measurements are important for good fit and you must anticipate a wide range of action for the dancer, especially in the shoulder, arm, bust, waist, and hip regions. If you have the correct measurements recorded on individual charts this will always be helpful. Prepare a chart for each dancer (see Figure 5-4).

The safest procedure is to purchase a ready-made pattern that has been styled and sized. If you have the correct pattern size, make sure of individual needs, and follow directions carefully, there is little chance for any difficulty. American pattern makers grade all patterns according to government standards and are therefore consistent. Unfortunately it is still up to someone to make the important changes according to special costume detail. These changes should not be too difficult once the costume structure is set. Get help if you are not sure of what you are doing.

## Fitting a Bodice and Improvising Other Pieces

Sometimes it is impossible to find the pattern that will satisfy the costume design. In that event it is up to the designer to improvise. The bodice is the key segment to most costumes as it is the stable unit to which skirt, pants,

**Figure 5-4    Measurement Guide and Chart**

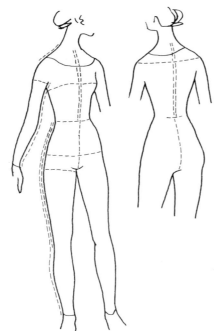

In taking the following fourteen measurements—which will serve for most costumes—have the dancer stand erect.

Measure around the body at the fullest part of the bust. Be sure the tape is at the same height in the back as in the front.

Measure around the natural waistline.

Measure around the fullest part of the hips.

Measure around the fullest part of the thigh.

Measure from the neck to the natural waist in front and also in back.

Measure from the neck to the crotch in front and also in back.

Measure from the neck to the shoulder to determine the shoulder seam.

Measure the arm circumference about an inch below the armpit.

Measure the arm length under the arm.

Measure from the natural waist to the ankle and also from the natural waist to the knee.

Measure from shoulder tip to shoulder tip across the back.

---

Name_____    Dance(s)_____

Telephone number_____    _____

Height_____ Weight_____ Bust_____ Waist_____

Hips_____ Thigh_____ Neck-waist (front)_____

Neck-waist (back)_____ Neck-crotch (front)_____

Neck-crotch (back)_____ Shoulder seam_____

Shoulder tip to shoulder tip (back)_____

Arm circumference about an inch below armpit_____

Arm length under arm_____

Waist to ankle_____ Waist to knee_____

sleeves, collar, cape, and other additions are usually attached. Remember the wide range of action that dancers need in the shoulder and arm area. To fit a bodice:

(1.) Cut two waist lengths of material, slightly wider than the actual measurement from shoulder tip to shoulder tip. Check to be sure that the direction of weave of the fabric is the same front and back.

(2.) Fold the pieces in half and press a crease down the center of each. Cut a flat quarter circle for the neck opening.

(3.) Open each length, pin shoulder seams, and drape on dancer.

(4.) Pin center fold at midline of dancer's leotard, same in back.

(5.) Making sure that material is straight, pin the front darts, then the back darts, and finally the side seams. Try to equalize the width of each seam.

(6.) Remove the garment, baste, and refit.

(7.) Sew all darts and seams, press flat. If you want a zipper, rip out length of seam and insert according to the folds.

To find the natural waistline, tie a strong and firmly twisted string tightly around the apparent waistline. Have the dancer hold the string, elbows out, and then lift shoulders high to release the bodice and let it fall naturally. The string will move to the natural waistline and you will be able to anticipate irregularities in the hang of the bodice. This is particularly important if you plan to attach a skirt.

Skirts can be full or narrow, short or long, gored or pleated. The simplest and most usable of dance skirts are the bias and circular ones shown in Figure 5-5. Straight or wrap-around skirts can be made of two straight pieces of material fitted down the side seams and darted at the waist for better fitting. There are many adaptations of this basic wrap-around either as additional skirt pieces or as undertrimming.

Here is a helpful hint for putting in a skirt zipper:

(1.) Most skirt zippers are on the left side, so sew up the left seam and leave the right one open. Press left seam flat and then rip out length needed for zipper.

(2.) With pressed folds as a guide, cut off tape at top to about 5/8 inch. Place front of skirt over zipper teeth, overlap a bit more than enough to cover zipper teeth. Pin, pointing pins diagonally up, about 1 inch apart, starting at top.

(3.) Place back of skirt with fold up against zipper teeth and pin from the bottom up.

(4.) Now sew, keeping the zipper closed except at the very start when you have to pull the tab down to assure straight stitching without hitting the tab. Start sewing at top of skirt front, 1/2-inch from fold. Withdraw pins as you reach them. Stitch down on front fold about 1 1/2-inches. Then get zipper tab out of the way. Stitch to the bottom, pivot, and stitch across, pivot and stitch up on the back fold to top of waist.

Figure 5-5    Skirt Sketches

Bias Skirt

Requiring two lengths plus 1/3 yard of 36-inch material.

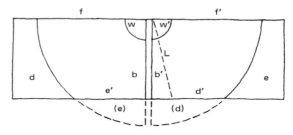

(1) Pin w and w' around the waist of the dancer.
(2) Pin f and f' to form the front seam.
(3) Pin b and b' to form the back seam (take in L for less fullness).
(4) Trim off bottom of skirt and use excess to complete back of skirt. Be sure
    straight edge d faces d' and e faces **e'**. (Piecing is unnecessary with wider
    material.)
(5) Trim excess at waist and sew on a straight-material waistband.
(6) Skirt may be open at front or back seam for greater range of action.

Circular Skirt

Requires two lengths of 54-inch material.

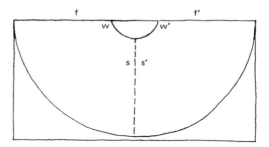

(1) W-w' is waistline; pin to dancer's leotard.
(2) Pin f to f' to form front seam.
(3) Trim bottom of skirt to desired length.
(4) For a skirt with seams down each side cut material in half as indicated by
    dotted line. Pin f to f'; s to s'.

The bodice patterns shown in Figure 5-6 can be adapted without too
much experience. Try muslin for the first one.

Another method for obtaining a pattern is from some other garment
especially one that fits well. This is simply a matter of taking it apart at the
seams and tracing its outline on paper, or even using it as a direct pattern fo

Figure 5-6    Bodices

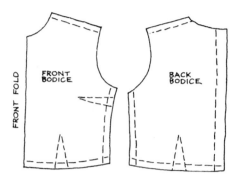

Join shoulder seams and then complete as much as possible before sewing underarm seams.

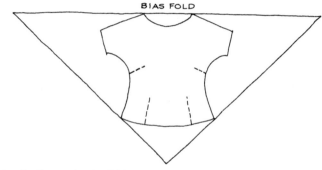

Here is a bodice made of a 36-inch square, cut on the bias—fold B. Pin shoulder and side seams, dart at bust and waist.

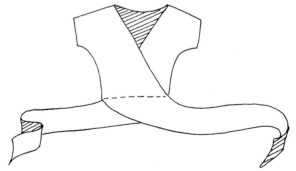

Here is a wrap-around bodice; the back is one piece and the front is in two pieces, each with extensions long enough to wrap around the body once and tie. Needs about 1 1/3 yards of 36-inch wide material. Pin shoulder and side seams, fit wrap-around, and dart as necessary.

95

cutting fabric. For example, a well-fitting leotard, bodice, or skirt makes a perfect pattern. A pattern for pants can be made by slipping one leg into the other and putting the pants flat.

## PREPARING THE FABRIC

Yardage requirements are always specified on pattern envelopes, but for dancers it is best to buy extra so as to ensure fullness for shoulder and hip action Guidesheets inside the package always include diagrams showing how to arrange pattern pieces on the fabric. Pay attention—this can save you on material.

### Preshrinking

Preshrinking is seldom necessary with quality fabrics, but costumes are often made of inexpensive and unprepared material. If in doubt, preshrink.

    Dunk cottons into lukewarm water, wring out, and iron. Dressing may be replaced by adding a little starch to the lukewarm water and ironing before the cotton is completely dry. For woolen fabrics, wet, and wring out a linen towel, and put it on the wrong side of the fabric, which is folded lengthwise. Set iron to "wool" and steam the cloth thoroughly. When the fabric is wet continue until the surface is smooth. Turn over and repeat on the other side (It must be a wet cloth; a steam iron is not sufficient.)

### Dyeing

The most readily available are the vegetable dyes, which are limited in color and intensity. Look in the yellow pages of the telephone book for sources of analine or basic dyes, which have a wide range of brilliant colors. The analine dyes are best for most costumes because the colors are clear, they fade and run very little, and they can often be used in cold water. Be sure to follow the directions, which are, basically:

(1.) Always mix dye to a smooth paste, then add salt or recommended fixing agent, strain through a cheesecloth or nylon stocking, and add to softened water, stirring thoroughly.

(2.) Prepare the fabric by dipping or washing in warm water and then immersing quickly in the dye solution.

(3.) This must be stirred *constantly*, making sure that there are no wrinkles in the material that would cause streaking. Follow instructions regarding temperature and time of immersion.

(4.) Remove from the bath and rinse carefully. Remember that colors are lighter when dry than when wet.

Some people use a large aluminum, stainless-steel, porcelain, or enamel-
ned vessel. Others use the wash-and-rinse cycle of their washing machine
fterward, be sure to run the complete cycle with bleach added). Rubber
oves are a must and a stirring stick, salt, water, softener, color remover, and
dinary bleach to correct mistakes are important aids.

Uneven dyeing is best because flat and even colors are uninteresting
nder lights. For example, try a heavy unbleached muslin dipped first in a red
nd blue mixture of ordinary vegetable dye for cotton, then redipped in a
asic royal purple. The result looks like a velvet brocade, especially if lit with
aree primary colors. A cheap sateen dipped in a deep orange analine dye and
nen tumble-dried will look like textured velvet. If you want an exciting blue,
ip the material first into a pale blue and then into a brilliant basic blue—the
esult will be a vibrant and rich color.

Spattering color can be done easily by dipping a firm brush into the dye
nd then either flipping or brushing it to splash on the fabric. This technique
useful to give an impression of age or dirt. It will have a sharp outline on
ry material and blend on a wet surface. Felt pens can be used to outline
atterns so that they will "read" better in a large theater. (Try dry bleach on
n already dyed fabric for a reverse-color effect.) Interesting patterns can be
nade by hanging a dampened fabric and letting the dye run down in varie-
nted streaks.

Spray-dye, if you use a good-sized spray-gun for large quantities, gives an
nteresting effect. Be sure that the dye is dissolved, heated to a boil, and made
ast with something like Permanent Mixture. The fabric should be spread out
r hung without folds and sprayed from a distance of about 3 to 5 feet.
ometimes an overspray of another color makes a fine surface, in which case
ou should proceed carefully so as not to blur the initial spray. Scene paint
an be used in the second spray for interesting texturing of the fabric. Be sure
o mix some liquid glue with the water added to the scene paint.

Stretch a wet fabric on a smooth surface and throw dry pigment onto it.
esigns can also be painted on with a brush. Obviously this would not be
nccessful with dyes requiring a high temperature to set. Sometimes nonwash-
ble felt-tip pens can be used with great success.

Tie-dye is achieved by gathering, folding, or bunching fabric, tying it,
nd then dipping it in dye, or pouring the dye onto it. For less blend tighten
ne ties and then experiment with the wonderful combinations from loose
es. Different tied areas can be dipped in different colors and the results are
ways a surprise, no matter how carefully planned.

Batik is an ancient Javanese method of resist dyeing. According to plan,
ertain parts of the cloth are coated with wax, which is then etched to
omplete the pattern. Only the exposed parts of the fabric will now take the
ye. The process is repeated each time a new color is desired. Sometimes a
naracteristic multicolored streak will appear where dye has penetrated the
racks in the wax. This is a time-consuming method but is very effective for
ne dance costume.

## Painting

Painting costume fabric may use a wide range of methods, including brush, spatter, spray, block print, silk screen, free hand, or stencil. Acrylic latex paints are excellent and will remain flexible even after laundering. Water soluble paints are also easy to use and can even be painted while the costume is on the dancer. Try painting unbleached muslin with a thin solution of dry color mixed with water and sized with liquid glue. Paint and art supply stores have a wide assortment of powders, pigments, glitters, and bonding agents. The tools and materials are readily available in most art supply stores; the imagination and interest must be supplied by the designer.

## Sewing the Garment

Almost everyone who sews has a different and favorite way of approaching the task. It is advisable for someone who is experienced and who understands the costume design to carefully outline a common approach for all assistants. Provide written and numbered instructions for each step in the construction process.

The designer has established the sketch; the fabric has been prepared and cut according to measurements and pattern; the garment has been basted and pressed on the wrong side of the fabric, all darts toward the center and seams flat open. Now the expert at the sewing machine makes it all fast, completing all of the previous labor.

## PERSONAL APPEARANCE

When the dancer steps into the performance area he is no longer an ordinary mortal who eats, sleeps, and perspires. He is, rather, an unusual paragon of neuromuscular skill, endless endurance, monumental flexibility and strength, exquisite sensitivity and conviction, natural talent for sincere projection, devotion to his craft and to his choreographer's intent! He has beauty of form and charm of face. He has presence, warmth, and humility.

At least that is what the choreographer hopes. Anything he can suggest or demand has been done. Now what else? The dance has been choreographed, rehearsed, staged; scenery, lights, costumes have been designed and provided; a potential audience has been gathered; programs and tickets were printed; ushers were delegated; the crew is alert. Everything awaits the performer. One last thing is necessary to complete the illusion—his face, his hair, his personal appearance.

The purpose of make-up is to reinforce facial characteristics of the dancer so that the whole person becomes visible. As viewed from a darkened auditorium, the dancer's face seems drained of all natural color in the strong artificial stage lights. And so it is necessary to replace color in the skin; to accent the eyes, the most powerful facial contact; and to outline the mouth, which tends to wash out entirely.

Each dancer has a particular set of features and his own unique coloring, so any generalization must be adapted to individual needs. The aim of most make-up for dancers is to unobtrusively accent the performer's natural assets—all in terms of the dance-image sought.

## Make-up

Unless the skin is very dark dancers will need a foundation of either greasepaint or pancake. The soft cream of greasepaint is easier to apply. After dipping the fingers in cold water, pat in small dots over the entire face and neck, blending into the hairline and low enough to accommodate all costumes to be worn. A pancake base is applied with a moist sponge and is smoother. It is not affected by perspiration and is much easier to remove. Under very bright lights however, greasepaint is best. A warm, not too dark suntan shade is best for most people but subtle variations can be selected to match skin and hair coloring. After the base is completed all highlights and evidence of facial contour are gone. Rouge is very important. Put a dot of moist, medium bright red on the most prominent part of the cheekbone and blend out with short *straight* strokes so that no line of demarcation is visible. Narrow-faced dancers spread the rouge high and wide, round-faced dancers bring rouge in lower, longer, and closer to the nose. Usually dry rouge is used for pancake and moist rouge for greasepaint.

A fine brown or black line on the upper and lower eyelid, near the eye at the lash line, is said to "stop the eye." Shadow on the lids adds brilliance to the eyes and also makes them visible. Without such shadowing the face often appears to have two gray depressions where eyes usually are. The shadow should be blended from the center of the eyelid off at the corner of the eye socket, at the nose, and below the eyebrow. If you are wearing several colors in a costume, a blue or lavender is best. Sometimes a tiny dot of carmine color is dabbed in the corner of the eye to give greater definition and luminosity. The eyebrows are penciled or brushed with short and gentle strokes, following the natural line of growth. Blend so that a hard line will not be evident. Black is usual for brunettes and brown for others. Sometimes the brows may be extended but only as a continuation of the natural line. Mascara, usually black, is applied to lashes with a wet brush. Newer brands do not smudge but remember to apply carefully with gentle up-strokes.

The wide range of lip coloring is not to be used for stage make-up, unless you are seeking unusual results. Usually the same color lip rouge is recommended as for the cheeks. Always follow the natural mouth line even if the natural form is small and needs to be made fuller. The natural shape of the mouth should not be changed or exaggerated. A powder slightly lighter than

the foundation color should then be applied generously and patted, not rubbe
on. Excess should be removed with a tissue or a soft brush. While there ar
differences of opinion about when the powder is applied, most dancers do
after eyes and mouth are finished.

Body make-up must be applied in cases where the skin color is markedl
different from the facial make-up or there are other obvious variations i
personal coloring. Remember that unusual lines of color differentiation, suc
as those between rich suntan and untanned areas, are as obvious under ligh
as are color decorations on costumes.

## Hair

The hair style should be determined by the choreographer and the designer. I
the hair best worn in a way common to all performers or in the individual
favorite style? Of course, the only way to have identical hair styles for mos
dancers is to resort to wigs. But even though some have long and some sho
hair, some curly and some straight, some dark and some light, there are way
of dressing the hair in relatively similar lines—they need not be identical. Fo
example, brushing the hair off the face and drawing it back with a rubbe
band or clasp will show facial lines with any length or color hair. Sma
hairpieces, nets, bands, and threads constraining stray ends are all usefu
Ordinary hairpins and bobbypins are as obvious as jewelry, beauty-patche
and bubble gum under stage lights. Let's have none of these.

The hair is often a neglected aspect of the effort to enhance the danc
image. How unfortunate that an otherwise well-integrated appearance i
sometimes topped by inappropriate mountains of curls or tousled face-cove
ing tresses that distract from the dance.

## The Final Check

When the dancer is familiar and comfortable in his costume and make-up he i
more assured. But it should also be right with the choreographer. Designe
choreographer, and sensitive observers should watch a'final rehearsal of cos
tumed dancers, making notes of discrepancies, needed alterations, and sug
gestions for improving the individual image as well as the dance picture.

The final lighting should be tried again, assuming that this has been se
before costume decisions were made. The scenery and background light
should be tried again. Everything that is planned for the final performanc
should be duplicated. Otherwise the final performance is by chance. Some
how it is never possible to be sure of the ultimate picture when dancers ar
clutching fabrics to themselves. Now it is more than color, it is line, drapery
texture, decoration, and the design as a whole that is apparent—on the mov
ing dancer, in the performance space, with the lights, with the accompani

ment. This is not technical or dress rehearsal—this is for designer, choreographer, and performer. It is the crucial test of all that has gone before. All components are in their place and now the question is: will they interrelate? The successful production depends upon the degree to which each component meshes and fulfills its individual role in augmenting the choreographer's movement image.

# 6

# Lighting Design

Played in flat, uncolored light few dances survive as anything but gymnastic exercises, which hopefully they are not. Theater requires a sense of wonder and mystery. A bit of color, some control of illumination, judicious arrangement of light and shadow—all contribute to the theatrical effectiveness of the dance, perhaps evoking ideas and emotions intended by the choreographer, perhaps evoking others not planned or expected.

Although a considerable mystique surrounds stage lighting, the principles of theater usage are fairly simple, or as simple as the designer's imagination will allow them to be. Visibility, atmosphere, and emphasis on place or person are the three controlling factors. All depend, as does scene design, on the intent of the dance. What is the dance supposed to convey? Is it drama, mood, or just a pretty picture? Are the figures as bright and cheerful as those in a Renoir painting, or are they perhaps engulfed in the tremendous baroque contrasts of a Caravaggio? Are they suffused with the amber glow of a well-varnished Watteau, or caught in a swirl of colors found not in nature but in the wildest excesses of German expressionism? Bright or dim, flat or sharply defined, white or colored, light serves the dance in direct response to the designer's imagination and the technician's craft.

The design process begins with an assessment of lighting requirements and ends with the preparation of a light plot containing the plans and directions needed to guide the technical crew in its work of rigging the instruments and running the performance (see Figure 6-1).

## MOOD

Assume that you are presenting a classic abstraction to the music of Vivaldi. Is there anything about the dance that suggests a mood, or is it simply a display of movement? The easy answer—and it may be the correct one—is that the abstraction represents clarity of technique and smoothness of line and so should be seen in light equally clear and smooth. If this is what you want, go ahead.

On the other hand, that Vivaldi music may hint at the gloomy things of winter, whether the dance has any reference to winter or not. Now you have to make another choice, just as arbitrary as the first. Does the idea of severe abstraction rule the lighting or does the implied emotion of the music? Emotionally, a fully lighted stage may not be quite satisfactory, but then is your concept of the music's emotional tone shared by the audience? Probably it is not, unless you provide the visual clues that suggest the mood—costume, scenery, and lighting. It is all so very arbitrary, but then your use of the Vivaldi music is also arbitrary.

Story-telling ballets and psychological studies are easier to justify as candidates for imaginative lighting. But again, a fully lighted stage may be the answer for a cheerful little tale about the football hero in the big game or a children's excursion to the beach or a comedy about the silent movies. Production pictures from the professional theater provide hundreds of examples of stories danced on a nice bright stage. Even the first act of *Giselle* is bright and cheerful, unless the designer wants to do all sorts of forecasting about tragedy to come, which he probably will not do because the ballerina and her handsome partner wish to be clearly and definitely seen. The second act dims

Figure 6-1    Lighting Schedule

---

Check all lighting and sound equipment . . . . . . . . . . . . . . (12-2 months)
  Experiment with available materials and
  facilities to determine possible effects.
  Anticipate new purchases, loans, rentals

Attend choreographer's rehearsals to study needs and
  relate to preliminary plots submitted    . . . . . . . . . . . (3-1 month)

Experiment and improvise lighting with dancers    . . . . . . . . . (4-1week)
  Discuss costumes, sets, and visualization

Technical rehearsal    . . . . . . . . . . . . . . . . . . . . . . . . (1 week)

Prepare complete lighting plot . . . . . . . . . . . . . . . . . . . (7-2 days)

Clarify cues and coverage at final rehearsals

---

the lights a little for the cemetery, adds a little blue, and becomes a sort of *Les Sylphides* among the headstones. The theater designer might trick up the lighting to add shadows and silhouettes and stray patches of red and dark blue; the choreographer and dancers would then bribe the electrician to make the lights a little brighter and add a nice follow spot. There seems to be a kind of war between designer and dancer. The designer longs to create a mood and a bit of beauty; the dancer loves that big white follow spot, even if there aren't many graveyards equipped with follow spots. Both sides compromise. The designer brightens everything a little and takes away the annoying slash of red; the performer agrees to an unobtrusive follow spot. Compromise rules the theater.

Theater is always a compromise, and since there are no absolutes, one compromise is as good as another if the audience likes the result. So pick a mood. Be happy or sad, mysterious or prosaic, or whatever you think the dance demands. That is the beginning of design.

## EMPHASIS

Most writing about lighting theory is concerned with the dramatic effect. What can lighting do to enhance the drama? Some of the answers are theatrical cliche's. Lady Macbeth sleepwalks in torch-lit corridors; the sun blazes through a covering of clouds when the heroine survives the near-fatal operation; dawn washes away the night of horror; night creeps into darkness as the killer slips through the gloomy street. In many instances there is no real choice, because the audience has been conditioned to associate lighting and event. If you insist on a daylight *Hamlet* or a grimy Strauss polka you can have it. The audience may wonder if the crew is running lights for the wrong show.

All too often the question of lighting as an aid to dramatic emphasis is forgotten, usually until it is too late to correct the choreography. In this area lighting design begins with choreography. Ideas about mood and color can wait until performance night if necessary; a change of gel may accomplish the required result. But a change of gel will not solve the question of emphasis. What is important? Certainly everything is not equally important, but if the choreographer insists that every movement, every expression is of vital interest to the audience the designer can simply write "full stage lights—no changes." This may be the right solution, or it may not.

Suppose you decide to isolate one dancer from a group. The dancer is a lonely outsider struggling to break through an invisible wall to join the gay party of young people. You can light up the whole stage, let the dancers work very hard, and overhear comments such as "What's that girl doing?" . . . "It's symbolic or something" . . . "Oh?" If at the beginning you keep either the girl or the group in a limited area, then the stage can be lighted in sharply defined areas and colors to show the isolation of the girl, the happiness of the group, even the invisible wall. You can do it, if you plan to use light to establish the separation and the mood. When girl and group share the same area at the same time, there can be no separation by pools of light. This is choreographic responsibility, but it is also part of the lighting problem. Once again the choreographer must be reminded to visualize the dance as it will appear on the stage.

The examples can be multiplied. Surrounded by medieval splendor costumed dancers whirl through a mad masque; as the music rises to a frantic climax a strange figure in black glides down the steps, into a shaft of flaming red light. Three figures bound by silver chains twist across the stage reaching for the warmth of a distant sun; at the final agonized turn their hands spring upward, into a beam of comforting yellow. The huge shadow of the cruel father divides the girl from her lover. A fairy in the forest plays in moonbeams.

A little imagination can convert a bland offering into exciting theater. Think about it, and think about it early, before the choreography becomes too fixed to change.

## COLOR

There are books that speak knowingly of the psychological effects of color. Red is exciting, blue is calming, green is peaceful, all that sort of thing.

Since the effects of color are variable, and are often the product of the individual spectator's experience, you may as well pick out what you like and forget the theories. In dance you are not so limited as you might be in realistic drama. A green sky may be just as acceptable as a blue one, and the sun can be pink, if there is no reason why it shouldn't be. The dance audience does not expect realism. So use color. It looks pretty.

There are a few exceptions. Moonlight is not red. Neither is it that blue favored in ballet, but the idea is acceptable because of theatrical convention and a willingness to think that moonlight really is bluish. Even this sort of exception is not an unbreakable rule. Somebody always plays around with purple cows and orange grass. The mood and the purpose of the dance permit the variations, or deny them. Art is always a product of choice and that choice is the artist's, whether anybody else likes it or not. The wise artist manages to please enough people to justify his decision.

Lighting color is often determined by costume color, and here again theory is available. Unfortunately the choreographer usually chooses costumes containing a variety of colors, and so that advice about red turning red into gray and blue transforming orange into dishrag brown, or whatever colored gels are supposed to do to fabric, turns out to be impractical in the theater. When everybody is in white, you have a better chance. The right course is to pick some colored gels and try them on the costumes. If the result displeases you, try something else.

Although catalogs list fifty or sixty colors, about eight recur so often as to be regarded as fairly standard for almost any production. The usual cool colors for general lighting are *special lavender*, a pink-blue flattering to faces, and *steel blue*, a pale blue that does not wash out those rosy cheeks. The often-encountered warm colors are *flesh pink*, the ballerina's delight; *bastard amber*, a pinkish amber; and *straw*, a useful pale yellow. These colors, used with cool shining from one direction and warm from the other, are the major five. For cyclorama and over-all toning the colors that recur are *medium blue*, *medium red*, and *medium green*. With just these colors the designer can create quite a variety of pleasing and dramatic effects.

The one important piece of advice about color is: try it. Try it on costumes and the paint scheme of any scenery and on the dancers' faces. Nothing will answer your questions more quickly and effectively than a demonstration of the actual effect of shining colored light on fabric or paint or the face of a patient dancer. But don't be afraid of color.

## VARIATION

Often, perhaps even most of the time, there is no reason to change the lighting during a dance. In other instances, changes add to the effectiveness of the performance. What can be varied?

## Intensity

Intensity is the most obvious example of what people think about when considering variation. With dimming equipment the stage can brighten from night to desert noon, twilight can fade into night, storm clouds rush across the face of the sun, the cheer of comedy drift toward the gloom of tragedy. The lamps in a crystal chandelier dim as the loved one dies; fearful shadows vanish when sunlight streams through the window.

Psychological hints of dark and light define some variations. Time is another determinate; the light of dawn is not that of noon or of night. Mood is a third factor; the haunted castle exists in darkness and shadow; the farcical hotel room is flooded with brightness. All of these can change from moment to moment or from the beginning to the end.

Are there any internal changes from light to dark during the course of a dance? How many? As always, the answers lie within the imaginations of choreographer and designer.

## Color

The lilac and pink of dawn is not the warm amber of late afternoon or the pale white of moonlight. Sometimes dawn must become morning or evening fade into sunset. Provided that instruments and dimmers are available the transitions can be made as the designer wills.

Neptune pursues the frightened mermaid from the ocean's dark blue depths through the green shallows and onto the sunlit shore, all suggested by changes of color, one blending into the next. Outlined in a shaft of saloon-lamp yellow a vicious woman jabs a knife into the victim's chest; slowly a mysterious green transfuses the air and the dead man rises; his hands circle the woman's throat as the light turns blood red; then man and woman sink to the ground together and the street returns to normal. Unreal lighting, certainly, but acceptable because of the theatrical situation.

There is also the arbitrary use of color, changing only for an interesting effect. In some ways it is equivalent to the quick cuts and odd angles in a motion picture dance routine—unnecessary, unmotivated, but interesting to the spectator. If you like it, and the dance does not suffer, you can try it, on rare occasions.

## Direction

The dance may suggest that light come first from one direction and then another. Such an arrangement might effectively illuminate the predicament of a girl caught between two lovers. First one attracts her, then the attraction, and the light, fades; the light from the other side of the stage springs up to tempt her into the arms of the second man. Or, invisible spirits torment a troubled man. One is represented by a red shaft from directly overhead, another flickers behind, a third glares on the right.

To be effective, this technique requires collaboration between designer and choreographer at the early stage of dance preparation so that light direction and dancer motivation are complementary. It would be very awkward for the dancer to direct his attention to one side of the stage, only to discover that the light shone from the other.

## Area

Let the dancer enter from upstage left, cross down right, and move all the way over to extreme left. Instead of turning on all the stage lights at the beginning why not start in darkness and bring up the lights in each area as the dancer moves through, keeping the rest of the stage dark? Perhaps two dancers are supposed to be separated by actual or psychological distance. As each dancer moves, the light in his area comes up, while the other remains in darkness.

All variations can be effective. Unfortunately, they can also be distracting, even when carried out expertly. There are no rules; the only guide is the designer's assessment of the value of any situation.

## SPECIAL EFFECTS

This may be a somewhat misleading phrase to apply to the miscellany of lighting techniques so often encountered in dance production. For want of anything better the term will serve.

### Dimouts and Blackouts

The dance ends. Perhaps the curtain closes on a lighted stage. If not, the choice is a dimout or a blackout. There is a difference.

A dimout is an orderly decrease in intensity, either fast or slow, at the discretion of the designer. The mood of the dance lingers for a few seconds, like a sunset fading into the night. The end is announced, but it is a gentle ending.

The blackout is an abrupt plunge into darkness. The switch is snapped, and there, without warning, what was light turns dark. For shock value the blackout is useful—the murderer rushes at the audience, the building explodes, the gallows-trap springs. Its other main use is a sort of theatrical punctuation to a comic sketch—the routine, the blackout at the punch line, the laugh.

## Follow Spots

Follow spots were probably invented because some star actress demanded that she be brighter than everybody else on the stage. No matter how the play suffered from this strange phenomenon of the golden girl glowing amid the motley crowd, the follow spot generated its obvious beam to establish the importance of whatever star walked the stage. And if there were two stars, then two follow spots.

Dancers seem to love that intrusive spotlight, even if it does wash the color from their faces and wipe out half the effect of carefully planned dramatic scenes. Of course, there are situations in which a follow spot can legitimately enhance a production. The most obvious case is that in which a soloist is supposed to be a soloist, that is, a performer demonstrating technical skill and personal charm. Sometimes a story or mood piece can use a follow spot to emphasize one of the dancers, but usually it should not be a vaudeville-star light but rather a carefully controlled and gelled spot that supplements the regular lighting in a manner so subtle that the audience is not especially aware of it, except, as always, when the dance requires an obvious effect.

When there are not enough instruments to cover all the various parts of the stage a follow can sometimes be used. For example, when the witch appears on her rocky platform, bathed in supernatural green, the follow may be the only thing available to provide the coverage.

Remember that a follow spot is a solo light. Its beam may be spread to encompass a fairly large circle, but not a circle large enough to pinpoint one dancer at stage right and another at stage left. The rule is: one soloist, one follow; two soloists, two follows—unless they keep very close together.

Maybe the theater doesn't even own a follow spot so you won't be tempted.

## Pools

Pools are roundish areas of light separated from one another. Interesting effects can be achieved as the dancers go through one circle, then into brief darkness, then appear again in another pool of light. The colors can be different or the same; areas may be large or small. This is one way to avoid the sameness, and sometimes flatness, of general illumination, which floods the entire stage. It is not for every dance certainly, but for some.

## Silhouettes

Dawn breaks. Ranged against the beginning violet light a row of spears rises black against the sky. Figures, vaguely seen, circle an ancient Japanese temple. Slowly, as the sun brightens, the pale light of dawn reveals helmeted warriors who wait for the battle of the Samurai to begin. Or, a woman stands on the edge of the sea. The sailor for whom she waits will not return. Only after the sun has set so finally on the lonesome ocean and the earth is dark, does she finally turn away, her desperate figure outlined against the uncaring sky.

Silhouettes are nice, if they do not last too long. The audience has not come to watch a shadow-puppet show.

## Shadows

Place a spotlight on the floor in front of a dancer and the shadow appears on the back wall, provided that the other lights are not too bright. Shadows are usually mysterious, but you can find all sorts of uses for them.

## Backlights

The movies love to use backlights to make a girl's hair glow or, if the front lights are not too bright, to add a pretty or perhaps mysterious effect. If you can pin a dancer down to a single area for awhile you might like the effect. And a strong backlight can be the only answer to the problem of the demon rushing out of the witch's cave.

## Cyc Lights

Cycs are good when they are good. Sometimes they are not good at all, and too much light makes them even worse. Preferably they are lighted from top and bottom, with the idea that color and intensity should be nicely blended.

Sky colors are common, but any color will do, provided that the colors and controls are available. And the colors can blend from one to another, from blue to red, or to an in-between pink.

Perhaps you might even try colored gels and patterns on a classroom overhead projector.

## Footlights

Probably no lighting is more typical of theatrical lore than those provided by footlights; and theatrical they are, bright and obvious, sometimes effective, sometimes distracting. Many theaters no longer provide footlights, since the modern trend dispenses with them except for musicals; so you may have to find some strips and place them on the floor at the front of the stage. Use color and dimmer control though.

Too bad they are disappearing, since they can remove unwanted shadows cast by overhead lights and, of course, they are indispensable for that old-time "you're in the theater" experience.

## Oddities

There are a few effects that appear with some regularity: black light or fluorescent material; a lobsterscope or strobe light flickering madly to make movements appear abnormal (for those silent movie scenes or rock and roll pieces); color wheels attached to a follow spot to change color obviously and deliberately; shadow boxes to cast shadows on the cyc; and a collection of psychedelic slides and machines and other oddities provided by theatrical suppliers. Black light, provided by specially coated fluorescent tubes, when combined with fluorescent scenery can provide the spooky underworld scene or thousand-starred sky or nighttime city, but keep the other lights dim. Some people like the Icecapades effect of costumes shining in the dark, and if you like it, go ahead.

## LIGHT PLOT

A light plot is a design on paper. Its purpose is to convey information, and a fumbling attempt at description is better than a vague promise to explain everything later. If you can't tell a leko from a scoop or the first pipe from the second then leave the technical decisions to those who can or—much better—learn in a hurry; it isn't that hard. Write down a few paragraphs of description, add a necessary ground plan or two to show the location of scenery and dancers, point out the special effects, and you have created a minimum ground plot, which can be handed to a technician to serve as a guide for 75 to 90 per cent of the work required before the first dress rehearsal. Any confusing points can be cleared up in the theater. A professional light plot is more complicated, but the choreographer-designer who produces a simple plot is considered a gem by the lighting crew. Begin with a minimum plot and graduate to the full presentation as knowledge and skill teach the techniques.

A good light plot should include the following parts:

(1.) A general description of the dance, especially of the mood. This may be the best indication of what you really want. It may even prove more useful to a crew than your technical instructions. An imaginative crew may sometimes clothe your ballet more gracefully than you deserve, with your requests for speckled light and the follow spot shining on the quartet. Even if you do all the work yourself, as occasionally you should, a written description reminds you of what you really want.

(2.) Indication of any changes of color, intensity, or any other variable. Even the best-equipped theater may exhaust its supply of instruments and dimmers if too many are needed. Now is the time to start worrying about the availability of equipment.

3.) Use of special lights and effects. That dramatic moment when the light turns red has to be specified. If the dance needs two follow spots, say so. Dress rehearsal time is too late to ask for what the theater cannot provide.

4.) Ground plan showing scenery and curtains. The crew may have to provide an extra light for the platform, or all that Spanish moss dangling from a batten may block the beam of the most important motivational spotlight. And please, after you have drawn the plan and given it to the crew, do not change the position of scenery during your studio rehearsals and forget to tell the crew about it.

5.) Ground plan showing the areas used by the dancers. If they really are "all over the stage," say so. Otherwise pin them down to general areas so that the needed light will be on and the unneeded light turned off.

6.) A general summary of the performance. This provides a fair idea of how the dance begins and gives the cues for changes, effects, and ending.

7.) A complete plot includes a *hanging plot*, which shows exactly where each light is placed, how it is gelled, and which dimmer controls it. Unless you are an expert of sorts you can eliminate this step, except for those items that you may wish to specify.

The following two sample plots may serve to provide an idea of what the lighting designer is supposed to offer the technician. Not every bit of information is included, since some decisions can be made in the theater. Color choice may wait for awhile; some of the effects may be arranged later; cues will be set at the technical rehearsal. But whatever can be included should be. Notice that both sample plots describe the choreographer's vision of the dance. What does it look like on the stage? That is what the technical crew wants to know. So tell them.

## Sample Light Plot for a Lecture-Demonstration

*Title:* Lecture-demonstration

*Music:* Various

*General:* A lecturer downstage right speaks for a few minutes and then introduces a series of dances. She speaks between each section. Slides projected on the cyc provide a different background for each dance. The program consists of four solos, two duets, and a group of eight.

*Specific:* The lecturer requires one light, which can be dimmed while she is not speaking. For the program the following lighting is suggested:

1.) *Flamenco.* Three minutes. An overhead spot center stage, probably special lavender. Side lights from the wings, red from SR and lemon from SL. Sort of a Spanish cave mood, exciting and mysterious.

(2.) *Black Swan Pas de Deux.* Five minutes. Bluish general lighting. Follow
spot in steel blue. When dancers are far apart each will be treated as a
soloist and the follow will be on the one actually dancing. Classic ballet

(3.) *New Shoes.* Two-and-a-half minutes. General, full-stage lighting. A little
comic piece.

(4.) *Viennese Waltz.* Three-and-a-half minutes. Follow spot only. Pink. Ex
hibition dancing.

(5.) *Absolve.* Two-and-a-half minutes. Scattered pools for two dancers who
move all over the stage. Some dimming up and down. Darker colors
preferably lavenders and blues. This is a psychological piece about two
lost souls.

(6.) *Illuminations.* Three minutes. The dancer speaks lines from a poem by
Rimbaud and then sort of writhes around on the floor. All center stage
A downlight in blue or green for the reading, changing to red sidelight
for the writhing. Very arty and obscure. Blackout at the end.

(7.) *Pattern in Red and White.* Four minutes. Abstraction performed by eight
dancers. They should not be too bright, or too dim, but sort of in
between. General lighting.

*Running:* Lectern is in front of the main curtain. On cue a light comes up on
the lectern and lecturer enters through curtain at center stage. At her cue the
curtain opens. The lectern light dims out and the lights and projection for the
first dance dim up quickly. After the dancer's final bow the stage lights fade
and the lectern light comes up again. Each dance proceeds in the same way
At the end the lecturer will give the final cue; the light will dim and the
curtain will close as the lecturer steps behind the curtain line.

Sample Light Plot for a Ballet

*Title:* The Haunted Palace
*Music:* La Valse by Ravel
*Time:* Eighteen minutes
*General:* The ballet is a dream piece based on the poem "The Haunted Palace" by Edgar Allan Poe. The period is 1840. In the ballroom of a crumbling
old mansion dancers gather for a party. Strange figures appear and the ghostly
atmosphere increases. Finally the dancers flee from the invading horrors and
the mansion returns to darkness. The lighting should start and end in deep
shadow. During most of the dance the lighting suggests the horror of the
place overwhelming the gaiety.

*Specific:* Projected scenery indicates the mansion. At one point the shadows of the dancers should loom large against the back wall. At the final appearance of the ghosts a red light shoots from the SR wing while the ballroom lights flicker wildly. Colors: over-all bluish cast. Red for the nightmarish scene. Projection in dark reds, black, gray, and violet. Costumes mostly black and white, with accents of dark red, orange, and blue. The chandelier, if available, uses plain white bulbs.

*Running:* Curtain opens on dark stage. Music begins. Light begins to pulse as though the darkness is transforming itself into a scene. The projection of the haunted palace slowly appears, and the pulsing light steadies. The dancers enter. Soon the strange figures enter; the lights flicker and dim somewhat. When the figures leave the lights come up again. A few minutes from the end the strange figures enter again, this time taking human partners for the mad waltz. Red spots shine from the wings and low-angle spots cast shadows on the back wall. The projection pulses as though about to disappear. At the climax of the dance the projection snaps out; the ballroom lights flicker wildly and then go out. Only the red side lights are left. The dancers run away, leaving the stage to the strange figures, who end the dance in steadily dimming light. As the music ends the lights fade out completely. The curtain closes on a dark stage.

# 7

# Scenery Construction

Scenery should be light enough to move and sturdy enough to handle, and there should be no nails sticking out in awkward places. Build scenery within these limits, follow standard construction practices, measure correctly, and the scenery will be of excellent quality.

## GENERAL PRACTICES

(1.) *Plan.* Know in advance what you intend to do.

(2.) *Measure.* Be certain of all dimensions. The size of lumber is misleading. A piece of 1 × 3 pine is not, as might be expected, 1 inch thick by 3 inches wide; it is, unfortunately, 3/4 inch thick by 2-5/8 inches wide. Measure often, never guess.

(3.) *Square.* Flats, platforms, steps, and other items are usually built with 90-degree corners. Too often temptation leads the carpenter to assume that two pieces of wood placed together will make a right angle; seldom is this true. So, for all square corners, use a carpenter's square.

(4.) *Repair mistakes.* A badly cut piece of lumber or a crookedly driven nail will cause trouble. Fix it now.

(5.) *Provide enough time.* Scenery can seldom be whipped up overnight. It takes time—for building, for painting, for assembly.

(6.) *Use imagination.* No book can tell you how to build those odd pieces your mind envisions. Think about it, experiment, and you may surprise yourself.

(7.) *Do not use the studio or stage floor for building.* Dancers do not like nails in their feet or paint on their costumes.

## FLATS

A flat is a wooden frame covered with material. Usually the frame is rectangular and the covering is muslin. However, the dimensions can be whatever is required and the covering anything from burlap to paper to plastic to balloon-dotted pegboard.

One flat can hide an entrance, two hinged together make a screen, three might represent a church, more can build a room. They can be solid or arched or whatever you want. They are useful and easy to build.

The following are instructions for building a flat 3 feet wide by 12 feet high.

Material

1 X 3 pine
1/4 plywood
Covering material
Glue
Nails

Preparation

(1.) Cut two pieces (A) three feet long. These are called *rails* and form the top and bottom of the frame. (See Figure 7-1.)

(2.) Cut two pieces (B) 11 feet, 6-3/4 inches. This length combined with the widths of the top and bottom rails makes up the required 12-foot height. These are *uprights*.

Figure 7-1    Preparation of Material for a Frame

1. Cut two pieces of 1" X 3" pine for top and bottom.

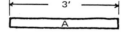

2. Cut two pieces of 1" X 3" pine for the uprights.

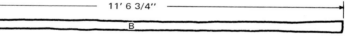

3. Cut one piece of 1" X 3" pine for a crossbrace in the center.

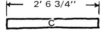

4. Cut four cornerblocks of 1/4" plywood.

5. Cut two keystones of 1/4" plywood.

(3.) Cut one piece (C) 2 feet, 6-3/4 inches. This *crossbrace* fits inside th'. uprights and is cut this length to make up the required width wh'.n combined with the uprights.

(4.) Cut four *cornerblocks* (D) from 1/4-inch plywood. These are abou t 10 inches by 10 inches.

(5.) Cut two rectangular *keystones* (E) from 1/4-inch plywood. These are about 6 inches long and the width of a piece of 1 X 3.

Assembling the Frame

(1.) On the workshop floor or large table lay out the cut pieces in a close approximation of the proper shape. (See Figure 7-2.)

(2.) With a carpenter's square, line up one corner at a right angle. Nail the upright B to a flat surface with two nails. Use the square again to re-fix the corner and then drive two nails into rail A. Drive nails only far enough to keep the lumber from moving.

(3.) Do the same for the other rail and upright. Notice that the square is used in every case. Occasionally, because of a slight angle in sawing or variation in measurement, the cut pieces do not line up exactly. The square corrects for minor errors, although sometimes there may be a slight gap where a rail and upright do not quite meet. If the gaps are large, try again.

(4.) Find the midpoint of the uprights. With the square, fit the crosspiece into the frame. The crosspiece does not have to be nailed down.

(5.) Using white glue, casein glue, or scene glue fasten cornerblocks to the corners of the frame. Leave a space from the edge of the top and bottom equal to the thickness of a 1 X 3. This allows one flat to be placed tight against another at right angles. Do not forget this, or you will certainly remember it later.

(6.) Nail the cornerblocks to the frame with small nails (blue nails are usual). The points will stick through the other side and should be bent over tight against the wood. The bending can be accomplished in one of two ways: (1) a metal plate is inserted under the wood and the nails are bent when driven through, or (2) the flat is turned over when assembled and the nails hammered down.

(7.) Glue and nail the keystones (D) in place, again remembering to allow space between the plywood and the edge of the upright.

(8.) Pull out the nails that hold the frame to the surface. Check for any nailheads coming through the wood where they should not. The frame is now ready for covering.

Covering

Muslin and thin cloth will be glued and stapled to the frame. Plywood

Figure 7-2    Assembling the Frame

1. Lay out the pieces.

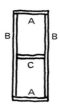

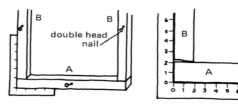

double head nail

2. Square and fasten to the work surface.

3. Maintain square corners even with gaps.

4. Insert crosspiece in the center.

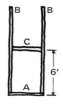

6'

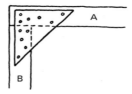

A

B

5. Glue and nail cornerblocks. Keep 3/4" from edges.

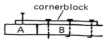

cornerblock

6. Bend over nail points.

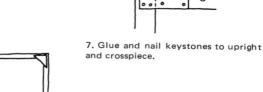

B

C

7. Glue and nail keystones to upright and crosspiece.

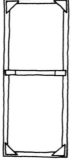

8. The frame finished.

117

plastic, and cardboard do not have to be glued. Flimsy material and paper should be mounted on cardboard or plywood, preferably with the edges folded over the ends of the support and glued or stapled before the whole thing is fastened to the frame.

If your situation requires scenery to be flameproof be certain that the covering material is flameproof or can be. Not all material can be treated. Flameproofing compound can be purchased at some hardware stores or ordered through a catalog; directions for use are included.

For muslin, the standard flat-covering material, the following procedure is generally followed:

(1.) Place the frame on the floor or work table. Lay the material over it to be sure that it will fit.

(2.) Start at the top. Fix the center of the top of the muslin to the center of the rail with a staple. Then staple the center of the bottom of the material to the center of the bottom rail. Do the same for the sides.

(3.) Staple the corners of the material to the corners of the frame. Hopefully the material will be stretched fairly evenly. If you plan to use scene paint with glue, leave some slack, because the material will tighten. Other kinds of paint will shrink the material to a lesser degree.

(4.) Before stapling the rest of the material spread glue on the top and bottom rails. Press the muslin evenly against the glue. Some glue will seep through, which is all right because the paint will cover it. Then glue the uprights and press the material down evenly. Do not glue to the crosspiece.

(5.) If there are wrinkles in the material or something else seems wrong pull out the staples and reset the muslin. When all is well press down the muslin so that it is securely held by the wet glue. Staple along the rails and uprights, using a staple about every nine or ten inches.

(6.) When all is dry the flat is ready for painting.

## SCREENS

Two or more flats or panels hinged together can make a screen. Ordinary screens open and close in only one direction. Others swing both ways and require special hinges. Sturdily built units will last through many productions and may be redecorated as the occasion demands.

### Procedure for a Three-fold Screen

(1.) Hold three panels upright and decide which way the screen is to fold. Mark an "X" where the hinges will be placed. Usually hinges are placed about one foot from the top and bottom, with an additional one provided in the middle for tall or heavy screens. (See Figure 7-3.)

Figure 7-3    Hinging a Three-Fold Screen

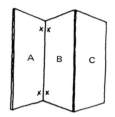

1. Mark X's where hinges will be.

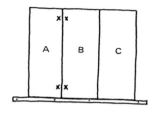

2. Nail down a long, straight board as a line-up board.

3. Place bottom edges of panels against line-up board, face side up.

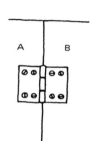

4. Hinge panel A to B on face side.

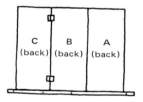

5. Hinge panel B to C on back side.

(2.) Nail a piece of lumber to the floor. This provides a straight edge to use in lining up the bottoms of the panels.

(3.) Place two panels (A and B) on the floor with the bottom edges against the line-up board. The X's for the hinges must be visible.

(4.) Lay a hinge over the crack between the panels. Try the hinge to see that it closes all the way. If it does not, turn it over so that it will. Make certain that the hinge is straight. With a pencil, outline the screw holes on both parts of the hinge. Using a nail as a punch, make a small hole about 3/8-inch deep in the center of each circle. This makes the job of fastening the screws a little easier. Insert the screws and tighten.

(5.) Raise the hinged panels to a standing position and try this part of the screen. Now is the time for any changes. If all is satisfactory put the screen back on the floor, turning it over this time, and add the third panel. The X-marks for the hinges should be in the right place. Hinge as before. Try the resulting screen to be sure that it swings the way you expect.

119

Procedure for a Screen to Swing Both Ways

In addition to two panels, you will need two screen hinges (explain the proposed use to the hardware seller or you may get the wrong kind), and screws to fit the hinges.

(1.) The special hinges go on the edges of the panels, not on the flat surface. (See Figure 7-4.) Lay one panel (A) on the floor. Take a good look at the hinges to see how they work. Place the hinges on the edge of the panel, about one foot from the top and one foot from the bottom. Make certain that the hinges are straight. Fasten the screws.

(2.) Stand up both panels and hold them back to back. Be sure that both are vertical and do not lean. Fasten the loose part of the hinges to the edge of panel B.

Figure 7-4    Hinging a Screen to Swing Both Ways

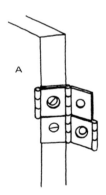

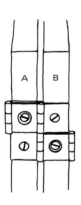

1. Fasten one side of hinge to edge of panel A.

2. Hold panels together. Fasten the other side of the hinge to edge of panel B.

## DROPS

Under the name *drop* can be included all the miscellaneous soft drapes, legs, borders, cyclorama, and backdrops that are used as scenery or masking.

Legs, borders, and main curtains are usually made of velour, a heavy fabric that hangs well and looks good under stage lights. For low-budget operations flannel, duvetyn, or corduroy is sometimes used, although the effect is inferior to that created by velour.

Cycloramas and backdrops to be painted are made from heavy muslin or light canvas. To sew this heavier material an industrial sewing machine may have to be used. Try to borrow or rent one. An ordinary home machine may not be strong enough.

Other scenic drapes and drops use whatever material the designer likes, within practical limits. There are a few cautions to observe. Some material is translucent or even transparent and so may not hide what it is supposed to. Some material is too weak for stage use, especially in a large expanse. Some material cannot be flameproofed or will be ruined by flameproofing. As always, the advice is: try it.

Material

> Fabric
> Upholsterer's webbing
> Grommets or cloth tape
> Weighting chain

Procedure for a Flat Drop

(1.) Cut panel A to the desired length, remembering to add extra material to make up a bottom seam about 3 or 4 inches wide and a small top seam. (See Figure 7-5.)

(2.) Cut panel B to the same length as A. Cut as many other panels as are required to make up the expected width of the drop.

(3.) Sew the panels together with strong, vertical seams. Check to see that any patterns or fabric finishes match.

(4.) Fold over the top edge for a small seam. This can be basted rather than sewn tightly. Sew upholsterer's webbing across the full top width.

(5.) Insert grommets in the top webbing. If grommets are not used then lengths of cloth tape can be sewn to the webbing. Both methods provide the means to tie the drop to the pipe from which it will hang.

(6.) Sew up the bottom seam. If the drop requires a weighted bottom, as do most draw curtains and masking legs, lay a length of chain along the bottom of the drop and then fold over the material for the seam and sew tightly. Fasten the chain to the material at several points to prevent slippage.

(7.) On the top webbing mark with felt pen the size of the drop. Also mark the center. This will save much time later.

Procedure for a Gathered Drop

The difference between the gathered drop and the flat one is that more

Figure 7-5    Making a Flat Drop

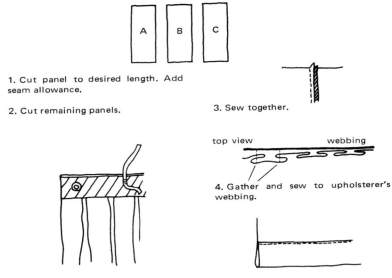

1. Cut panel to desired length. Add seam allowance.

2. Cut remaining panels.

3. Sew together.

top view                    webbing

4. Gather and sew to upholsterer's webbing.

5. Insert grommet or sew tape to top.

6. Sew bottom seam without pleats.

material is required to make up the same width and the excess material i gathered or pleated as it is sewn to the webbing at the top.

(1.) Cut panel A to desired length. Provide extra material for a bottom seam 3 or 4 inches wide and a smaller top seam. (See Figure 7-6.)

(2.) Cut the remaining panels the same length. The combined width of all the panels should be 50 to 100 per cent more than the expected width of the drop. For example, if 15 feet is the area to be covered, then it wil take 5 widths of 3-foot material simply to stretch all the way across, plu another 3 to 5 widths to allow for the gathering.

(3.) Sew the panels with a strong, vertical seam.

(4.) Fold over the top seam and baste. Lay the panels over upholsterer' webbing, which has been cut to the desired width of the finished drop Gather the material in even pleats and sew to the webbing. The best wa to do this is to gather and sew both ends first, then the center. Keep o gathering in the center of each resulting section. This will help keep th amount of material even.

(5.) Insert grommets or tie cloth tapes to the top edge for hanging.

(6.) Sew the bottom seam, with or without a chain enclosed for weight. Thi seam does *not* have pleats.

(7.) Mark the size at the top. Mark the center.

Figure 7-6    Making a Gathered Drop

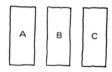

1. Cut panel A to desired length, plus allowance for seams.

2. Cut additional panels (B, C, etc.) to make total width.

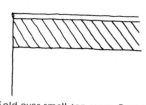

3. Sew panels together.

4. Fold over small top seam. Sew upholsterer's tape across the top of the drop.

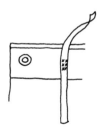

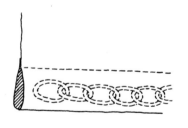

5. In the webbing insert grommets or sew cloth ties for tying drop to pipe.

6. Sew bottom seam. If weight is needed, insert a length of chain and sew in several places.

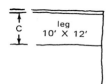

7. Mark size of drop in top corners. Mark center.

**TEPS**

teps require a fair amount of work and a great deal of attention to detail. ome degree of experimentation may be required to determine the dimen- ons for a particular dance, since a standard tread size may be too small. Find

**Figure 7-7    Building Steps**

---

### Preparation

1. Cut the treads from 1" X 12" pine.

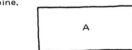

2. Cut the risers from 1" X 12" pine.

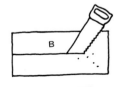

3. Cut legs from 2" X 4" fir.

4. Cut leg braces from 1" X 3" pine.

5. Lay out pattern for support on the 1" X 12". Note that all riser facings are 6 1/2" high EXCEPT for the bottom one, which is 5 3/4".

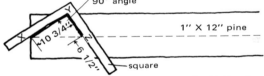

5-1. The first step. Place square's corner at point Y. Revolve so that point X (10 3/4" from Y) and Z (6 1/2" from Y) are on the same line, or the pattern will not come out right.

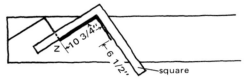

5-2. Repeat for second step. Continue for third step.

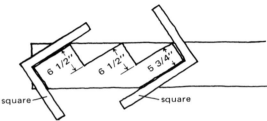

5-3. Finish with 5 3/4" bottom riser support (5 3/4" riser plus 3/4" tread equals a 6 1/2" step).

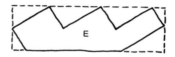

5-4. Cut along lines.

5-5. Lay the cut piece over another piece of 1″ X 12″. Draw the pattern. Cut the second piece.

Assembly

1. Nail support to legs. Allow 3/4″ from edge for back brace.

top view

3/4″ space

Allow 3/4″ from edge for back brace

6½″

side view

square

E   6½″

5 3/4″

2. Nail bottom riser B to supports.

3. Nail bottom step tread A. Nail middle tread B. Then nail middle riser A. Repeat for top.

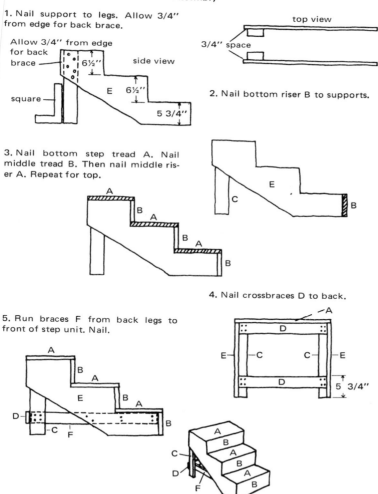

4. Nail crossbraces D to back.

5. Run braces F from back legs to front of step unit. Nail.

out before building, not later. The following instructions are for steps 1-1/2 feet high by 2-feet wide:

## Material

| | |
|---|---|
| 1 × 12 pine | 2 × 4 fir |
| 1 × 3 pine | Nails (6 penny) |

## Preparation

(1.) From the 1 × 12 cut three pieces (A) 2 feet long. These will be the *treads*, the pieces on which the foot steps. (See Figure 7-7.)

(2.) From the 1 × 12 cut three pieces (B) 2 feet long and 5-1/4 inches wide. These are the *risers*, which give the height.

(3.) From the 2 × 4 cut two pieces (C) 1 foot, 5-1/4 inches long. These are the legs that hold up the steps.

(4.) From the 1 × 3 cut two pieces (D) 1 foot, 10-1/2 inches long. These will be the braces for the legs at the back of the unit.

(5.) The support (E) for the whole unit is cut from the 1 × 12. Follow the pattern. Notice that each rise will be 6-1/2 inches, except for the bottom one, which will be cut at 5-3/4 inches. A little drawing with a pencil will show why the bottom cut has to be less than the higher ones; that is the only way that all of the steps come out the same height when the treads are added. Use a square, measure carefully, and cut carefully.

(6.) Cut 2 braces (F) from the 1 × 3 pine, as long as you need to attach them.

## Assembly

(1.) Nail one support to one leg. Keep the leg 3/4-inch from the back edge of the support to allow the crossbraces to fit inside. Use the square to be sure that the legs form a 90-degree angle with the support. Nail through the support into the leg. Now see that the leg makes a 90-degree angle with the floor. Do the same for the other leg, remembering that both legs fit inside the support. Do not allow one to be nailed on the inside and one on the outside. (See Figure 7-7.)

(2.) Nail the bottom riser B to the bottom face of the support.

(3.) Nail the bottom tread A to the riser and support. Nail the middle riser in place, then the middle tread. Do the same for the top.

(4.) Nail crossbraces D into the legs across the back. Nail the top tread into the top crossbrace.

(5.) On the inside of the unit run 1 × 3 braces from the back legs to the front step. Nail.

## PLATFORMS

The term *platform* includes ramps and boxes as well as rectangular and odd shapes—anything that can be used to stand on. Careful measurement and cutting are necessary if the platform is to rest solidly on the floor. Also, care must be given to nailing or fastening with screws, or a dancer's bare feet will certainly discover the lapse. To build a platform 4 feet wide by 8 feet long by 2 feet high, proceed as follows:

### Material

> 1 X 12 pine
> 1 X 3 pine
> 2 X 4 fir
> 3/4-inch plywood
> Nails (6 penny)

### Preparation

(1.) From 1 X 12 pine cut four pieces (A) 8 feet long. These will form the long side. A 1 X 12 actually measures 3/4-inch by 11-1/2 inches. Two together will be 1 foot, 11 inches high. The top, of 3/4-inch plywood, brings the platform to within 1/4 inch of 2 feet high. (See Figure 7-8.)

(2.) From 1 X 12 pine cut four pieces (B) 3 feet, 10-1/2 inches long. These form the short sides and fit inside the long (A) sides to make up a 4-foot width.

(3.) From 2 X 4 fir cut six pieces (C) 1 foot, 11 inches long. These will form a sort of frame to hold everything together.

(4.) From either the 1 X 3 or the 2 X 4 cut one piece (D) 3 feet, 10-1/2 inches. This will be the crossbrace to keep the plywood from sagging under the weight of a dancer.

### Assembly

1.) Place three of the 2 X 4 pieces (C) on the floor. Lay two of the A pieces over the C's so that one C-piece is in the middle and the others are 3/4-inch from the edges of the ends. Nail the 1 X 3 sides onto the 2 X 4 braces. One long side should now be a solid unit. Do the same for the other long side.

2.) Fit the B pieces between the completed A's. They will rest against the C braces. Nail. Now the base of the platform is complete. Measure to be certain that it is the desired size of 4 feet by 8 feet.

Figure 7-8   Building a 4' X 8' X 2' Platform

Preparation

1. From 1" X 12" cut four pieces 8' for long sides.

2. Cut four pieces 3' 10 1/2" for short sides.

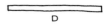

3. From 2" X 4" cut six pieces 1' 11" for upright braces.

4. Cut a crossbrace 3' 10 1/2".

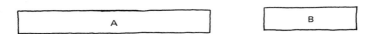

Assembly

1. Nail long sides into upright braces. Allow 3/4" to fit in B pieces.

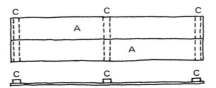

2. Nail short sides into frame.

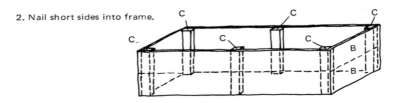

3. Nail crossbrace to middle uprights.

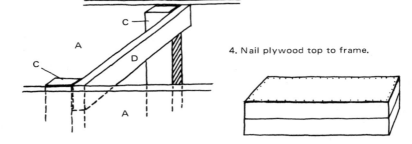

4. Nail plywood top to frame.

3.) The D crossbrace is nailed into the center 2 × 4 brace. This forms a resting place for the plywood top; so it should be even with the top of the B sides, not above or below.

4.) All that remains is to fasten the plywood top. Nail one corner. Nail another corner. You may have to twist the base slightly to make the plywood coincide with the base. If you neglect to do this the platform will not be square at the corners. Nail the other corners. Slight misalignment makes little difference in the finished product, but large errors indicate that something is wrong. If all is well finish nailing the plywood to the base, using about one nail per foot. Include the crossbrace. If you have the time and energy, screws are probably better for the top, since they have less tendency to come out than nails. The dancers might prefer them.

RAMPS

To build a ramp 3 feet wide by 4 feet long by 1 foot high, use the following material and procedures:

Material

    1 × 12 pine
    3/4-inch plywood
    Nails (6 penny)

Preparation

1.) From 1 × 12 pine cut one piece 4 feet long. (See Figure 7-9.)
2.) Draw a diagonal line from one corner to the other. Carefully cut along the line. The resulting pieces (A) will make the sides of the ramp.
3.) From 1 × 12 pine cut one piece (B) 2 feet, 10-1/2 inches.
4.) From 3/4-inch plywood cut a top piece (C) 3 feet by 4 feet.

Assembly

1.) Place the A piece against the B and mark the angle.
2.) Cut the top edge of the B piece at the marked angle.
3.) Nail the A pieces to the B. A larger ramp would use corner braces to make it sturdier, but a small one can do without.
4.) Sometimes the top is laid onto the frame and nailed. If it is necessary that the bottom of the ramp be flush with the floor and the top of the ramp flush with another platform, then top and bottom edges of the plywood must be cut at an angle that will allow them to form a straight line with the surface they touch.

Figure 7-9    Building a Ramp

---

### Preparation

1. Cut one piece 4' long from 1" X 12" pine.

2. Cut diagonally to make two pieces.

3. Cut one piece 2' 10 1/2" from 1" X 12" pine.

4. Cut plywood top.

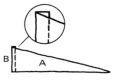

### Assembly

1. Place A against B and mark the angle.

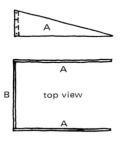

2. Cut a beveled edge across the top of B.

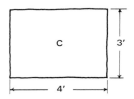

3. Nail sides to B.

top view

4. Nail top. For beveled-edge top, lay the top across the frame, mark angles, cut the bevel, then nail.

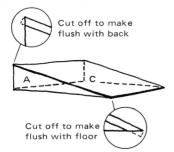

Cut off to make flush with back

Cut off to make flush with floor

## MISCELLANEOUS PIECES

Occasionally there may be a need for a rock, a ground row (which is a painted silhouette or design that stands by itself in the background), or some other bit of symbolic whimsy. Seldom will any good blueprints be found to assist in the construction. The thing to do is to imagine what the finished product is supposed to look like, then make an underpiece that roughly resembles the unit, cover it with some kind of material, and paint. If your imagined rock looks like a beer barrel with horns sticking out of it, nail some horns, or a reasonable facsimile thereof, to a beer barrel, cover, and paint. That is the way to acquire those decorative accessories.

### General Material and Procedure

The understructure can be anything that will support the product or, when necessary, a dancer. It may be a platform already on hand, or two boxes surmounted by a bucket and a coffee can, or a frame built of wood. The idea is just to make something that will hold together and offer a core for the covering.

In many instances the first covering will be chicken wire. This can be pushed around, crumpled, and handled to create three-dimensional shapes. Nail or staple the wire to the support and fasten wire together at various points to keep it from slipping.

The second covering is usually muslin or burlap dipped in glue, wallpaper paste, or a thin solution of plaster of Paris. This is applied in strips or patches over the chicken wire, handled and molded to suit the artist's fancy, and allowed to dry.

Other alternatives call for the use of papier-mâché, which is really paper mashed up and soaked in glue or paste, or Celastic, a sort of chemical version of the same idea, more expensive but stronger. Numerous arts and crafts books explain the papier-mâché process in detail; Celastic directions come with the product advertised by theatrical suppliers. And there are plastics and styrofoams available from dealers in such material. Again, look in dance, theatrical, and art magazines for suppliers. Don't forget the telephone book.

Quite often a store handling party goods, florist supplies, decorator items, and used display-window equipment may supply just the prop you need. If you have more money than time, you may find a store ready to supply what you need.

The final step in converting the prop for stage use is painting. There are two ways to paint: (1) apply paint as well as possible and (2) apply paint as well as possible artistically. For thousands of years the former method has served the theater; the second deserves more use. About the techniques of painting there are only a few standard pieces of advice to offer; all the rest comes from practice and vision. When possible use paint that will wash off brushes and people; do not use oil-base paints and varnishes except for those rare occasions when shiny scenery is wanted; use drop cloths to keep the floor clean, or paint outside on the grass; clean brushes after use. An adequate paint job is within the capability of most dancers; a good one takes more time and talent; an excellent one is a desirable rarity.

Procedure for a Practical Rock

Rocks are either decorative or practical. If they must be used by a dancer the construction will be sturdier than it would be for a piece that lies dormant on the stage floor. The trick to making a rock is to provide an underframe that closely approximates the finished product before all the bumps and curves are added. Rocks can be formed from platforms, boxes, steps, cans, barrels, or anything else that will provide a support for the covering material. The artistry consists in the delicate arrangement of a mass of chicken wire and cloth and the final painting. Fortunately the audience is so far removed from the stage that the artistry does not have to be of Rembrandtian caliber.

You will need framing material—lumber, boxes, etc.—plus chicken wire, muslin or burlap, and glue, wallpaper paste, or plaster of Paris.

(1.) Construct a frame that resembles the finished rock. This requires nailing some lumber together as though it were some sort of platform, or assembling odds and ends into a sturdy base held together with nails, wire, welding, or whatever will do the job. Make sure that any place that must bear weight has support beneath it. Step or jump on the finished product to make certain that it will not collapse. (See Figure 7-10.)

(2.) Cover with chicken wire. Stretch and mold the wire over the frame so that it looks rocky. Nail the wire to the frame at selected points so that it will not slip. Fasten loose edges together with pieces of wire. Stand back and look at the thing. Check those places that will be used to stand on; bare feet will not appreciate the insistent probing of a wire sticking up from a step.

(3.) Dip the muslin or burlap into a solution of glue, wallpaper paste, or plaster of Paris. The material can be in strips or pieces. Apply the wet material to the frame. Again, watch out for those rough places where a bare foot might land.

(4.) Allow the prop to dry. Then paint it to look like a rock. The easiest way to achieve an adequate result is to coat with a base coat of the color that predominates and then spatter with darker and lighter specks of paint. Some darker shade of the base coat can be used in the hollows and under ridges to add to the three-dimensional effect.

Procedure for Strange Pieces

Someone might be inspired by a surrealistic painting of Yves Tanguy, another

Figure 7-10    Making a Rock

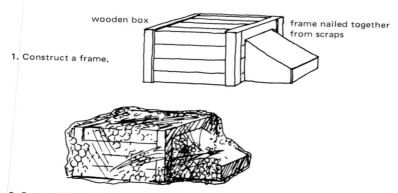

wooden box

frame nailed together
from scraps

1. Construct a frame.

2. Cover with chicken wire. Keep parts that will be stepped on somewhat even.
Fasten down anything that might stick out.

3. Dip material into plaster or glue. Apply to frame.

person by a cactus garden, still another by a Mayan ruin. If some of these
creations must be built instead of projected on the back wall or painted on a
flat, the problem becomes one of building and painting a three-dimensional
object. The techniques are the same as those used in making a rock. Imagine
the finished product, build a sturdy frame, cover, and paint. Remember that
you do not have to provide a unit that must withstand museum-visitor scru-
tiny; only the dancers have a close-up view and they should be too busy to
care about inaccurate restorations of idols or lumpy cactus. As long as the
result is a decent approximation of the original, and strong enough to survive
rehearsals and performances, the audience will accept the offering. Besides,
they may not even know what the thing is really supposed to be.

To make odd-shaped three-dimensional pieces you will need the same
material used for a practical rock: framing material—lumber, pipe, etc.—plus

chicken wire, muslin or burlap, and glue, wallpaper paste, or plaster of Paris.
(1.) From lumber, pipe, cans, cardboard tubes, or whatever is available, construct a frame in the rough shape of the finished piece. Nail or wire together securely so that the frame will not fall apart. Plywood or bent wire may be used to form protrusions and extensions on the basic frame. (See Figure 7-11.)

Figure 7-11    Making a Strange Piece

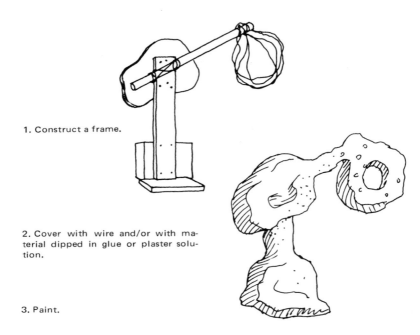

1. Construct a frame.

2. Cover with wire and/or with material dipped in glue or plaster solution.

3. Paint.

(2.) Cover with chicken wire stretched and molded to the wanted shape. Fasten the wire to the frame with nails or staples or other wire.
(3.) Cover with muslin or burlap dipped in glue, wallpaper paste, or a solution of plaster of Paris. Papier-mâché may be substituted, or one of the plastics.
(4.) If the piece is supposed to be futuristically smooth, coat the finished product with thin layers of plaster or papier-mâché to fill in the wrinkles and holes. Sandpaper to the desired smoothness.
(5.) Paint.

## PROJECTED SCENERY

The dancer's most useful scenery is often a picture or a pattern projected onto a wall or the cyclorama, even onto people. The methods are simpler than might be expected, and the result is well worth the time, labor, and expense. An ambitious producer might provide motion pictures or whirling displays; for most occasions a photographed 35 mm. slide or a painted glass plate will serve.

The equipment needed is readily available. A 35 mm. slide projector is sufficient in many cases. A classroom overhead projector is an excellent device to use with painted glass or acetate slides or colored gel. Until you use one in a production you will never realize how useful either kind of projector can be.

Motion picture projectors of course require a reel of film to run through them. The preparation of a suitable film is sometimes rather complex, and there is always some outlay of money, but the results are worth the effort. If the projector can be placed fairly close to the screen and a very large picture is not needed, an 8 mm. film, especially super 8, is cheaper than 16 mm. and gives a satisfactory result. It is worth a try, especially a highly imaginative try.

The preparation of the slide or film demands thought and care. The audience sees the result, not the intent. The original drawing or painting, whether provided by dancer, designer, or some published source, should be chosen carefully. The film should be relevant to the dance and should not look like one. By all means use projected scenery; just be sure that it is a decent accompaniment to the dance.


To Make a Photographic Slide

1.) Find or paint the desired picture. The larger the picture, the better the reproduction.

2.) Photograph the picture on 35 mm. film, if a 35 mm. slide projector is used. If a larger projector is used—a $2'' \times 2''$ for instance—photograph with a camera using that size film. If you are concerned with distortion and want an exact rectangle or an exact shape you will have to photograph the picture from the same angle that the projector will project on the wall.

3.) Project the slide. If it is satisfactory in focus, shape, and clarity, have several copies made, in case one or two are destroyed or faded during rehearsal. Mount in glass covers. The unwanted parts at the top and sides can be blocked off with opaque paint.

4.) Mark the slide with the name of the dance and any other code needed to identify it. Be sure that the mark will read correctly only when the slide is held in the position ready for insertion into the projector.

To Make a Glass or Acetate Slide

(1.) Paint the picture on the slide. Oil paint mixed with varnish can be used, as can the special paint designed for use on acetate or glass. The result may be somewhat disappointing, since both paints tend to form washes and streaks that will appear on the projected picture. Or perhaps the effect is a good one. However, some experimentation will result in a satisfactory image. If you are concerned with distortion, the slide should be painted to correct for it. The only practical way to do this is to place the projector where it will be during the performance, lay the plate over it, and sketch the outlines of the picture so that it looks right. Then fill in the details.

(2.) Use opaque paint to block off unwanted details. Ordinary oil paint will not do the job; rubber-base house paint or an art-store paint made for the purpose is required.

To Make a Composite Slide

(1.) On a base of glass or acetate or plastic gel from the lighting department, glue pieces of transparent material made from gel or anything else that will not dissolve or crumple in heat. Pieces of glass or thin silk may be glued to the base, or fingernail polish may be applied, or whatever else will allow light to pass through. A felt pen may be used to draw lines. Tinfoil or aluminum foil glued to the support will block the light completely for those heavy lines or patches of darkness.

(2.) It may be easier and more effective to assemble the slide if the support is placed on the projector and the result observed on the wall as the various items are added.

Other Techniques

Some slide projectors have a zoom lens. Suppose you want to see a ship approaching from the distant horizon. Start with a small image on the screen; slowly zoom in the lens and the ship seems to come closer and closer. The reverse action can be used to create the illusion of a space traveller leaving the surface of a mysterious planet. Rapid pulses—quick zooms in and out— can suggest a giant beating heart or a fantastic, unsteady landscape.

Two carousel projectors equipped with dimmers can be used to fade from one picture to another or to overlap pictures. Dimmers prevent the on-and-off flashes as the slides are changed.

Moving patterns can be made with a glass bowl placed on a classroom overhead projector. Pour water, dye, and mineral oil into the bowl and watch the color swirl. Blow across the surface, or drip more dye and oil into the mixture. Float another glass dish on the dye-oil mixture and see odd patterns appear. A little alcohol may be needed to prevent boiling if the light is too hot. The psychedelic lighting companies advertise in magazines like *Theater Crafts* and *Dance Magazine* and in the underground newspapers. Send for their catalogs and pick up useful ideas about techniques and materials.

If no projectors are available, try shining a spotlight on some of that plastic wrapping from the kitchen, or on bits of mirror and colored glass pasted onto plastic or cardboard. Reflect the patterns on the walls or on the dancers.

Then practice with the projectors and rehearse with the dancers. Do not wait until the night of the performance, or you will be in trouble. It takes time.

## ENCOURAGING WORDS

If you tremble at the sight of a hammer and saw you can avoid worry by eliminating any new construction or painting. However, if you try, you may find that providing a little scenery is not beyond your talents.

Do try projected scenery. Anybody can take a picture and project it on some kind of surface. And a transparency painted for use on a classroom overhead projector can be a simple project. Until you use pictures you will never realize how a production can be enhanced by a small amount of imagination and effort.

# 8

# Publicity, Tickets, Programs

Publicity sells the show. If the prospective audience is not told that the production is coming and can be seen at a certain place and a certain time then the dancers will play to a select group of friends and co-workers. So tell everybody about it, in every possible way, whether it be a formal newspaper story or a stunt so wild and memorable that the whole community talks about it. Tell your story, and tell it again. Show business is a public affair.

Publicity begins before, not after, the event. While dancers usually have a ready-made audience of parents, friends, and colleagues they need even more people in the auditorium on performance night to make the whole affair worth all the time and effort. A publicity campaign drums up interest.

Unfortunately, choreographers and dancers are too busy with their own particular tasks of designing and performing the dance to spare the time necessary to write stories, make posters, and contact all possible channels of exposure. A publicity director is required, one who can initiate and carry through the details. Helping him can be committees of people willing to design and construct posters and fliers, to check mailing lists and address mailed material, to write and distribute stories, to speak to editors and radio and television producers, to talk about the production, to provide photographs, to do all the mechanical work (see Figure 8-1). Seems like a lot of work is needed, doesn't it? It is.

Figure 8-1    Publicity Schedule

Planning with director and choreographers  . . . . . . . . . . . . (4-3 months)

Preparation of copy about coming events, to be ready for
   inclusion in programs, brochures, news stories,
   or informational fliers  . . . . . . . . . . . . . . . . . . (12-4 months)

Preparation of material for fliers to be
   sent to mailing list  . . . . . . . . . . . . . . . . . . . . . . (3-1 month)

Preparation of copy for news releases. Obtain photographs,
   biographies, dancers' home addresses, special items  . . . . . (2-1 month)

Preparation of feature stories, news stories,
   and advertisements . . . . . . . . . . . . . . . . . . . . . . . (1 month)

Announcements to radio and television stations . . . . . . . . . . . (1 week)

Design, construction, and distribution of posters  . . . . . . . . . (3-1 month)

Design and preparation of program copy . . . . . . . . . . . . . . (2-1 month)
   Check with director, choreographers, and performers.
   Double-check name spelling, all credits, program
   materials. Plan for duplication and check proofs

## CHANNELS OF PUBLICITY

In a world bombarded by advertising and public relations it is necessary for those concerned with this production to spend time and effort in searching for practical ways to let people know about the event. The most readily accessible avenues are:

Printed stories in newspapers and periodicals.

A selected mailing list for sending fliers, postcards, posters.

Announcements on radio, television, public gatherings.

Bulletin-board announcements, posters, pennants, signs, banners, table-mats, counter-cards, automobile bumper stickers.

Special events, stunts, or planned drives for calling attention to the production.

Notices of coming attractions in earlier program formats, or in the programs of other community events.

### Newspapers

Newspapers require an immense amount of material. Most of what is printed is provided by staff writers or from syndicates, which deliver a variety of stories and features to the subscribing paper. Sometimes stories offered by groups planning a public presentation are welcome. The papers want *stories*, not lengthy unpaid advertisements; so write a good story that will interest the reader. Take a look at a newspaper before you write it. Newspapers are not English composition classes or friends; they are written in certain ways. If you cannot discover the style through reading, then study some of the many books available on reporting. An editor may rewrite a bad story if it is of sufficient interest to his readers or if someone on the paper pushes for publication for private reasons, but the chances are better if the writing is good enough to stand alone. So work at it.

It hardly seems necessary to recommend clean copy, typed doublespace, on one side of the paper, with a clear identification of who sent it, including name and telephone number. Certainly all copy should be accurate, sent to the correct person, with his name spelled right, at the correct address, and with enough postage. It helps if it arrives for consideration before the deadline! Always check spelling, especially of names, places, and titles.

Use the famous who, what, where, when, and how. They tell the audience what they need to know.

The *who* of the story may be a performance company or a school dance group; or it may refer to a choreographer, performer, or sponsor; or it may be a studio, community center, recreation department, or club.

The *what* is the kind of production: lecture-demonstration, studio performance, part of a tour, showing of student dances, a happening, a videotaped showing. Is it a premier? Is it in fulfillment of some graduate degree?

*Where* involves the place of the event: the name of the performance place, the address, telephone number, available parking space, and directions for getting there.

*When* states all details of date, day, and hour.

*How* instructs the interested person to call by phone or in person for tickets, gives the prices, and indicates student or block rates.

The chances of publication are sometimes better in a small paper than in a big one. A small-town editor is more willing than a metropolitan staffer to publicize a local show. Try them all. There are neighborhood papers and shopping newspapers that cater to local readers, there are school and club papers and newsletters, Sunday school and fraternal organization programs and mailers. Even if the complete story, or, as it should be, set of stories, is not published, an announcement may appear in a calendar of events or listing of entertainment. It doesn't cost much to try—just work and a little postage.

In general:

(1.) Begin the story with a well-balanced headline that clearly indicates the content of the story.

(2.) Write, at the top of the page, the suggested date for release, such as "For Immediate Release" or "For Release April 30." If there is more than one page be sure that each is numbered, that the source and title are on each page, that all pages are clipped or stapled together. Clearly indicate the ending of the story.

(3.) Make the story brief, with short stabbing sentences. All highlights should appear in the first paragraph and then be elaborated later. Be sure that all the information is included. Local names sell the story.

(4.) Resist the temptation to send notices that interest only a few people. Develop good rapport with the editors by always sending newsworthy items, well-written and concise. It might also be nice to express your thanks when he does use your material.

(5.) Consider the possibility of a series of notices timed with events leading up to the production. Stories about the dances to be presented, the choreographers, performers, music or sets, costumes or staging, or even unusual aspects of the agency involved may be interesting. It might be appropriate to discuss the nature of dance as a performing art in the event of a formal concert.

(6.) If you have difficulty in getting appropriate material printed it might be useful to call this to the attention of the editor. It sometimes helps to add a pleasant request for reconsideration. Never demand anything.

(7.) It is most important to pay attention to the deadlines for receiving different kinds of stories. In most cases it should arrive about one day in advance of the deadline. But it is apt to get lost if it arrives too soon.

(8.) A letter or a memo to an editor proposing a story or an interview is often well received. Briefly include some of the facts that could be developed for reader interest. Offer time for interviews or photography.

(9.) If photographs are sent they should be glossy prints 4 × 5 to 8 × 10. The usual request is for simple, clearly outlined features with no "arty" effects such as an unusual focus or camera angle. Two or more dancers, in costume, either in a setting or in *simulated* action against a white background, in a well-lit studio, are usually preferred. These are not the pictures that the dancer or the choreographer favors, but the policy of the newspaper editor must be considered. Find out what this policy is. Each print submitted must have clear identification typed and taped to the back of the print. Never type or write directly on the print because impressions show and sometimes the paper cracks.

(10.) Papers printed by the offset process can use glossy prints easily, but others, especially those with limited circulation, should be provided with mats made from your own engraving. When sending copy and a mat, always include a reproduction of the mat with its captions attached. However, mats cost money. Ask the newspaper office how to get a mat.

A feature story is usually a weekend feature that is exclusive to a particular paper. Such a story might have the by-line of the choreographer, leading dancer, or director. It could be an interview with a critic about dance as a performing art, or with a teacher about dance in the schools, about this particular production, or about some of the local performers. The names of local people are vital, no matter how unimportant their roles. If you are sending these stories to a large paper try to indicate the area of greatest relevance, such as arts, education, society, disadvantaged youth, etc.

The news-tip is a brief reminder to an editor that something worthy of his reader's interest is about to occur. Brief, accurate, and truthful facts should be outlined, advance copies of the program included, and interviews suggested. Remember that you must convince the editor that the affair is of interest or in some way newsworthy. With large newspapers these tips should be sent to the appropriate editors.

The best form of free newspaper advertising is the critical review, even if the critic seems unkind to your production. Usually critics will come, even to minor events, if asked politely by letter. It sometimes helps to enclose tickets and to arrange for a meeting with the dancers or choreographers following the performance.

Advertisements themselves cost money, more perhaps than you think. So first check the cost of space, typesetting, and illustration. For productions with limited budgets, newspaper ads are a luxury that can seldom be afforded. But a newspaper ad is effective because of its widespread and objective evidence of an event. The notice can be clipped and saved for future reference. Here is a direct attack presenting the important facts of who-what-where-when, and how much. Don't be tempted to write long and glowing accounts of the production—leave that to the critics. Catchy slogans or lines with fresh impact are better than long and tedious descriptions. Some symbolic trademark for the dance group, a logotype with unusual letters or illustrations, may be exciting to use and will become associated with the group if it is used consistently.

Designing a good advertisement takes time, concentration, and skill. Keep looking at advertisements and choose or adapt from one that you like. You can rearrange the words to fit your own situation.

It is important to decide on the essential information and to find ways of making it exciting so that an audience will be enticed into coming to the performance. After the words have been selected and a design made it is time to consider how you want it printed. Sometimes it is helpful to type the copy on blocks of paper or cardboard and then manipulate them until you find the right relationship and pattern. Sketches, photographs, and designs can also be tried in different relationships to the words. Try for an over-all balance, not necessarily a centering of each block. Then make a copy of the actual size that will appear. A one-column ad only an inch high may not be large enough for everything. (See Figure 8-2.)

Ads in entertainment sections of newspapers can be most effective, even if they are only a few lines, because many people are accustomed to looking

Figure 8-2    Newspaper Advertisement

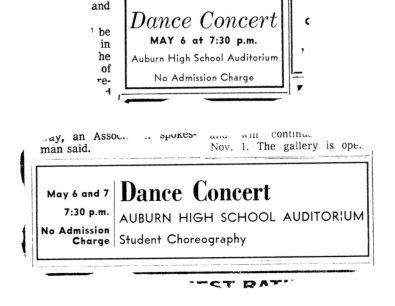

there to know what is going on. If you are planning a series, it helps to make the ads distinct and uniform and to have them appear at regular intervals.

## Radio and Television

A *notice* may be sent to all radio and television broadcasters who publicize community or educational events. Compile and keep current a list of all possible stations, as well as program directors, producers of talk or news programs, and calendars of events. If names are not known, it is usually sufficient to address by title: News Director or Producer, "Town Topics," or some other identifiable title. In television programs the producer's name is always listed in the credits and should be written down by any prospective user of his services. Radio notices will usually be addressed to the personality heard on the program.

Be sure to keep the notices short and accurate. Read them to yourself to see that they make sense and sound as though they are spoken and not written sentences. Include—though not as a part of the notice to be read on the air—a brief statement about the organization and its program, as well as a telephone number for further information.

An *interview* may be suggested, provided the guest can contribute something of interest to the audience. Choose the proposed guest carefully, picking someone who is literate, presentable, and able to speak easily and without hesitation. After all, the speaker represents your organization. The interviewer should be provided with information on the guest and the production, not in long rambling pages but in concise and factual paragraphs. Some questions may be suggested. And do not forget the hard information about event, time, and place.

Music from the production may be suggested for inclusion in radio programs if the music fits the format. A disc jockey will not play ballet music, nor is the "Old Favorite Song Hour" inclined to feature the latest electronic sound synthesis. When music has been especially composed for the production this may be promoted as an event of interest. Of course, it is always necessary to check the copyright and to secure the permission of the composer or publisher. With any tape or record that you supply always send neatly typed information about the production.

Time units of 10, 20, 30, on up to 60 seconds can be bought; while very expensive, they are effective. This is the time for superlatives. Each word must be just right and a catchy phrase or a funny line is preferable. Of course, the what, when, and where should be emphasized and repeated.

## The Mailing List

A neat, well-organized, and currently accurate mailing list is a valuable source for contacting a select audience. Of course there are many kinds of mailing lists—even the telephone book will serve—but the most effective is made up of people with an active interest in dance. This would include the dance or physical education departments of colleges, universities, junior colleges, high schools, community or recreation centers, YMCA, YMHA, and YWCA, dance studios, public libraries, art galleries and museums, and listings of those who have attended previous dance events (always make available a place for members of the audience to add their names to the current mailing list). Personal lists from performers, choreographers, and production staff are certainly of current value.

Typical mailing pieces include: printed or mimeographed fliers enclosed in an envelope or folded and stapled; postcards, which may have a return piece to serve as a ticket order; duplicated letters describing the production; leaflets; "gimmick" pieces, which may range from cutouts of ballet slippers to engraved formal invitations to the production. (See Figures 8-3 and 8-4.) A survey of your own advertising mail will show the great variety of techniques used in mail order advertising.

Figure 8-3    Mimeographed Program Announcement

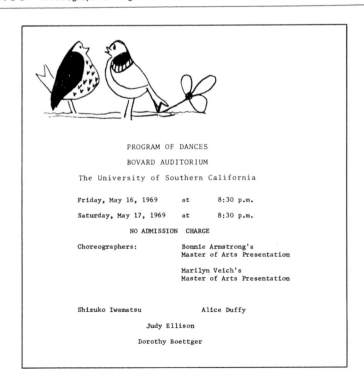

Figure 8-4    Printed Announcement Folder

---

# a dance production

*Musical Comedy and Modern Dance*

**Presented by the Dance Students of U.S.C.**

## SATURDAY MAY 24

**Matinee 2:30**                                    **Eve 8:15**

Bovard Auditorium 36th and University

| ADMISSION | TICKET INFORMATION |
|-----------|--------------------|
| General $1.00 | Student Union |
| Block of 10 .75 each | Room 209 |
| High School .50 | RIchmond 8-2311, Ext. 610 |

*Sponsored by the Physical Education Department with the cooperation of the University Extension Division*

---

Some schools have their own print shop, but if you are dealing with a commercial printer, work tends to be costly. Discuss the possibility of a package deal with him, to include posters, tickets, fliers, programs, and other materials. If you can find a helpful printer, willing to work for you on successive productions, you are fortunate.

Mailings require postage, so that means money. Resist the temptation to over the entire community. Choose the prospects, then try to sell them. If the list is long some saving can be made by using bulk postal rates, which will be explained at the post office. Be sure to understand all the postal restrictions *before* you print the material.

How is the budget holding out?

## Bulletin Boards

The purpose of an announcement placed on a bulletin board is to attract attention. Amid the clutter of the usual board nothing can attract attention; so first, strip away the extra material, provided, of course, that you are authorized to do so.

Pictorial and colored material stands out. Action photographs of the

145

dancers, or colorful posters, or even a typewritten sheet of paper mounted on a piece of poster board with ribbon or gold seals, will catch the eye long enough to make some impression.

Since posted material is easily removed, it is a good idea to restrict pictures and posters to those that can be lost without trouble and tears. This is no place for irreplaceable items.

## Displays

A glass case could contain costumes, scene designs, photographs, or anything else that might provide an interesting display. Only you can determine whether the case provides the necessary amount of safety. If you are not certain, do not risk the loss of such items.

## Posters

A standard method of advertising productions is the printed poster. Posters can easily be duplicated by a number of techniques once an effective format has been designed. The advantage of color and illustration is obvious, but too much of either will be distracting. A simple but striking design, an action figure, a reproduced photograph, an abstraction, or a color overlay will be a point of emphasis for directing attention to the what-where-when of the production. Take a good look at magazine advertising and collections of prize-winning posters. Borrow what you like.

If students or friends volunteer to make posters, be sure that some general plan is followed; otherwise, well-meaning creativity may produce confusion. Obviously there is no rule about such things; it is just that someone must check the content, form, and taste of the plan and the product. Consult a good book on poster-making for clarification of techniques and general principles.

## Specials

Table-mats, counter-cards, printed-stickers, banners, or pennants are all things that enthusiastic committee members enjoy making. These can be effective if something of the basic poster or flier design is repeated along with the pertinent information of what-where-when.

## Notice of Coming Events

Even a small notice included in the program of earlier dance productions by the same group or in other community production programs reaches a proven audience. If possible, include some information that will generate interest and enthusiasm for the event (see Figure 8-5).

Announcements and Special Events

Short and well-planned announcements in community and recreation centers, schools, clubs, social gatherings, and studios may reach a potential audience.

**Figure 8-5    Notice in Earlier Dance Program**

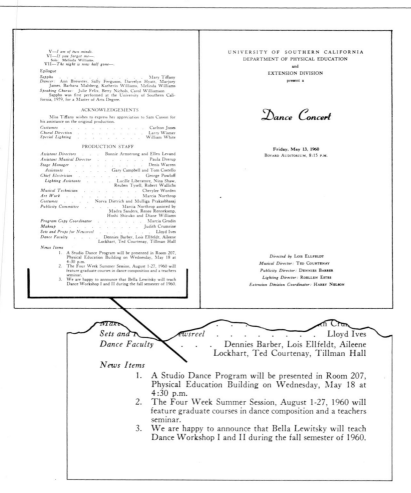

V—*I am of two minds.*
VI—*If you forget me—.*
    Solo: Melinda Williams.
VII—*The night is now half gone—.*

Epilogue

*Sappho* . . . . . . . . . . . . Mary Tiffany
*Dancers:* Ann Brewster, Sally Ferguson, Darrelyn Hyatt, Marjory James, Barbara Malsberg, Katherin Williams, Melinda Williams
*Speaking Chorus:* Julie Felix, Betty Nichols, Carol Williamson
    Sappho was first performed at the University of Southern California, 1959, for a Master of Arts Degree.

ACKNOWLEDGEMENTS

Miss Tiffany wishes to express her appreciation to Sam Casson for his assistance on the original production.

*Costumes* . . . . . . . . . . . Carlton Jones
*Choral Direction* . . . . . . . . Larry Wismer
*Special Lighting* . . . . . . . . William White

PRODUCTION STAFF

*Assistant Directors* . . . Bonnie Armstrong and Ellen Levand
*Assistant Musical Director* . . . . . . Paula Drerup
*Stage Manager* . . . . . . . . . Denis Warren
*Assistants* . . . . . Gary Campbell and Tom Costello
*Chief Electrician* . . . . . . . . George Powloff
*Lighting Assistants* . . . . Lucille Liberatore, Nina Shaw, Reuben Tysell, Robert Wallichs
*Musical Technician* . . . . . . . Cherylee Worden
*Art Work* . . . . . . . . . . Marcia Northrop
*Costumes* . . . Norva Dietrich and Mulliga Prakasbhasaj
*Publicity Committee* . . . . Marcia Northrop assisted by Madra Sanders, Renee Rennekamp, Hoshi Shizuko and Diane Williams
*Program Copy Coordinator* . . . . . . Marcia Grodin
*Makeup* . . . . . . . . . . . Judith Crumrine
*Sets and Props for Newsreel* . . . . . . Lloyd Ives
*Dance Faculty* . . . Dennies Barber, Lois Ellfeldt, Aileene Lockhart, Ted Courtenay, Tillman Hall

*News Items*

1. A Studio Dance Program will be presented in Room 207, Physical Education Building on Wednesday, May 18 at 4:30 p.m.
2. The Four Week Summer Session, August 1-27, 1960 will feature graduate courses in dance composition and a teachers seminar.
3. We are happy to announce that Bella Lewitsky will teach Dance Workshop I and II during the fall semester of 1960.

UNIVERSITY OF SOUTHERN CALIFORNIA
DEPARTMENT OF PHYSICAL EDUCATION
and
EXTENSION DIVISION
present a

*Dance Concert*

Friday, May 13, 1960
BOVARD AUDITORIUM, 8:15 P.M.

*Directed by* LOIS ELLFELDT
*Musical Director:* TED COURTENAY
*Publicity Director:* DENNIES BARBER
*Lighting Director:* ROELLEN ESTES
*Extension Division Coordinator:* HARRY NELSON

*Sets and ~~~~~~~~ ~~~wsreel* . . . . . . . Lloyd Ives
*Dance Faculty* . . . Dennies Barber, Lois Ellfeldt, Aileene Lockhart, Ted Courtenay, Tillman Hall

*News Items*

1. A Studio Dance Program will be presented in Room 207, Physical Education Building on Wednesday, May 18 at 4:30 p.m.
2. The Four Week Summer Session, August 1-27, 1960 will feature graduate courses in dance composition and a teachers seminar.
3. We are happy to announce that Bella Lewitsky will teach Dance Workshop I and II during the fall semester of 1960.

Some specially developed event or stunt may also be organized. At one high school, members of the publicity committee dressed in old dance costumes and paraded around the school campus. One student led a small fox terrier in a pink tutu, and others, with signs having the what-where-when clearly indicated, chanted, "Look what's coming, why not come?" Winding up the parade in grand style, a big black poodle wiggling along in a white tutu pulled a little red wagon carrying a two-faced poster proclaiming the program. It may be a little silly, but it works. There is no limit to the possibilities of an imaginative and interested committee!

## TICKETS

Some performances will be open to the audience with no seat reservation or cost. Free tickets or invitations may be issued bearing the important what-where-when information, simply to make sure that people know the details of the event. However, if you anticipate income it is necessary to design and control the entire ticket procedure. And tickets are equivalent to money, so be careful.

Tickets for reserved seats must follow a numbering system based on the seating plan for the theater. Obtain or make a seating chart and consult it in printing and selling tickets. By making a copy of the chart for each performance and scratching off the reserved seats sold, the person in charge of tickets can keep track of advance sales, and the chart also can be used in the box office for sales just before the performance.

Tickets may be printed or duplicated by a variety of methods. They can be hand-cut and lettered or they can be purchased in a stock roll. These stock rolls of tickets are numbered but have no printed designation of the event so that they look incomplete and cheap. But they do provide a means of keeping track of how many tickets were issued.

The information on each ticket will vary according to the production and the decisions of the director. But if the tickets are printed it is advisable to have ticket and stub, numbered and priced. Desirable additions will include place, date, and time of event (see Figure 8-6). Different colored tickets for seats reserved in different parts of the house are helpful to members of the audience and to ushers. Options such as using many colors of paper or ink often involve higher costs. Again, it is the eternal balance of available money and priority of need.

Close control of tickets is imperative, otherwise the whole plan is in jeopardy. A complete record must be kept of all tickets, including complimentary ones for guests and critics. Whoever is in charge of ticket sales, his assistants, the ticket sellers, and the ticket takers at the time of performance must all be efficient and trustworthy. In some cases they are bonded.

A prompt accounting of all ticket sales and attendance should be included in the final report to the director by the one in charge of ticket sales.

Figure 8-6 Tickets and Stubs

```
┌─────────────────────────────────────────────────────────┐
│  Seat    USC Department of Physical Education    Row     │
│                        presents                          │
│              A Modern Dance Production                   │
│           DANCE IS FOR EVERYBODY           Seat          │
│  Row  Bovard Auditorium              Saturday            │
│       8:30 p.m.        $2.50      March 20, 1970         │
└─────────────────────────────────────────────────────────┘
```

```
 101  Seat   Department of Physical Education        MARCH 20, 1970  Bovard Auditorium  Row  J
             presents                                                                        
 Cent'r Sec. ORCHESTRA  DANCE IS FOR EVERYBODY  ORCHESTRA  8:30 p.m.           Sec. Cent'r
             A Modern Dance Production
        MAR        Bovard Auditorium
  Row   20       University of                                              Seat  101
                 Southern California
                 SAT. NIGHT, 8:30 p.m.
        1970    Orchestra, $2.50
                No Refunds—No Exchanges
```

## PROGRAMS

The program is a guide given to members of the audience, with selected information about the production. The information in the program varies according to the point of view of the director and choreographer, serving as a bridge from their intent to the audience's perception.

The minimum information within a program will include:

(1.) The kind of production, such as dance concert, folk dance festival, or dance happening.
(2.) The place, date, and time of performance.
(3.) The sequence of events, titles of dances.
(4.) Program notes or necessary comments.
(5.) The names of choreographers, performers, and production staff.
(6.) Credits to composers, designers, and assistants.
(7.) Intermissions.

If it is considered important that the audience understand the details of the event then it is important to design titles, program notes, and explanations to this end. It may, however, be considered more appropriate to establish an atmosphere or mood—a setting within which the audience draws its own conclusions. Or the program may be restricted to a list of events and credits. Here again there are so many possibilities that final decisions must simply be in accord with the discrimination and belief of the person designing the program. Unfortunately, such decisions are often made on the basis of past experience or traditional form rather than on a careful consideration of what best suits the situation.

The layout is also a matter of decision in terms of the particular situation. Whether the program is to be printed, mimeographed, xeroxed, hand-lettered, or duplicated by some other process, it is necessary to anticipate a size and shape for the document. Sometimes a single sheet of varying length and width will seem appropriate; or a single folded sheet with its resulting four surfaces for words and design may be desired; or it may be a single fold with a single sheet insert that is favored; or it may be any one of the endless

Figure 8-7    Program for Dance Concert

ther variations in size, shape, and format. It is logical, however, to first
determine the material to be used and then to manipulate it within the most
useful and attractive form.

The title of the program, the date-time-place, the name of the group
performing, and the sponsoring organization usually appear at the top or on
the first page of the program. (See Figure 8-7 and Figure 8-8.) The sequence
of events is usually outlined, with immediate credit given to the composer of
the accompaniment, to performers, choreographers, and special assistants.
Sometimes credits are kept to a minimum in this part of the program and
given at the end.

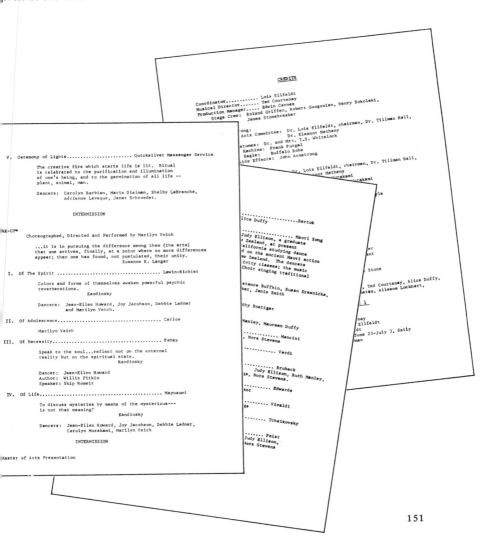

Figure 8-8    Studio Dance Program

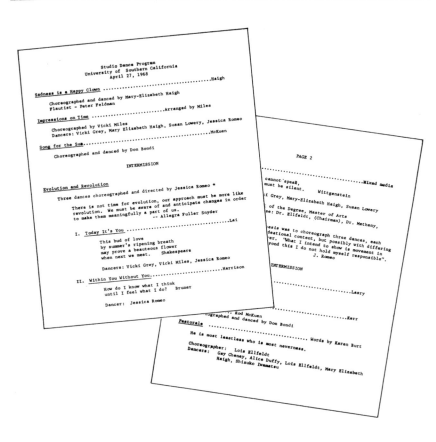

Acknowledgments and credits, always spelled correctly, should be given to everyone concerned with the production. Information about coming events can be of great publicity value. Additional information in the program may refer to the nature of the dance to be seen, the sponsoring agency, the choreographers, dancers, designers, or members of the production staff. Programs on fairly heavy paper, and of a size that is convenient for the spectator, will eliminate paper rattling during the performance. If the cost is too high, try to sell some advertising.

A drawing for the cover and/or other parts of the program may add considerably to the over-all impact, but sometimes it is done just because it is a "thing-to-be-done." The extent to which an imaginative and fresh design can enhance the program can hardly be overemphasized. Try to be aware of the many programs that you see when attending different shows in the theater, museum, gallery, and other public meetings. Keep a record of unusual or interesting ideas for programs so that you can refer to them when initiating your own designs.

Program notes should be used only when the choreographer is convinced that they are needed to direct attention to certain facts or to set a mood. This use of notes actually represents a philosophic point of view and reflects one's stand on the value of verbal description to clarify a nonverbal form.

# Before
## Performance

# 9

# Lighting: Practical Work

The creative work of lighting design gives way to what too many people regard as the plodding mechanics of lighting. But just as a choreographer has to work with dancers to carry out an interesting idea so too does the designer work with equipment and crew to realize his idea. Both tasks are challenging, both are necessary.

The mechanical part of stage lighting is divided into seven separate tasks:
(1.) *Preparation*—inspection and readying of equipment.
(2.) *Rigging*—placement of instruments and cables.
(3.) *Gelling*—cutting and framing the color medium.
(4.) *Plugging*—mating cables to switches and dimmers.
(5.) *Focusing*—pointing and shuttering the light.
(6.) *Cue-setting*—deciding and charting light usage.
(7.) *Running*—operation of equipment.
The first five operations are usually carried out before the technical rehearsal; the last two are ordinarily determined during technical rehearsal. Changes can be made when needed.

None of the work is particularly complicated, possibly excepting focusing, which presents a number of problems, but all require some degree of thought and care if the result is to be proper and safe.

## PREPARATION

Before setup-time arrives all material should be checked for completeness and for safety. Better to discover trouble early than to find out through blown fuses or sudden fires that equipment is defective.

## Lighting Instruments

Although the units are usually rugged enough to withstand abuse, there are certain elements that can be damaged. These should be inspected:
(1.) *Lens*. A cracked lens is liable to drop on the stage or somebody's head. It has happened before.
(2.) *Cords*. Replace dangerous wiring. Frayed leads at the instrument or at the plug are too dangerous to be ignored.
(3.) *Yoke*. Tighten bolts enough to make sure that the instrument will not fall from yoke or C-clamp.

(4.) *Lamp*. The lamp socket may be empty because someone "borrowed" the bulb for another spot. Or the existing lamp may be burned out. Replacement now saves worrying later.

## Cables

Extension cables are a frequent source of trouble, either because the wire is too small or because a short circuit exists in some part.

(1.) *Wire size*. The amount of current that a wire can transmit depends on its size. For heavy loads a heavy wire is needed. Ordinary household cords are usually too small for stage use unless the stage lights are also small, perhaps not exceeding 500 watts for each cord. If the cable becomes hot when the light is turned on, substitute another with larger wires. If in doubt, ask someone who knows.

(2.) *Plug*. Check to see that the wires are securely attached to the terminals and that they are not twisted so that they touch, or can touch, either the other wire or the metal part of the plug.

(3.) *Connector*. Wiring is sometimes pulled loose when an unknowing hand jerks at the wire instead of the connector. Unscrew the top, look, and reattach.

(4.) *Splices*. Any splices should be neat, solid, and safe. If they are not, cut the cable and refasten and retape the wires so that each wire is separately and completely covered by tape. If the budget permits, replace bad cables.

(5.) *Boxes*. If the cable ends in a box with two or more receptacles, the screws and other.fasteners should be checked. Sometimes a nut inside the box will work loose, allowing the cable to move back and forth freely. A rattle indicates that the nut is completely off. Unscrew the holding screws, look inside, tighten anything loose, and replace the screws. It is a simple job.

## RIGGING

Usually, lights are hung from a pipe. For this reason most spotlights and floods are provided with C-clamps, which can be fastened to a pipe. After the location has been determined, either from the light plot or the designer's direction, the instrument is held up to the pipe, the mouth of the C-clamp placed around the pipe, and the bolt tightened with a wrench. Tighten as much as needed to hold the unit securely, but not so much that a sturdy truck driver must be summoned to loosen the bolt. When focusing time arrives those lights may have to be moved.

If the instrument is not provided with a C-clamp then use whatever means is provided or improvise with wire and screws. Add a piece of wire or rope to make certain that nothing can fall accidentally. This is especially true for clamp-on units.

Light stands usually provide a place at the top where the bolt from the instrument yoke can be screwed in. If there is not such a bolt hole then the instrument can be fastened with a C-clamp or other clamp. A few weights piled on the base may be required to keep the stand from falling over, or, if the stand does not have to be moved, the base may be screwed or nailed to the floor.

Any makeshift arrangements—nailing or wiring lights to a pipe or piece of wood, propping with sandbags, hanging from rope, or whatever else seems necessary at the time—should be as secure and safe as possible. There may be times when proper procedures cannot be followed, but those lights should not be wigglers and slippers. If the lights hang above the audience be even more careful; audiences tend to sue more often than dancers when unexpectedly struck by a falling hunk of metal.

When the lights are in place and fastened to pipe or stand or whatever, some arrangement must be made to connect the cords to the power source.

Many light pipes are provided with receptacles connected directly to the switchboard or plug board. If there are enough you are very fortunate. Usually you need some extension cables to provide power. A full light plot will show whether the instrument is plugged into a pipe receptacle or goes into an extension. When a full plot is not available, as usually happens, the rigger decides how the light gets its power.

Sometimes the right thing to do is to plug the light into the nearest receptacle. This is the easiest way, but it may be the wrong way. Pencil-and-paper figuring determines the decision. For example, that receptacle may be connected to a 1000-watt dimmer, but you are using a 1500-watt spotlight; so you have to run an extension to a power source capable of supplying the extra power. Or you may need four separate circuits when the pipe has only three. Or one of a pair of spotlights is connected to a nearby receptacle while its mate is thirty feet away and yet has to be on the same circuit. So you use extension cables.

Extension cables should be long enough, which seems quite obvious, except that many people forget to allow enough slack at both ends to relieve tension on the cord as well as to permit moving the light if necessary. A little spare cable on both ends is always useful; wire doesn't really stretch as much as you would like it to.

As each cable is run it should be marked at both ends with some kind of identifying number. You won't remember which cable is which; so wrap a piece of masking tape around the ends and mark well with a felt-tip or ballpoint pen.

Individual cables are required when the lights they feed must be individually controlled. If light #1 shines only when light #2 is supposed to be off, then each light must be separately powered or both will certainly come on. If two lights work together, at the same time and at the same intensity, they can be fed by a single cable, provided that the cable is large enough to carry the current without excessive heating.

After the cables are run they should be arranged neatly and fastened t
the pipe with cord or tape. Cord tied with a shoe-tying knot is much easier t
undo than sticky tape. If connections are loose they may be fastened with
few wraps of friction or electrician's tape, not masking or cellophane tape
First be sure that twist-lock connectors are twisted so that they hold tight.

Those cables trailing from the end of a pipe or sprawling across the floo
should be fastened every couple of feet with cord so that they make a nea
bundle that can be handled as one item and not as a random collection o
loose wire. When the tied bundles reach the patch panel, or dimmers, o
switches, the excess should be coiled and again tied into a neat bundle tha
can be tied up or shoved out of the way. Better a neat bundle than a trap fo
somebody's neck or a nest waiting for an errant foot. Remember that back
stage areas are usually dark during a performance and those cables migh
catch what they are not supposed to. Keep cables out of the way.

GELLING

Sheets of colored transparent gelatine or plastic—both called "gel"—should b
provided by the designer. These will be cut to fit the frames for spots an
floods. Before cutting any gel make sure that you can tell one color fror
another. If there is any doubt, cut all of one color at the same time, mar
well either by color, name, or number, insert in the frame, and specify th
light for which the frame is intended. There are quite a few colors, althoug
the number commonly used is small enough to be learned with little trouble
Probably six recur so often that they can be recognized after a little exper
ence: special lavender, flesh pink, bastard amber, steel blue, straw, and me
dium blue. The others had better be kept in a separate bundle.

Cutting

Stop to think of the most economical way to do the job, or you may have t
run off to buy an extra sheet of gelatin. The easiest way to begin is to lay
gel frame across the sheet and move it around until you have determined th
maximum number of pieces that can be cut. Or you can be more mathemati
cal and calculate the number. Circular pieces should be cut near the edge s
that there is a chance that the rest can be used in a square frame.

Cutting can be done with scissors, mat knife, or paper cutter. Or th
frame can be held tightly against the gel and the gel pulled up so that it neatly
tears itself against the metal frame. Or the gel may be folded, tightly creased
and then torn. The first method is recommended; the second and third requir
careful attention.

Patching

Sometimes you may have to patch a gel, either because of a tear or because
the available piece is not large enough to fit the frame. Fortunately, gelati

n be patched easily, often permanently, by wetting the edges and pasting
e pieces together. No glue is needed, just the wet gel. Provide enough
verlap to give a good bond—half an inch is sufficient, and either more or less
on't hurt too much.

Plastic medium, such as Cinemoid or Roscolene, requires transparent
pe or careful application of a heated soldering iron.

## oring

fter cutting the gel, provide the remaining pieces with names or numbers
d store in a roll or book for future use. The extra strips may go into a box
be used for patching or fire effects or stained glass windows.

## raming

he cut piece of gel is inserted into a metal frame, which is usually a piece of
etal bent in half. There may be several sizes of frames in use, according to
e variety of spotlights and floods. Be sure that the right frame size is used.
little masking tape at the top edge will keep the gel from falling out. When
metal frame is not available, a substitute can be cut from cardboard and the
l fastened to it with masking tape. In an emergency a gel can be directly
stened to the light with tape. Of course it often flutters down onto the
age at an inopportune moment, but it can be done.

## LUGGING

ugging, sometimes called *patching*, is the connection of lights to a power
urce. In its simplest form it may be only taking the cord from a table lamp
d plugging it into the wall. From there on the job increases in complexity.
mewhere, hopefully, there is a plug board or patch panel that provides a
mber of receptacles into which things can be plugged, or there is some kind
provision for the connection of permanent wiring to dimmers or switches.
hoever runs the light board at your theater will have to show you, since
ch is different.

In studios you may be caught with only a few wall plugs, and if this is
ur fate then the lighting is going to be simple and on-and-off. Try to
omote, from whatever source, some kind of central board (see Appendix A,
production in a studio).

Another session with pencil and paper may be required before plugging
the lights, not only to determine what you really want to operate and
hen everything turns on and off but also to consider the capability of the
mmers and switches.

## immers

immers can carry only a stated load, and so only a limited number of lights can be connected to a single dimmer. Try to connect 1500 watts of spotlight to a 1000-watt dimmer and you will find very quickly that either a fuse blows or the dimmer begins to smoke. Count the number of watts in those spot lights.

The capacity of the dimmer, that is, the number of watts that it can handle, is usually marked somewhere on the dimmer or its case. A name plate may read: Cap. 2000W, which means 2000 watts is the maximum amount that it will handle. Perhaps the nameplate will read: 2 KVA, which is another way of saying 2000 watts, because KVA means, for our purposes (though not really), 1000 watts; thus 2 KVA is twice 1000 watts. Again, if you are not certain, ask someone who knows.

First, add up the wattage of the lights fed from the cable you are about to connect. There may be one 500-watt spotlight and a 750-watt spotlight which adds up to 1250 watts. If the dimmer is rated 1500 watts or 1.5 KVA you are all right. If the dimmer is rated for more than 1500 watts you can even add more lights, up to the maximum. A 1000-watt dimmer will take one light or the other, not both.

## Switches

Switches may be switches or they may be *circuit breakers*. A breaker is a device used as a substitute for a fuse. When too much current passes through the breaker snaps off, or *trips*. When the load is lessened, or when a short circuit is fixed, the breaker can be turned back on. It is a protective device like a fuse, but easier to use. Since it is so much like a switch it is often found on theater boards and on dimmers, providing switching in the normal manner as well as protection from circuit overloads and troubles.

Breakers are marked somewhere in *amps*, and, very roughly, will carry load in watts equal to the number of amps marked multiplied by 100. Thus breaker with 20A marked someplace on it will carry 20 × 100 or 2000 watts before it trips off. Actually, the load can be somewhat greater, but for theatrical purposes the estimate is close enough.

Switches are on-and-off devices and provide no protection against over loads. Hopefully there will be fuses somewhere in the circuit to prevent trouble.

## Doubled Circuits

The plugging problem comes when a large number of lights must be connected to a small number of dimmers or switches. Thought should be given to the question of the maximum use of available controls. Does each cable need an individual control? The answer to this question depends on two factors capacity of the control, that is, how many watts the circuit will hold; and whether the lights go up and down at the same time or separately. Obviously if one cable is already carrying a full load for each dimmer, another cable cannot be added. If the lights connected by one cable are supposed to dim at one time and those on a second cable at another, then they must be plugged to individual circuits or the dimmer will operate both at the same time.

This is when you remember all those warnings about getting the choreographers to work out a compromise about who gets the green special and who the red floods. Since it is a little late to worry, do the best you can.

## Changes

Provided that the theater offers a patch panel, it is possible to change connections during a performance by pulling out one cord and inserting another. All this should be planned in advance, paying proper attention to the cautions about load capacity and the need for separate controls for lights that must be worked separately.

Mark the cords plainly, and on the cue sheet state what gets plugged into what and when it happens. It is a troublesome procedure, but when there are more lights than controls, patching becomes necessary.

## Dimmer or Switch Choice

Suppose that the board provides twelve dimmers. Instead of randomly connected circuits there should be some sort of order imposed on the process. If you have planned six general areas those areas can be controlled by the first six dimmers, arranged so that area 1 is on dimmer 1, area 2 on dimmer 2, and on down the line. The remaining six dimmers can be used for the specials, following whatever pattern appears to be easiest to control. (See Figure 9-1.)

Figure 9-1    Dimmer Board

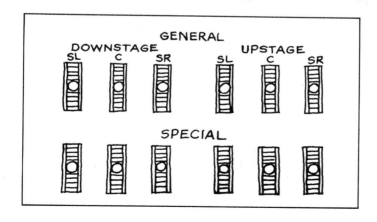

## FOCUSING

Focusing directs the light where it is wanted and away from where it is not. Often this requires more instruments, dimmers, and switches than are available. Therefore, something is doubled on a circuit, something eliminated, something changed. Once again compromise intrudes upon art, and once again the need for preplanning the effects and cooperating with the other choreographers becomes obvious.

### General Lighting

Begin the focusing with the general lighting, since the need for visibility takes precedence over the special effects. If the general lighting is properly done there will be a more or less uniform spread of illumination across the entire stage, adequately providing for most of the program's needs.

First, divide the stage into areas, the number of which depends on the size of the stage and the number of spots available. Six is about an absolute minimum, just as a corps of six in *Swan Lake* might be a minimum, although far from perfection. Each area overlaps so that there will be no dark spaces between, and each is lighted by two spotlights, one from stage right and the other from stage left. (See Figure 9-2.)

Figure 9-2    Lighting Diagram

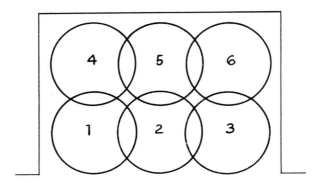

The downstage areas—in this example, numbers 1, 2, and 3—are lighted from spotlights placed somewhere in front of the stage, usually from a balcony or a beam or pipe suspended above the audience. Preferably the vertical angle from spot to stage should approximate 45 degrees: a lower angle tend to wash out the small degree of shadow needed under eyes and chin to avoid a bland flatness of face; a higher angle may cast shadows heavier than desired

The upstage areas—4, 5, and 6—receive their light from spots placed on a pipe closer to the stage, often one just above the apron. The angle in this case will be fairly steep, more than 45 degrees in some cases, but the shadows are more easily tolerated here than a little closer to the audience. The same directional arrangement is followed—one spot from SR and one from SL.

Start from either side. Take out the gels so that the light will be as bright as possible. Assign someone to stand on the stage so that you can see the effect of the lights.

Point the middle spotlight—#2 in the example—at the model standing in the middle of the center area 2. Now move to the other side of the balcony or pipe and focus the other middle spotlight (#5) toward the same place. (See Figure 9-3.)

**Figure 9-3    Focusing Downstage Areas**

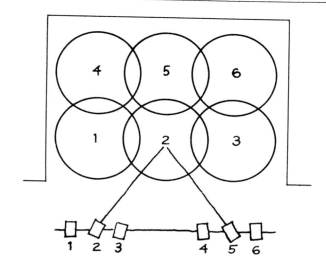

Carry out the same procedure for the other downstage areas. Focus spots #1 and #2 into area 2, then #3 and #6 into area 3.

Ask the patient model to walk slowly across the stage. Any dark spots between areas can be seen. To correct any differences point one spotlight from each pair a little away from the center of its area. If all does not seem perfect—and it seldom will—remember that the audience will think that is the effect you want. They don't know, and, after all, the dancers are going to be great.

If the areas are too large to cover with the available spots, add more, or leave the edges of the stage dark, or forget it.

### Shuttering

The next step is to remove unwanted light from the wings or front edge of the stage or wherever else it has crept. An ellipsoidal spotlight—or *leko*, as everybody will call it—has shutters, which are metal blades designed to block the light. When the metal tips that protrude from the spotlight casing are moved, the light is cut off in a sharp line. A little practice will turn you into an expert.

If shutters are not enough, or there are none, you can try to shift the focus enough to avoid the unwanted spill.

### Gelling

Slip the gel frames into place. The downstage general lighting is now focused.

### Upstage Areas

Upstage focusing often requires a man or woman on a ladder. The pipe is up in the air and many theaters are not equipped with a catwalk or ladder conveniently close to the spotlights.

Bring out the ladder. Clasping wrench in hand to untighten and then retighten the bolts, mount to the top. Be sure that the pipe is at the height where it will be for the performance, or the job will have to be done again. Start on one side; focus the center the same way as before for the downstage areas. (See Figure 9-4.) Tighten the bolt and descend.

Figure 9-4    Focusing Upstage Areas

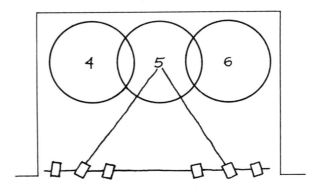

Move the ladder and climb up to focus the other side of the pair covering the center area. Go through the operations until finished. Again call upon the patient model to walk across the stage to find the dark spots. When you make the final adjustments to smooth the gaps between areas and to tip the spots away from cycs and curtains where they should not be pointed, you can also place the gels in their holders.

Now turn on downstage and upstage general lighting. Once more the model walks around. You have a choice of adjusting the bad places from the front lights or the back pipe.

When you are finished, the stage should be lighted fairly smoothly and be without obvious dark or bright patches to distract the audience. Forget about perfection though, unless you have both the equipment and the patience to achieve that glorious state. The audience will overlook minor flaws.

Sometimes you may be forced to use the balcony or audience pipe to light the upstage areas as well as the downstage. The main trouble with such a location is that it is practically impossible to avoid spilling over the backdrops or the cyc, unless the dancers are a considerable distance away from the back. If there is no alternative, focus the lights in the same way as was done for the downstage areas and forget about the unwanted spill. Idealism is fine, but reality prevails.

Occasionally, striplights hung from above or footlights are used to smooth out the over-all levels. These are just turned on—dimmed, hopefully— since they cannot be focused. They are useful, but dangerous because they may smooth out the lighting so much that the result is very bland.

The general lighting should now be done.

All of this has been done in this particular way to provide some kind of modeling for the face and body and to avoid the effect of flatness seen so often in flashbulb pictures of a person staring at the camera. The directional positioning of the spotlights helps, as does the high angle. The use of warm gel from one side and cool from the other helps to create the illusion of shadow through color. It is worth all the trouble required to focus properly.

## Specials

All those specials come next. Here you will discover the reason for preplanning choreographic effects, unless you are fortunate enough to own a large stock of instruments and dimmers. One spot may have to serve as a special for several dances, functioning as a red demon light for one dance, a pulsing downlight for another, and a stray sunbeam for a third. Possibly the gel might be changed when the curtain is closed; refocusing is generally impractical.

Whoever has first call on the specials should come onto the stage to direct the first operation. If there is any scenery involved, it should be on the stage. Let a dancer go through the movement and then determine the proper direction for the light. Hang the light and focus it.

Before settling for that single position requested by the first choreographer, bring out the other choreographers. Let them decide whether that special might also serve their dances. Perhaps a small adjustment will make that possible, thus avoiding the need for extra cables, spots, and dimmers. A couple of feet one way or another seldom makes much difference.

## SETTING CUES

At the technical rehearsal the nearly final lighting decisions are made. There always seem to be later changes, although they should be kept to a minimum. For every light controlled by a dimmer the intensity level is determined. Some lights may be bright, others dim, others not used at all; and there may be changes during the dance. While the dancers walk through the movement—*walk* through, not give a finished performance—choreographer and designer consider the effect desired and settle which lights should be on, how bright they should be, and when they change. If there are no dimmers, then the switchable circuits will have to provide the only control.

When the dimmers or switches are set, the readings on the scales are written down. Memory will not serve; paper and pencil are absolute requirements. Each time there is a change in lighting pattern the new dimmer or switch readings are recorded. This information becomes the cue sheet.

### Cue Sheets

For every dance a cue sheet is prepared. This indicates: (1) circuits used, (2) intensity of each light controlled by a dimmer, (3) all changes, and (4) special instructions to the crew. Ideally, a cue sheet is so complete a guide that the lighting crew needs only the stage manager's signal to perform all dimmer, switchboard, and special duties. The form is a matter of personal preference. For simple productions it may be a simple description:

> DANCE 1 "Holiday"      Open dark stage, then bring up—
> 5 mins.                All balconies full
>                        Dimmers 1, 2, 3, 6, 7 to half
>                        Blackout at end

This sort of thing is useful for people who know what they are doing and who know the opening and closing cues. Often it may serve as a preliminary memorandum for preparation of a fuller cue sheet.

The usual production requires a more specific chart, as shown in Figure 9-5. The chart shows that before the curtains open (PRESET), dimmer 1 is at an intensity of 10 on its scale; dimmer 2 is at 9, dimmer 3 at 10. The other dimmers and switches are off. Therefore, there will be lights turned on before the curtain opens.

The first change comes at the stage manager's signal: "Go, cue 1." Dimmers 1, 2, and 3 remain the same. Notice that there is no need to repeat the previous intensity number on the cue sheet—only changes are indicated; this makes the chart easier to read than one filled with numbers. Dimmers 4 and 5 are brought up to a reading of 10 on their scales, and switches 1 and 2 are turned on. According to the "instructions" column, another circuit, number 6, is plugged into dimmer 1.

On the signal "Go, cue 2," dimmers 1, 2, and 3 are turned down to 0 and

Figure 9-5     Cue Sheet

LIGHTING CUES

DANCE   HELLO, GOOD MORNING

| CUE | DIMMERS | | | | | SWITCHES | | | | INSTRUCTIONS |
|---|---|---|---|---|---|---|---|---|---|---|
| | 1 | 2 | 3 | 4 | 5 | 1 | 2 | 3 | 4 | |
| PRESET | 5 | 5 | 7 | 10 | 10 | OFF | OFF | OFF | OFF | |
| 1 | 10 | 10 | | | | | | | | WHEN CURTAIN IS COMPLETELY OPEN |
| 2 | | | | | | ON | ON | | | |
| 3 | 0 | 0 | 0 | | | | | | | QUICK CUE IN MUSIC— WATCH CLOSELY |
| 4 | 10 | | 8 | | | OFF | OFF | ON | | PLUG CYC RED INTO DIM 2 SWITCH OFF 3 ON CUE |
| 5 | 7 | 7 | 7 | | 7 | | | OFF | | |
| 6 | B | L | A | C | K | O | U | T | | CUE FROM CHOREOGRAPHER |
| | | | | | | | | | | |
| | | | | | | | | | | |

switches 3 and 4 are turned on. There are no changes in dimmers 4 and 5 or switches 1 and 2.

Cue 3—blackout—requires that all dimmers and all switches be turned off at the same time.

Sometimes there are two additions: an arrow points up or down, reminding the crew which way the dimmers are to be moved, and the time required for a dim up or down may be indicated. Usually placed inside the box giving dimmer intensity the time is indicated by a phrase such as "ten count," which means that 10 seconds elapse between the cue signal and the time that the dimmer reaches its assigned intensity.

The initial chart may as well be a pencil copy because of the need for later changes. For the performance, a new cue sheet, very legible and clear, may be prepared.

## Cues

Before the state manager can speak those words "Go, cue 1," he must know when that cue is to be given. There are several possible methods.

169

The *sight cue* is a cue determined by dancer movement. For example, when the dancer in red lifts her hand or when three dancers twine together and one looks up, cue 1 is given. Sometimes the actual movement is slight, and it may not even be noticed by the dancer until that movement is emphasized as a cue. Sight cues require that certain movements be consistent; if the movement is changed or forgotten the light cue may never be given and all complaints to the light crew will be rightfully ignored.

A *music cue* allows the cue to be given in response to music, provided that the particular measure or chord is clear enough to provide an unmistakable signal. Some music is confusing because of repeated phrases resembling or identical to the cue itself; electronic music is often impossible.

A *time cue* is set by a stop watch, which is started when the music begins. After the alloted number of seconds ticks off the first cue is given, and the next cue follows on its stop-watch point. Unfortunately, some dancers do not follow stop-watch time and so the light cues may appear arbitrary when compared to the movement.

A *signal cue* requires a light or buzzer operated by the choreographer who observes the dance. The signal may be given orally by someone who "knows the dance." Except in emergencies do not rely upon such signals. That somebody, whether dancer or choreographer, always seems to wander off at the wrong time or becomes so involved in the dance that the cue is never given. One trial is usually enough to convince everybody that this method is inadequate.

Eventually the cues will be memorized. But remember, the choreographer and dancers have lived with the dance for weeks, even months; the light crew are strangers and should not be expected to remember everything after a single rehearsal or even four or five rehearsals.

Once the cues are set do not change critical movements or music. The lights will go up and down according to the written instructions on the cue sheet, no matter what unplanned surprises the dancers may offer. Consistency in cuing is a necessity.

## RUNNING

Operation of the equipment requires a little practice and much concentration. Most of the mistakes will arise when the lighting crew is distracted by an over-friendly dancer or is busy eating supper or catching up on school work. Therefore, concentration is the first rule.

There is really nothing that can be written about running a dimmer board or switch panel, since each will be different. Practice with what you have until it becomes automatic; that is the secret of smooth operation. At the stage manager's first signal: "Warn, cue 1," hands and mind are readied; at the signal "Go, cue 1," the cue sheet instructions are carried out.

Concentration and practice—those are the rules of running.

# 10

# Move-in, Technical Rehearsal, Dress Rehearsal

The day finally arrives. The trek from studio to stage begins. Practice rehearsals become dress rehearsals, and opening night pushes its way into the schedule. Now all sorts of things will happen, and a few people will wistfully hope for a convenient case of flu or a minor, though incapacitating, accident. But the time has come.

## MOVE-IN

People and equipment must be moved, schedules arranged and rearranged, all sorts of details considered, dozens of problems solved. As always, advance preparation saves physical labor and mental upset.

### Preparation

First, everyone in the company should know when moving time is. This seems elementary, but there is always someone who forgets. To avoid any misunderstanding, let the day and time of moving and setup be clearly posted on the wall and that posting reinforced by a dittoed schedule presented to each choreographer and dancer and crew member.

Next, assemble the equipment. Gather all tapes and records, tape recorders and phonographs, drums, woodblocks, flashlights, and everything else. Even if the costumes and scenery disappear enroute the rehearsals can proceed if you have the music and sound. The tapes and recordings should be those that will actually be used in performance. One of the frustrations of any rehearsal is a missing tape or one that is somewhat different, even if the difference is small. Dancers and crew alike depend on learned cues; so, no excuses about not having time or not being able to find the right music to record.

Gather the costumes. The problem will arise with those costumes that are unfinished, or, worse, unstarted. Again, there should be a list to check for each dance and each dancer. Take the finished costumes and those that require only minor work. The others, depending on the work methods, can be left behind or taken to the theater for finishing.

The necessary props can be placed in boxes or bags, with those for each dance gathered separately in a container clearly marked with the name of the dance and the items contained. Larger props can be tagged with the name of the dance and a tentative storage location.

Make-up and personal items come next. Some directors will go so far as to request their dancers to bring shoes to the great gathering, just to prevent that occasionally heard murmur "I forgot my ballet slippers." Even big girls sometimes forget.

All of the above can form the first installment. They are the basic requirements for the dance and should be in the theater as soon as the rehearsals begin.

Scenery and any lighting equipment should be gathered and inspected to see that everything is ready. Some additions to the scenery may be done in the theater—but the fewer, the better. Usually stage managers discourage painting, since paint tends to splash and puddle in unwanted places and wet paint wipes off on curtains and costumes. Painting should be done in the shop or, if permitted, on a grassy lawn where nature will eliminate the traces. It really is much easier to finish the entire scenic job in a shop or some place away from the theater.

Do not forget the tools, and the needles and thread, and the safety pins and bandages, and pencils and paper, and drinking cups and keys.

The move may require a truck. Who has a truck? Who will drive? Who brings it back? Does the driver know where to go? Who loads and unloads?

By now there should be some neat piles of material gathered in the studio or in the shop, all tagged and entered on a list so that there can be no mistake about what is ready to go.

## Schedule

A long time ago you devised a schedule. Somewhere on a theater calendar there are a few penciled marks containing the expected time of arrival, rehearsal hours, and performance dates. Does the present schedule coincide with the old one? If not, have you told everybody concerned? Stage managers and crew are often unhappy to learn of the changes only after they have been waiting a few hours or even a day or two. You are no longer independent of the theater staff and crew.

Submit another schedule. Include:

(1.) Time of arrival
(2.) Time of setup
(3.) Times of all rehearsals
(4.) Time of performance

Include any arrangements about picture-taking, visits, equipment deliveries, or anything else that may come as a surprise to the theater people, as well as to the dancers.

There are a few cautions. The first is to provide enough time. This means starting early, or else those technical and dress rehearsals will run past midnight. The second, which is too often disregarded, is to allow time for the technical crews to set up and test equipment. They cannot do this if a dance group insists that it must rehearse on the stage. No longer can the dance groups act as though they were in their own studio. If you want scenery and lights and curtain then the crew must have the time needed to provide these things. The third reminder is that the technical crews need time for rest and meals. A nice full schedule, with each dance group fitted into neat hourly blocks with no breaks, neglects the needs of the crew. So, whether you like it or not, the schedule has to allow time for crew breaks.

After the schedule has been set, demand that the dancers follow it. There will be all sorts of requests for extra time to do this or that, and some will move in on the stage whether scheduled or not. If the discipline breaks down the production will suffer. Theater is a cooperative affair.

Finally, are you sure that your schedule does not conflict with the use of the facilities by somebody else? There may be other productions, or classes, or programs, or workmen repairing pipes, or janitors cleaning the place, or other crews taking away band risers, or all sorts of things you have overlooked. Have you thought about possible conflicts?

## Transport

Cast and choreographers may carry much of their production material if the move is a short one. It may be well to borrow a dolly or hand truck or even a child's little red wagon, stack up those bundles and boxes, and plow across the country like the forty-niners storming the gold fields. The peculiar procession may help stir up interest among those who watch; it might even sell a ticket or two.

A trek across a great distance requires some motorized assistance. For heavy loads and items too large for a car, or even a station wagon, a truck is required. Perhaps it can be borrowed, or possibly the school or organization owns one. The other alternative is to rent one. Since rental is usually paid by the hour it is a very good idea to have everything already assembled and a crew standing by to load and unload. And do not forget to tie down any scenery or boxes that might fall out; traffic tickets are seldom included in the budget.

Before the departure signal is given make sure that everybody knows the destination. On a trip away from familiar grounds a route map may be required, one that includes the correct way to get from the street to the stage door. Just in case of trouble the driver should be provided with a telephone number to call for further directions.

## Arrival

Too many troupes arrive like a herd of cattle stampeding for the food trough. It might be best to enter quietly and proceed at a discreet pace until such time as the stage proves safe for chatter and clatter. You may not be alone.

## Dressing-Room Assignment

There are several ways to arrange the cast. The oldest theatrical tradition just throws everybody together in one or two common rooms. Convenience sometimes dictates the gathering of each dance group into one area, thus keeping cast and costumes together. Another alternative places those with quick changes near the stage and those with fewer problems at a greater distance. Hopefully you do not have to cater to Stars.

Post the assignments on the doors and be prepared with a good explanation for any objections. Also, be prepared to change if the objection is valid. A contented dancer is more valuable than a mere bookkeeping entry.

## Costume Storage

Hang up the costumes in the proper dressing room, separating those that still require work.

Occasionally there may be no place to hang costumes. Some items may be laid across chairs. For others, lay some paper on the floor and carefully arrange the costumes in full-length layers to keep wrinkles at a minimum. A simple pipe rack is a good investment.

## Preparation of Space

Sometimes the theater staff will clean the stage and keep it clean. More often the stage will be janitorially unattended, just waiting for the next user to sweep and mop. Be prepared to work the janitor shift. There is no point in arguing for something that will not happen. Come prepared with your own mop and bucket.

Set up the tables needed for sound equipment. Occasionally there is a conveniently raised area where this can be done, and maybe there is a conventional sound booth provided with good communication to the stage manager and the nervous choreographers. Most often there is a begrudged square of space in the wings, which really cannot be spared because a dancer's spectacular exit leap lands right on top of the tape recorder. Move the table around so that it is as much out of the way as possible while still allowing the operator to see enough to start and stop on cue. Also check the sight line to the audience. When you have done the best that you can, indicate with tape or chalk exactly where the table is to be.

Arrange for quick-change screens, and block out everything that interferes with the dancer's space in the wings or exits. In other words, any space unavailable to the dancer should be filled or marked carefully. This prevents unpleasant surprises later.

First-Day Activities

Provided that the production is not rushed into technical or dress rehearsal, the first day of move-in is generally devoted to a melange of unfinished activities. Some of the scenery is rigged and marked; a little lighting is tried; costumers sew and iron; the dancers try the stage; the choreographers watch from audience distance.

In comes the master of sound and music, burdened with a miscellany of equipment for setup. In addition to his sound equipment he will need room for work light, flashlight, scissors for cutting tape, tape splicing material, tape leaders and marking pen, pencil and paper for writing down cues, and the rehearsal and performance tapes. Or maybe he has records and record player; or he may have drums, autoharps, flower pots, gongs, wood blocks, and a set of Japanese tea cups. Everyone make way, and make space! Extension cords usually have to be run. These should be out of the way of the dancers, even covered with a rug or canvas. Protect the dancers and protect your equipment. Hook up everything and see if it works. If it doesn't, check the theater power first. You may be plugged into a socket that has to be turned on at the switchboard. Check the lights. Hopefully, you have one of those high-intensity lamps or some kind of a table-light that can be hooded so that its beam spills onto the work surface and not onto the stage. When the stage is dark, either at your request or during one of the dark times, go out front and see if the work light is obvious. If it is, wrap colored gelatine over it or make an aluminum-foil hood.

The wise director tries to keep the first day short for the dancers and convenient for the crew; the days remaining before opening will be full enough to make up for any minutes lost during a relaxed beginning. Resist the temptation to work a twelve-hour schedule, no matter how you hate to see those precious hours fly away. Time is required for the dancers to get used to the stage and for the crew to begin its work. Seldom can both groups use the stage at the same time; so why should they try? Remember that schedule.

Do collect the choreographers, if you are not the sole creator, and hold technical conferences with the crew. You may have to rethink some of the choreography and design. The time for change is now, not opening night, but it is too late for major changes.

Allow for rest and meal breaks. The dancers need them and the crew needs them. Nothing tends to promote anger and consequent slackening of effort more than overlooking these needs. The crew is especially resentful at lack of free time. Remember, the crew is working, not performing, and there is a difference. And please, do not hold the crew during the scheduled rest period or after rehearsal time with some excuse about needing just a little more time to carry in scenery or set another light. If the crew members are also dancers the requirement for time off is even more important.

When you become nervous about those "wasted" minutes join every-

body else for coffee or supper. You might as well. Of course, if you are
teacher you can grade papers or write exams. Beyond the dark walls life plod
along.

## TECHNICAL REHEARSAL

This is a rehearsal for the technical crew. It is a stop-and-start affair, usin
dancers only as puppets moving across the stage to test scenery and lightin
patterns. Hopefully they are rehearsed. Only at the end, if there is still time
do the dancers assume any individual importance and even then their tas
remains secondary to that of the designers and technicians.

### Purposes

Technical rehearsal is a trying time, in both senses of the phrase. Scenery i
placed and used; lighting is tested and reworked; sound is coordinated; cue
are set; crews practice. Whatever has to be done to turn studio practice int
performance is arranged, rearranged, and rehearsed. Seldom is any fun in
volved, but the work is necessary and it is *technical work,* not dance practic
If the dancers need practice take them someplace else.

### Scenery

For each dance the total scenery is set in place. This includes curtains, drops
sets, and anything else used for effect or decoration. The dancers then walk
through any movements that might be affected by the additions to the bare
stage. If there are any doubts settle them now. If a dancer cannot hop onto a
high platform work out the problem now. It should have been solved weeks
ago. If anything interferes with the dance move the scenery, adjust it, o
change the dance movement. But do something. Do not sacrifice the dance
for the scenery, but do not give up too easily—a change in position may
provide an acceptable solution.

Mark, on the floor, where the scenery or set goes. Use masking, drafting
or colored tape to mark at least two corners, or some other part, that indicate
where the piece is to go. Write on the tape the name or code number of the
dance as well as the piece of scenery to be used. Otherwise you may have a
stage filled with anonymous pieces of tape.

Also mark the height of any hanging pieces. A ring of tape at a known
position will provide an adequate signal for stopping the raising or lowering of
a rope.

Make a diagram of the setup in the stage manager's book.

## ighting

opefully, much of the lighting will be roughly focused and gelled. The
echnical rehearsal smooths what has already been done and sets the cues.

The procedure generally follows a pattern:

1.) Choreographer, designer, and stage manager stand on the stage to talk
over the cues and technical problems.

2.) The opening cue is set. How does the stage look as the curtain opens?
Write down the dimmers and switches used and the intensity readings.
Let the dancers walk through the movement seen in that particular cue.

3.) The next cues are described by the choreographer and set by the lighting
crew. The dancers walk through the movement that leads up to the
setting and then continue long enough to check focus and setting.

4.) The final cue is set. What happens as the curtain is about to close? After
it closes? Should it be a dimout or a blackout?

5.) Now the whole process is repeated. This time another factor is added—
the point at which the cue changes. If a light dims or the cyc comes on,
what in the dance gives the signal for the change? The stage manager and
crew usually learn a movement pattern. For some reason movement
seems easier to remember than music, especially electronic or monotonous music that must be listened to carefully. So set a definite movement as a signal and keep that movement standard throughout the rest
of rehearsal and performance time. If the signal is the girl in red raising
one finger be sure that she does not raise two fingers the next day or
that light cue may never come. The music should be played to help with
the identification.

6.) Run through the entire process again. Let the dancers walk through the
dance. They can skip over long passages during which no lights change.
Call a warning for the approaching cue, call the cue, try it. Do not let the
dancers continue past a missed or very bad cue. Go back and try again.
Repeat the bad places.

7.) Rework the impossible things. Write down a clean copy of the cues.

8.) If time permits, let the dancers run through their dance while the crew
tries to work the show. Remember one thing that choreographers hate to
think about—the crew does not know the dance, and they are not going
to learn it in half an hour of technical rehearsal.

## urtain

ecide on when the curtain opens. What comes first—lights, music, or cur-
ain? When does the curtain close? Is it fast or slow? Are the dancers back of
he curtain line for that closing curtain?

## Music and Sound

Gather the musicians and creators of nonrecorded sound. Find a place for them and their instruments. Are they out of the way? Can they see enough of the dance to provide the proper accompaniment? Is the resultant sound right?

For recorded music the proper levels must be set. The music has to be loud enough for the dancers and for the audience, but not too loud and not too soft. Possibly there may have to be separate loudspeakers for the audience out front and for the dancers backstage. Some tape recorders are not powerful enough to give good sound in an auditorium or even in a large studio. The original recorder may have to be plugged into an amplifier, which will then run larger loudspeakers. Do not offend the audience with fuzzy sound or inadequate volume levels.

Set the cues. Decide whether the music comes before or after the curtain or lights, before or after the dancers are in place. If the tape stops or fades during a dance or at the end what is the point of the stoppage or fade?

Practice changing tape or record. Preferably the entire sound track for the production will be on one tape, or at least there will be one tape for each part separated by intermission—a collection of short tapes always causes trouble.

As a final caution, use the complete tape for the rehearsals. A duplicate should be on hand for emergencies or for practice. It is long past the time when the choreographer can get by with substitutes.

## Stage Manager's Script

All the cues and special instructions go into some kind of script, which the stage manager has been preparing throughout the technical rehearsal. Anything that the crew has forgotten to record, or cannot, is retained in some kind of written plot. It is so very easy to forget details, so they should be written down. (See Figure 10-1 for an example of a production cue sheet.)

## Basic Philosophy

In summary, it should be said that the technical rehearsal comes close to answering questions only imagined by designer and choreographer. If dance and design and technical aspects do not work there is still time for change, although the time is limited.

And there should be a repetition of a basic warning. Do not allow the desire for perfection, or even its approximation, to cancel those rest and meal times. Technical work is difficult; it requires the crew to stand for long hours and to do a fair amount of physical work; it forces designers and crew chiefs to continually move back and forth from stage to auditorium. In short, it is tiring.

**ure 10-1    Production Cue Sheet**

Production Cue Sheet

| Staging and Curtain | Sound | Lighting |
|---|---|---|
| Dance: OPUS 3<br>**1** | Tape starts | |
| Fast curtain<br>**2** Pre-set: 3<br>Flash lights | | |
| **3** Overhead projection #1 | Sounds offstage | |
| **4** | | Balcony spots and<br>overheads to ¼ |
| **5** | Tape stops | |
| **6** Lower frames | | |
| **7** Carry on boxes | | SL + SR spots<br>on full |
| Back curtains<br>**8** open on | | |
| #2-3 overhead<br>**9** projections | | All lights dim<br>to off |
| **10** | Tape starts | |
| Projections off; start<br>**11** slides (4 second sequence) | | |
| Cyc to blue<br>**12** Movie starts | | |
| Back curtains close<br>**13** All off | | Dim up SL spots<br>to ½ |
| **14** Dancers on with screens | | Overheads up<br>to ¾ |
| **15** Action continues | | Slow dim-out |
| **16** Action continues | | Up full for call |
| **17** Curtain close | | House up full |

Then, too, there is the matter of consideration for the crew. Choreographers have seen the dance for weeks, even months, time after time. The crew may be seeing it for the first time. How good were your dancers the first day of rehearsal? How much did they remember even after the first month?

Finally, the choreographer must remember that the technical rehearsal is not intended as dance practice. If you try to make this a dress rehearsal you heat everybody, including yourself. Keep it technical.

## DRESS REHEARSAL

For many dancers, dress rehearsal represents the pinnacle of interest. A good dress rehearsal is a close approximation of performance, but it does not contain the element of fear present when an audience has assembled. A good dress rehearsal therefore is essential to a dancer, as well as to the crew, because it demonstrates the best of what can happen. The trouble is that so many things go wrong. Lights go on at the wrong time; the tape breaks; the curtain closes late; costumes drag; the lead dancer finds herself on the wrong side of the stage; everything bad happens. Yet parts of the performance may never be better. The excitement may never again be recaptured. Altogether it is a wonderful and terrible experience.

### Purposes

The primary purpose is to provide a complete, uninterrupted runthrough for dancers and crew. The word to be remembered is *uninterrupted*. No matter what goes wrong, unless it is a complete disaster, plow through the dance from beginning to end. Fix it later.

A second purpose is to discover any unexpected problems. All too often the production is still being assembled. There may be lighting not set in the technical rehearsal, or a curtain cue changed or costumes never worn before, or even a replacement dancer appearing for the first time. All sorts of things happen. Let them, but fix them later.

A third purpose is to allow the choreographer to see the entire production for the first time. Up to this point the dance has never been complete. The good and the bad become apparent, but resist the temptation to make major changes; it is too late.

Finally, production photographs may be taken, both during the dance for action shots and at breaks for posed pictures. Usually action shots are more expressive of dance and dancers. By using fast film, even color if there is enough light, and an exposure meter, a good record of the production can be obtained. In addition, movies or videotapes of the complete rehearsal may be made. The film or tape will help in assessing the production later on, it will provide a record of the choreography, and it will be a valuable document for students who take part in future dance productions.

### Discipline

Since dress rehearsals are often tense affairs, cast, crew, choreographer, and visitors must observe some rules of behavior. Lateness, excess noise, improper attention to the work, and temper tantrums are out of place. All occur; none should.

Try to start on time and try to finish as quickly as possible. Most delays are the result of choreographer failure to round up the dancers soon enough or of choreographer reluctance to stop wasting time and to start their rehearsal. Control the choreographer and many problems will be resolved.

Plan for the dancers who are not on the stage. Keep them somewhere out of the way, not in the front row where they talk, crinkle papers, and wander back and forth to block the view of the stage. Keep them in the dressing rooms or assigned to the back rows.

Treat the rehearsal as a performance and insist that it be run as one. This is no time to play childish games.

## Make-up

Until this time the dancers have resisted the use of theatrical make-up. There seems to be a psychological need to convince the subconscious that all the learning and rehearsal encountered so far is really part of a game played for self-amusement and not a prelude to exhibiting before the public. The use of make-up signals a new phase in the relationship of performer to production. Make-up transforms the individual into a masked performer, thus submerging personal responsibility into a group activity. So much for the philosophy.

The producer is interested in two things: one, the appearance of make-up under stage lights from audience distance; and two, the neatness of the dressing rooms. The first calls for the appearance of the dancer on the stage, an inspection of the result, and suggestions for change. If the dancers mingle seminaturalistic make-up with stylized "ballet-dancer" make-up the audience will notice and wonder why it happened. Use one method or the other, not both, at least not in the same dance, unless there is a legitimate reason. The second problem is an aesthetic one. Some people are not bothered by tables and floors littered with crumpled tissue and spilled powder; others are. It is quite simple to provide each dressing-room space with placemats of paper or cloth, which can be gathered after each use and thrown away. A clean dressing room is probably more conducive to a feeling of professionalism than sometimes thought.

## Costumes

The costumes should be ready, fairly clean, and ironed. Each should be hung in an assigned place. For those that are used in quick changes a safe spot should be found, not, please, over a fly line or a dimmer handle or on the floor. The stage crew are not dressers for a sloppy dancer.

Dancers encountering difficulty because of costume complexity or lack of time should be provided with a helper or two. Wigs and hair pieces are simpler to handle with assistance, as are costumes composed of a miscellany of floating pieces of fabric. Provide the help.

Quick changes can be done in the dressing room, if the costume is ready and a helper is standing by. Or they can be done in the wings, in public if it does not matter to the dancer, or behind a screen if it does. Try to time the change, and if it seems that it might interrupt the flow of the performance plan the change before the rehearsal begins and then see if the plan will work If the change interferes with the dance, rework the costume, the change, or the dance. The audience does not want to wait.

## Running the Show for Continuity

The dress rehearsal, especially the final one, is a performance and should be treated as one. This means that everything is run from backstage, with minimum interruption from those out front. Include all cues, all curtains, all intermissions. Unless absolutely necessary, do not depart from the order of dances that will be presented at the opening performance.

## Calling Crew and Dancers

About half an hour before the scheduled starting time the stage manager or assistant warns the cast: "Half-hour to curtain." The light crew gathers to test the lights to see that everything works and they set the first cue. The other crews make a final test of their equipment.

About fifteen minutes before the start the stage manager warns the cast: "Fifteen minutes." Visitors are chased away from backstage. This is sometimes a touchy matter, but visitors should be outside or in the auditorium, not backstage, no matter who they are. The curtain man closes the curtain. The house lights are set as they will be when the doors are opened for the audience.

Then comes another warning. "Five minutes." The stage manager and assistants make an estimate about the actual readiness of cast, crew, and stage. Up to now the assumption has been that the rehearsal will start on time. If there is any doubt let the producer know and then the crew and then the cast. Find out if the delay will be encountered on opening night, or if the trouble is temporary.

## Cuing the Crew

Before giving the first cue, make sure that the dancers are ready. It is always embarrassing to start a show and then discover that one little girl is still next door at the coffee stand or another is on the wrong side of the stage. Somebody has to know.

The stage manager stands in the center of the stage and looks around for a last check. Then he walks off stage, consults the book, and gives the first cue: "House lights." From then on the cues are given as they come, beginning with the curtain or the music or the lights, whichever has been selected to open the performance.

Each cue is preceded by the word "Warning, cue _____," which should be given sufficiently in advance so that the crew can make its mental and physical preparations. Then comes the quiet command: "Go, cue _____."

If a light cue is missed, or goes wrong, the stage manager quietly says: "Slowly go into cue _____." Do not race to fix the mistake, unless it interferes with the dance. Gentle change is usually better than an abrupt admission of guilt.

For cues that are not written the stage manager assumes responsibility. Place little trust in the words of a dancer or a friend of a dancer; they too often are late with cues or forget them. The stage manager and lighting crew are usually more accurate than even a choreographer; they are looking at the production, not the dance.

During the rehearsals cues can be given in a louder voice than will be used at performance. It helps to set the cues for everybody, including those dancers who may hear. The cues are not supposed to be secret.

## Pulling the Curtain

This simple little task can cause terrible trouble. Improperly done it tells the audience to prepare for amateur night with Miss Lucy's Limberlegged Lassies. Well done it becomes an authentic part of the performance. The secrets of success are: (1) the proper manner of pulling the rope and (2) timing.

Rope-pulling seems simple enough, and it is. All you have to do is pull smoothly with both hands, one after another, not with one hand alone or with both at the same time. The trick is to keep the curtain moving along evenly, not jerking a foot at a time as a hand yanks down, flies up for another hold, and yanks again.

Timing is partly practice, partly alertness. The dance itself dictates the speed. There are dances that need a quick ending, others that gradually fade from view. That is the choice of the choreographer. Quick curtains are often dangerous. They can pull lights out of focus, spray dust at the audience, trap dancers inside swirling folds of cloth. So, practice to avoid those dangers, and slow down. Most curtains require some sort of count; the curtain opens or closes completely as the puller counts "one, two, three, four, etc." Again, practice is required. Finally, there is the problem of the slow curtain. All too often the dancers are wavering through an arabesque too long held or some other such awkward position while that curtain wanders across those miles of empty space. The curtain puller is faced with a decision. Either the curtain must be pulled at the speed determined by the choreographer or closed more quickly to protect the dancers. An estimate of choreographer ego is the only guide. For some, the only answer is to allow the dancer to topple to the stage like a cracked Coppelia. Fortunately, most prefer to speed the curtain.

And close the curtain all the way. Do not leave a foot-wide crack through which the audience can peep at those backstage mysteries.

Those cursed with motor-driven, constant-speed curtains just have to push the button at the right time and hope for the best.

## Operating the Equipment

It seems obvious that all the lights should be used, and the scenery, and recorders, and everything else. Amazingly enough, some foolish optimists, or amateurs, insist that the right tape recorder will arrive on performance night or that a special platform will be delivered sometime in the future or that the dramatic overhead spot will be focused in time for opening.

Why isn't everything there? If it isn't there for the final dress rehearsal, forget it. The dancers and crew deserve at least one runthrough under performance conditions, and if something is missing at the final rehearsal it should be missing for the performance.

## Intermission

When the first section ends the stage manager says: "House lights." The house lights come up. The stage manager marks the time in the book, both as a reminder of the beginning of intermission and as a guide to timing the entire show.

The work lights go up. Any work needed backstage for the next piece is done before the crew takes any kind of break. Occasionally this may take the entire intermission period, so it becomes evident why stage crews need some rest. Additional time may have to be provided, however much the producer wants to move the show through the complete rehearsal.

The dancers change for the next part or rest or run around aimlessly. Keep them off the stage. The choreographers check their notes. There are usually conferences with designers, stage managers, crews, and anybody else who might be affected. It might be wise to provide refreshments.

After a standard lapse of time the second part begins. The lapse should not be extensive—try to keep to fifteen minutes. Notes and long conferences should wait until the end.

## Setting the Curtain Calls

After the entire rehearsal, each dance group is called out and the curtain calls are set. Make them short, not fancy, or you may find the applause reluctant or nonexistent in a few second's time. Make the final bow very apparent, or else the poor curtain-puller and light-operator will not know when the display has ended. No false endings.

At the curtain call the front lights, if there are any, should come up to bathe the dancers in a shimmer of glory. To do this the operator has to know when to start. That means the choreographer must make it very clear when the cue comes. How long is the curtain closed? Do the dancers come out onto a dark stage, take positions, and wait for the light? Do they run on? Do they remain in position under the last-used stage lights? Whatever happens, demonstrate it to the crew. And do not change it overnight.

Plan a procedure for repeated curtain calls, in case there are any, and make the action clear to dancers and crew. Audiences hate to watch a mad scramble to reach positions recently vacated.

## Notes to Cast and Crew

Mix a few encouraging comments in with the bad.

Anything that might be personally embarrassing, unless it happens to be a funny incident that can be enjoyed, should be discussed with the offender in private. There is an overabundance of masochists, as well as sadists, in theater, but most of them are quite sensitive to personal disapproval. However, do not spare those who deserve criticism. First, make sure that they do. Ask why something happened and then comment. The answer may be legitimate.

Notes are primarily for correction of mistakes and for encouragement. It is usually too late to demand a new interpretation from a dancer or new scenery from the designer or a new cue sheet from the lighting crew. Some changes can be made, and should be, but be judicious, not arbitrary. After all, the program has been in the process of preparation for a long time and the decisions should have been made by now.

## Care of Everything

Typically, there are bits of costume strewn around the stage, shoes and purses littering the auditorium, props forgotten in the rest rooms, scenery propped against an alley wall. Somebody has to gather up all this stuff and put it where it is supposed to be. Possibly the cast might pick up their own things, if they have been doing it during studio and stage rehearsals.

Anyway, hang up the costumes, put the shoes in the right dressing rooms, put the tops back on the make-up tubes, shout at the dancer who is absconding without her purse. Dancers, after all, are children, no matter how long they have skipped through life.

## Final Technical Adjustments

There usually are some. Some can wait until the next day; some cannot. Technical crews grumble and mutter unkind words, but then they do not share the glory of the spotlight, and the pay is not so good either.

Be sure that the changes are minor and will not interfere with the dancers' expectation of what will be on the stage. A slight change in the focus of a light is one thing, but the sudden installation of a battery of psychedelic projectors might tend to upset someone's concentration.

# Performance

# 11

# Performance

At last the big day arrives, when the audience becomes part of the production. In front of the house and behind the curtain a new set of conditions applies, all because of the need to assemble and entertain those who want to watch the dancers.

## FRONT OF THE HOUSE

Tickets are sold and collected, patrons are directed to seats, intermissions are provided, money is protected. If no tickets are involved the procedure is much easier and may be handled by one person; but most organizations seem to want to sell tickets, and that takes a staff.

## Box Office Problems

At least an hour and a half before curtain time someone should be ready to sell tickets and to answer the telephone. Given a list of reservations, the tickets, seating charts, a supply of money for change, and information about curtain time, length of show, cast, and crew, the ticket seller is ready.

He will be faced with certain choices.

1.) If a customer is at the window and the phone rings, which takes precedence? The usual reaction is to answer the phone and leave the customer waiting. The better choice is to serve the waiting ticket buyer and let the phone ring. After all, the customer has taken the trouble to come down; the caller may not bother.

2.) Which reserved seats should be offered? Those that have been set aside for critics, cast, friends, and whomever should be kept until released. The others may as well go by rows, unless the customer wants some particular place that may still be available. The one rule is: *do not argue.* If the seats are available, give the customer what he wants. If not, pass out the best remaining, assuring him, "These are the best we have. If you do not like the location we will exchange them for others." It usually works. If an argument ensues ask the customer to step over to see the house manager at the theater entrance. At least that clears the window.

3.) What is the best way to make change? Lay the bill to be changed in a place separate from the other money. This prevents the possible complaint "but I gave you a ten dollar bill, not a five." Then start the count with the price of the ticket and add the change piece by piece. For example, a ticket costs $1.63 and a ten-dollar bill is tendered. First place the bill in a safe location. Put the ticket on the counter and say. "One dollar, sixty-three cents." Add the pennies: "Sixty-four, sixty-five." Add the remaining small change. "One seventy-five. Two dollars.' Then come the bills. "Three, four, five, and ten." Push the ticket and change to the customer. "Thank you, enjoy the performance." When the customer leaves put the changed bill in the cash drawer. You will find it much easier to add the money piece by piece than to subtract the ticket price and then give the change, and the customer feels more secure.

(4.) Are checks acceptable? Ask for money, but take the check. However make a note of the ticket and if it is returned give back the check, not money. It is unlikely that you will have trouble, but it can happen.

There are other problems that can be avoided by some precautions. Do not leave the box office door open, or even unlocked. Do not allow anyone in the box office, except for those with the authority to enter. This means that friends shall stay outside. Do not pass out free tickets without previous authorization. Do not mix private money with production money. Keep money distant from hands that might reach inside. Never hurry. Take time to look at tickets; take time to look at the money offered; take time to count change. Do not disparage the production; even if you do not like it, the customer may.

## Ticket Taker

He welcomes the patron. A simple "good evening" is sufficient.

After inspecting the ticket to be certain that the date is correct, he tear it in half. He gives half to the patron. If the seats are reserved he give directions to the proper aisle or location. When seats are not reserved he says "Take any seat you like."

He drops the other half of the ticket in a box to be kept for a later tally

## Ushers

The ushers should be pleasant, though not gushing, and, of course, present able. The usher takes the ticket, checks the location, and leads the patron to the proper seat. She—and female ushers usually have less trouble—stops at th proper aisle, stands with her back to the stage, and says something like, "A' is the seventh seat in. Almost in the middle." She gives the ticket back, along with a program.

If there is a mix-up in the seating, the usher should compare the ticket and suggest that someone move, unless neither customer objects to the avail able location.

Latecomers can be asked to remain at the back of the auditorium or to take side seats until there is a break in the program. It is not fair to those who arrive on time to be interrupted by a gang of people climbing over them and blocking their view of the stage. For those who object to waiting there is probably nothing to do except to escort them to their seats as quickly as possible.

When seats are not reserved the whole job is a lot easier.

## Phone Calls

There is always someone who calls on the phone and demands to speak to a member of the audience immediately. This is called an "emergency."

Obtain the name and number of the caller. If these are not given, simply state that it is not the policy of the theater to relay anonymous calls, and hang up. A legitimate caller has nothing to hide.

The caller should be asked if the call can be returned at intermission or at the end of the show. If the answer is no, there are alternatives. If the person is known to the theater staff he can be found and preferably given a note with the caller's name and number. If he refuses to answer, this message can be transmitted immediately. When the person is not known to the staff the message can be given from the stage during a break between dances; theatrical tradition requires that the name be paged at intermission or at the end of the show, not during the performance.

Unfortunately, sometimes there are emergencies. Even so, seldom will a performance be interrupted. After all, can you stop a show, announce a phone call, and then start it again? There have to be some rules. And if things are really bad a police car will drive up with the message. Just tell the caller that you are doing the best you can.

## Disturbances

An usher should ask the disorderly person to come to the back of the theater to talk about the trouble. This will work in some cases. A second request can be made by the ticket taker or someone with more authority. A third request should be made by the police. One rule never break—do not grab a customer, or even touch him. Some people use any excuse to sue. Leave big trouble to the police.

## Intermission

While the first part of the program goes on, the intermission activities are prepared. If you plan refreshments, those delegated should set up the tables as quietly as possible. A single table can cause a traffic jam, so use two or more.

Everything served should be of good quality, even when free. When a charge is made the cost should not exceed the usual charge outside. Intermission refreshment is basically a public service. If you have a good reason fc charging high prices and providing small servings then make it quiet clear tha the excess goes into a special fund. Profiteering with water briefly exposed t an orange or with a penny cookie sold for a dime does not belong to anythin but the most crassly commercial operation.

Beverages should be prepared in advance. Insulated urns keep hot drink hot and preserve the ice for cold ones. Avoid bottles; they add to the cost an to the mess and will always clatter on the concrete during the quietest danc When bottles are used the server should pour the contents into a paper cu and keep the bottle. Make sure that the cups are large enough.

Provide change. Take care of the money. Throw all used cups and pape into nearby trash cans. After intermission take everything away.

There are several other responsibilities. As the applause for the first pa thunders into the night, the ushering staff opens the front doors so that th customers can exit quickly. Turn on some lights. When the crowd exits circu late any messages that may be waiting. Provide necessary information abou rest rooms and telephones. Don't just disappear.

Near the end of intermission check backstage to be sure that the nex part of the show is ready to go on, then blink the lights or ring a bell c somehow inform the audience that it is time to return. Signal the stag manager when most of the audience is inside. Turn off the lights and close th doors.

## BACKSTAGE BEFORE CURTAIN

Hopefully there will be no last minute pounding and painting in a frantic rus to beat the deadline. Pounding tends to make the audience suspect that all not well backstage, and wet paint always manages to find its way to a curtai or costume. Resist the temptation.

Do not forget the small details of backstage preparation: a check of th dancers and crew, equipment test, backstage quests, dancer preparation, an general things to do.

### Dancer and Crew Check-in List

Post on a prominent surface, such as an unavoidable door or wall, a list c everyone concerned with the performance. Then every dancer and crew men ber initials his name as he comes in. The stage manager can consult the lis and begin calling those who have not arrived at the appointed time.

### Equipment Check

Before the audience is admitted, all stage equipment should be checked. Tr the lights and the curtains and any trick scenery.

## Backstage Guests

Hundreds of people seem to flutter around backstage before a show and at intermission and, unfortunately, even during the performance. Many of these will be friends and teachers and choreographers and other important people. However, such visits should be discouraged, and certainly all visitors must be invited to leave ten or twenty minutes before curtain time. The dancers need a period of concentration before an entrance and the crew may need a little time to check cues. Fortunately, most people will leave when asked.

## Dancer Preparation

The dancers can use the stage until about five minutes before curtain time, *except* when the stage crew needs a clear stage for any last-minute work. Sometimes the stage crew will have to place scenery or prepare a drop; they have trouble when a choreographer insists on a runthrough just before the curtain is supposed to open. Choreographers really ought to believe that the time for rehearsal is past, even if the dance is not quite ready. Precurtain time is for warm-up, not rehearsal. Sometimes the choreographer calls all the dancers together and reassures them with such suggestions as "make your mistakes with conviction," or "try to remember where the wings are," and "remember the curtain call."

## General Problems

The lead dancer has the flu and cannot come; a costume rips; a zipper won't work; shoes vanish; a bare foot finds the only nail on the stage; the dimmers won't dim, scenery falls to pieces; a thunderstorm breaks. Whatever can happen has happened and it will again. The usual bad things are overlooked; if things are really bad you can make a speech to the audience and explain. The theater can drive you crazy if you worry too much. Just remember that the audience is willing to accept almost anything, if they can find something to like.

## THE SHOW GOES ON

finally. But first—tell the dancers that the curtain is about to open. Otherwise you may be startled to discover that someone is still in the dressing room, and you don't really want to start without a full cast, even if the missing dancer is the one who forgets to step off on the right foot. And tell the crew.

193

### The Start

The stage manager stands near the curtain and makes sure that the dancers are all in place and that the crew is ready. He then goes to his place in the wings and gives the first cue. The proper lights come up, the music starts, the curtain opens—or whatever sequence has been chosen. If the beginning is a disaster, close the curtain and start again. It has been done before by the best professionals.

### Running the Show

Provided that the stage manager keeps track of the cues and makes sure that the dancers are all present to go on at the proper time, backstage activities should be a practiced routine. The dancers are on their own; they claim the attention of the audience. The crew follows one cue after another.

When a cue is missed, as inevitably it will be, either skip it or *slowly* rectify the error. Just remember that the audience does not know what to expect. Whatever you give them will be accepted as the rehearsed effect, no matter how terrible the blunder may seem to you. The theater exists only through the toleration and ignorance of the audience. Even the greatest performers and finest technicians make bad mistakes. And shows have gone on with flashlights and candles when the lights failed.

Once again, check to see that all dancers are present before the curtain opens. They have a bad habit of taking too long to change between dances or collecting on the wrong side of the stage or even forgetting that they are in that dance. So count them.

### Pauses

The audience hates to sit in the dark for long periods of time and in the dark fifteen seconds is a long time. For short pauses between dances the front curtain should be illuminated. For long stretches, when scenery-moving or costume-changing will take more than about a minute and a half, turn up the house lights—a soft glow is preferable to full brilliance.

If the break drags out, make a little speech to the audience to explain that the tinfoil cobweb has collapsed and will require a little extra time to reconstruct, or whatever of interest has occurred.

### Intermission

Bring up the house lights.

While the crew is setting up the next part of the program and the dancers and changing and resting, visitors will swarm backstage, always in the way and always a bother. At least try to keep them out of the dressing rooms and off the stage. This is not play time.

Keep the dancers off the stage until the crew work is finished. It is quite difficult to drag a platform through a platoon of swan maidens. After the work is done, the dancers can have a few minutes to warm up.

When enough time has elapsed inform the house manager, who will then call back the audience.

Collect the dancers and crew. Make sure that the stage is ready.

Lower the house lights and start the next part of the performance.

## AFTER THE SHOW

At last the curtain closes. The house lights go on.

Dancers and choreographers accept the congratulations due them. Good cheer and relief invade all those tired muscles and worried minds.

Unfortunately, there are a few pieces of work still to be done; sometimes they can be postponed, sometimes not.

### Dressing-Room Clean-up

Collect the costumes and make-up. Prepare them for transport back to whatever destination has been arranged. Check the items against the list of what was brought over. It is very easy to overlook a shoe or bracelet.

Throw away the trash.

### Scenery and Props

Anything that can be removed immediately should be. It is very easy to leave something, explaining "we'll get it later." Somehow scenery tends to linger on the stage for a long time. Take what you can now. Other people may be using the stage soon after you leave!

Throw away the junk.

### Cast Party

Some people like them. It gives everybody a chance to talk about the show and to unwind a little. Do some planning in advance. Try to pick an accessible location—the beach may be beautiful by moonlight, but how does everyone get there and back? Who pays the bills?

The general windup still waits.

# 12

---

# Windup

After the performance is over, dancers, choreographers, technicians, assistants and everyone else seem to melt away when they have no specific responsibilities for picking up and transporting something back to home base. It may be necessary to reverse the whole order of "move-in" as described in Chapter 10. It is logical to progress again from preparation to schedule to transport, arrival, and final storage.

Remove as much paraphernalia as possible immediately after the performance because facilities and equipment must often be made ready for other performers or for classes.

## REMOVAL OF EQUIPMENT AND MATERIALS

Everything that was bought, rented, borrowed, or owned by the group should be removed from the performance area, checked for its working condition, and returned to its source. Some of this may entail special know-how and wrenches, so be sure that you have arranged for capable assistance.

Remember that everything that you brought in must be disposed of, unless you are donating it to the stage. Even then you should consult the stage manager, or someone in charge of the space—maybe they don't want it. In any event, it must be put out of the way of whatever happens next.

Don't forget the stray pieces of scenery propped up against the trees outside, the plastic mobiles still hanging for the last set, the signs on walls and doors, extra tables and photographs at the front entrance, odd shoes and costume bits strewn back of curtains, tape floor markings, extra programs and cue sheets, and those daisy cut-outs pinned to the curtain. Whatever the condition of the area when you arrived, leave it neat and clean. Maybe you can set a precedent.

## RETURN AND STORAGE

When things are returned haphazardly there is a tendency to stuff costumes, hammers, extension cords, props, eyebrow pencils, tapes, and scissors into the nearest space or box, fully convinced that in a week or two—when you have recovered—you will put everything where it belongs. Don't you believe it! Do it now or you will soon forget what is where and it will become a part of a soiled, smelly, broken, and wrinkled junk-pile.

Costumes should be put aside to be mended, washed, or cleaned and then hung in plastic bags; accessories should be sorted into recognizable groupings for storage; gelatins should be arranged according to color and carefully rolled and covered; make-up should be checked and put in a covered carton. Everything should at least be put in boxes with other things of a like nature, so that the follow-up storage business does not start with a tangled mass.

What about having neatly typed or lettered lists to post on the walls of storage rooms or cabinets, with contents marked on each storage unit and the inventories to be kept current? Do it now or it will all join the inevitable number of things to be done "someday."

## CRITIQUE

It is most helpful to discover and record the reactions of choreographers, dancers, assistants, musicians, technicians, designers, publicists, and audience. Often the assets and liabilities of a production will be evaluated at postperformance meetings; certainly there will be implications as well as recommendations for future events. These suggestions should be organized and made available for future directors and administrative personnel. (See Figure 12-1.) Any evaluations by critics could well become a part of the report.

It will be valuable to everyone to evaluate the performance on the basis of original intent, the many necessary compromises, and the final performed product. Don't let the immediate relief of "it's over" disguise the need for careful examination of all aspects of process and product.

Perhaps the most valuable critque will be prepared by the director, who has had full responsibility for the production. He is apt to have a broader perspective of all the interactions. His reaction will refer to the initial statement of purpose as discussed in Chapter 1. Did the end-product of this long and involved process fulfill its original aim?

Sometimes the resulting performance is a success even though it seems unrelated to the original plan. If this happens you are simply lucky. Of course there are implications that you might not wish to recognize. It is more usual to judge the success or failure of any such venture in terms of the degree to which it coincides with the original purpose.

## BUDGET RECONCILEMENT

The final budget report of actual income-expenses as compared with the original budget proposal is the key to this problem.

Too much or not enough? It is usually not too much, but it could be. What would you do with the extra money? It all depends upon what kind of budget, requisition plan, or administrative control has been set up. Sometimes the surplus may be kept in some account and applied to future needs;

Figure 12-1    Sample Staff Critiques

Staff Consensus:

1. Insufficient performance space for the dances as choreographed.

2. Later date would be preferable for all concerned.

3. Need for greater integration of choreography, costume, and scenic design. Too many changes in the choreography.

4. Time wasted at dress rehearsal, need for better planning and scheduling.

Dancers:

1. Need for more rehearsal time in costume and with sets and props.

2. Need more practice and help in make-up.

3. Remember first-aid equipment for blisters and pointed tweezers for removing splinters.

4. Replace zippers with hooks and eyes.

Choreographers:

1. Earlier design and construction of costumes and sets so that dancers may rehearse sooner. Fewer changes in the choreography.

2. Greater attention to the details of titles and program notes. Need to start sooner.

3. More time for rehearsing curtain calls and all entrances and exits.

Musicians:

1. Earlier check-up of audio equipment so that a better ratio of tone and volume may be attained for the taped sound. The usual equipment in the school theater is not adequate at this time.

Costume Designer:

1. Need uninterrupted time, at least ten minutes each, to get accurate measurements of all dancers.

2. Must have access to lights that will be used before making final choice of material texture and color.

Publicity Director:

1. Must have at least two uninterrupted meetings, at least thirty minutes each, with all choreographers and dancers, one to two months before production.

2. Need at least two responsible assistants to keep track of the volunteer committees working on posters, fliers, and the mailing list.

Stage Manager:

1. Need better control of visitors backstage, before, during, and after the performance.

2. Attempt to get the same crew for performance as for the technical and dress rehearsals.

3. Dancers must clear the stage when the crew uses the stage for working on lighting and scenic equipment.

4. Plan more time for technical rehearsal; need more attention to transitions. There was no aid in cues for the dances between the first and second intermission.

or it may go into a general fund, in which case the director will rush out to purchase something to use up the extra income. It stands to reason that the business manager, or the director, will attend to all unpaid bills, even to the last box of mothballs and cleaning charges.

If the expenses exceed the income you may suffer refusal of future budget requests, be obliged to seek assistance from the community or friends, even be held personally responsible! Be sure that you have understood the procedure in the very beginning, and be prepared to act accordingly. This is the time of final reckoning.

## PRODUCTION RECORD

The critique is concerned with opinion, the production record with the hard data of tickets sold, yards of material purchased, ticket stubs missing, feet of lumber used, packages of band-aids bought, bills paid and unpaid, and money still available to be used.

If you have been sufficiently clear and firm in your directions there should be final reports coming in from many of those concerned with the details of production. There should be some kind of reports from stage manager, house manager, publicity director, business manager, and choreographers. There may even be other reports that will be useful in preparing a complete record of the performance. Here again, as in the critique, it is helpful if someone can sift through all of these and form it into one record. Otherwise there will be stacks of individual reports, repetitious and tedious to read.

## FOR THE FUTURE

In spite of the urge to shout "never again," almost everyone involved with a dance production awaits the next time. One yearns for another chance to *really* plan and organize the entire event. Somehow the possibility of an involved and successful interaction of all concerned is a symbol of true happiness. No matter how confused the last experience was, the next one will be run according to schedule. It really won't, you know, but even a little planning and control of events is better than just letting it happen.

# Appendix A

# Minimum Facilities and Equipment for Production in a Studio

TRADITONAL STAGE AT ONE END OF THE STUDIO

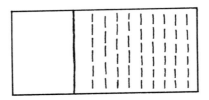

*(1.) Performance Area*   This is obviously dependent upon the size of the studio, the number of performers, and the size of the audience to be accommodated.

*(2.) Background*   With this arrangement of studio space it is necessary to have a suitable background. This may be a curtain, drapery, single or multiple screen, blank painted wall, or stretched muslin cyclorama. Neutral colors are best, especially if stage lighting is contemplated. Black or dark gray are the best choices, but use what you have. A white muslin cyclorama that could be covered by a black-pile traverse curtain on a heavy duty curtain track would be useful.

*(3.) Wings*   Wings, as exits and entrances to stage left and right, can be made of screens, flats, or hangings from the ceiling. These should blend in color and texture with the rest of the stage draperies. Precut flats and platforms are available but are more expensive than those you can make.

*(4.) Front Curtain*   If there is a curtain it should be on a heavy-duty curtain track for ease of manipulation. It could well be of the same material and color as the background curtain, or it could blend with the rest of the studio. All of the draperies and curtains should be made of fire-resistant or flame-proofed material.

*(5.) Audience Seating*   Chairs, benches, mats, or bleachers should be set up as far back as possible from the performing area. If all seating is on the same level, try to leave extra space between seats and arrange the next row of seats behind the spaces in front. A view of the performance area becomes more

limited the farther you move back. Platforms of increasing height would be useful for seating to the rear. All such arrangements should first be cleared with the fire inspector.

If there are mirrors in the studio mask them with drapery or sheets of heavy paper, preferably the same color as the studio walls. Sometimes the bulletin boards will also need covering.

*(6.) Lighting* In any serious production stage lighting is a necessity. This means that all windows and doors must be covered and masked from outside light. Venetian blinds or black traverse draperies are probably best.

Obviously the size of the studio and the distance of the performance area from the audience will determine what the lighting equipment should be and where it should be placed. A few wide-beam flood lights and ellipsoidal or Fresnel spotlights, hung on stage trees at each side of the stage or on an overhead pipe, would be minimum for short distances. PAR bulbs (150-watt display bulbs) in holders will often work well. One or two spotlights on stands for each side of the performance area would be helpful for cross-lighting and for special effects and may sometimes be used as a follow spot.

While a dimmer board may imply luxury, it is really a necessity if you plan for more than "turn it on—turn it off" or "pull the big plug out and put the small one in." Portable boards, easy to handle and taking very little space, are now available, either by purchase or rental. They can be set up near the performance area so that lighting technicians can see the performers. The board should be provided with sufficient current to run the intended number of lights and the board should have sufficient outlets, switches, and dimmers. A board that has ten or twelve circuits, each controlled by a switch if not a dimmer, is not difficult or very expensive to build. Just remember that it is a job for somebody who knows what he is doing.

Gelatin or plastic are the most satisfactory media for providing colored lights on stage. Gelatin is fragile, water soluble and must be held in a supporting frame. It comes in some eighty colors and in 20 x 24-inch sheets. Plastic is more durable, waterproof and can be used, in small pieces, without a frame. But whichever you use it is seldom that you need more than ten to fifteen colors. The usual shades are special lavender, flesh pink, bastard amber, steel blue, medium blue, straw, medium red, and medium green. For special effects try violet, medium blue-green, light magenta, dark magenta, medium amber, dark red, and combination variegated shades. (Color sample books are available from most theatrical lighting suppliers.)

Have the advice and assistance of an experienced theatrical electrician or engineer when setting up any theatrical lighting system. Amateur advice may be well-meaning, but dangerous. Any stage lighting facility demands special panels, cross-connect units, cables, and outlets as well as expert opinion on location and angle for placement of theatrical lighting instruments. Without this aid there will be considerable trial and error and possible insufficiencies in lighting potential.

## ARENA OR CIRCULAR STAGE

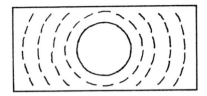

An arena stage is best in a large studio where there is ample room for seating an audience around the performance space.

*(1.) Performance Area*  The performance space can be of any shape. Unless on a raised platform it tends to merge with the front row. If platforms are used make sure that they are stable and don't squeak when dancers move on them.

*(2.) Background*  Solid backgrounds are obviously impossible, but three-dimensional sets, suspended pieces, and floor pieces are all possible and quite appropriate.

*(3.) Entrances and Exits*  At least two special aisles should be reserved for the dancers' entrances. Nearby there should be screened or draped areas for costume changes. Ramps are especially useful if the performance area is raised.

*(4.) Curtains*  Curtains or draperies are seldom useful, though a large parachute or similar drapery, hung so that it does not interfere with audience vision, could be designed for special effects.

*(5.) Audience Seating*  Arrange the chairs in circles or ovals. There should be at least four aisles, at each quarter of the circle, for audience access and safety. If there are more than fourteen seats in each quarter there should probably be more aisles. The usual regulation is that no member of the audience shall have to cross more than six people to reach his seat. Again, it is recommended that you have the advice of the fire inspector.

*(6.) Lighting*  As in any other performance area, all doors and windows must be darkened. The same equipment used for a traditional stage set-up can be used here, but it will be placed in different positions. Obviously the lights must be angled down from the ceiling so as not to shine on the audience. Sometimes this angle of light coverage is hard to determine and may call for a different kind of instrument. It will always be to your advantage to have the

dvice and assistance of a theatrical electrician or engineer. The standing spotlights will probably not be useful here; clustered lights on a pipe directly over the surrounding limits of the stage area are more appropriate.

A dimmer board is a necessary aid and should be high on the priority list. The same gelatins or plastics for color used in the traditional stage lighting area will be used here.

## CORNER OR CURVED STAGE AREA

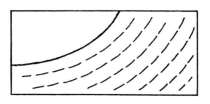

Perhaps the most successful of all performance-audience arrangements in a rectangular-shaped studio is this long corner set-up.

*1.) Performance area* Set up a stage area on the corner farthest from the studio doors. Actually, this will be a diagonally angled area, in terms of the studio shape, but it can lend itself to interesting movement design.

*2.) Background* The imaginative uses of screens and suspended draperies are endless. Flats set up on the right-angled walls can be interesting and decorative. Projections on these surfaces are particularly exciting. But be sure that none of the audience is seated directly in the line of the projection, unless you want somebody's shadow on the wall.

*3.) Entrances and Exits* Unless there are appropriate studio doors, you will probably be limited to open entrance and exit on just one side. Screens and draperies can be used to mask another area opposite for a semblance of access.

*4.) Screens* A set of double screens near each wall can provide the illusion of greater performance space.

*5.) Audience Seating* The most desirable aspect of this arrangement is the increased viewing-space for the audience. Chairs can be arranged in a series of curves parallel to the performance space, with two, three, or four access aisles. As usual, the chairs at the rear are best raised onto platforms but of course must be secure and stable.

*(6.) Lighting*   With this corner arrangement it is necessary to have lights from above the audience or from stage trees near each wall. Since the performance area is much the same size as those previously described, the same kinds of instruments may be considered minimum. Masking outdoor light, seeking the advice of experts, using the dimmer board and color media are much the same as in other area formations.

## A VERY MINIMUM SET-UP

*(1.)* Enough chairs for the expected audience.

*(2.)* Screens to hide the dancers for entrances and costume changes.

*(3.)* Lightproof coverings for the windows.

*(4.)* Enough lighting to enable the audience to see the dancers. Probably 12 PAR spotlight bulbs equipped with gel frame holders, cable to reach a central control point, and switches to turn them on and off are about minimum. The PAR bulbs and gel frames are obtainable at most hardware stores.

*(5.)* Dancers who know what they are doing.

# Appendix B

# Sources for Goods and Services

SOURCES FOR AUDIO EQUIPMENT, SOUNDS, ACCOMPANIMENT, MUSIC

Audio Effects
    1600 North Western Ave., Los Angeles, California 90027

Cheviot Corporation
    Box 34485, Los Angeles, California 90034
        (Ruth White's MUSIC FOR DANCE)

Dance Caravan Products, Inc.
    250 West 57 St.
    New York, New York 10019

Educational Activities, Inc.
    Box 392, Department D
    Freeport, New York 11521

Freda Miller Records for Dance
    Box 383, Northport, New York 11768
        (records for modern dance)

G. and T. Harris Sound for Dance
    236 West 55 St.
    New York, New York 10019

Hoctor Records
    P.O. Box 38, Waldwick, New Jersey, 07463
        (records for dance and exercise)

Idento Disc Inc.
    3033 North Sheridan, Chicago, Illinois 60657
        (records for ballet, character, tap, jazz, Spanish)

Leo's Advance Theatrical Co.
    125 N. Wabash, Chicago, Illinois 60603
        (records and sheet music)

Masque Sound
    331 West 51 St., New York, New York 10019
        (sound and amplification equipment)

MusiCues Corporation
    117 West 46 St., New York, New York 10036

Orion
    614 Davis St., Evanston, Illinois 60201
        (high fidelity records)
Record & Tape Sales Corp.
    821 Broadway, New York, New York 10003
        (imported and classical records)
The Record Center
    1614 North Pulaski, Chicago, Illinois 60639
Russell Records, Inc.
    P.O. Box 3318, Ventura, California 93003
Tams-Witmark Music Library, Inc.
    757 Third Ave., New York, New York 10017
Theatresound, Inc.
    68 East 153 St., Bronx, New York 10451
Thomas J. Valentino
    150 West 46 St., New York, New York 10036
        (sound effects, records)
Wonza Productions
    1270 Fifth Ave., New York, New York 10029
Yale Audio of Florida
    2732 Florida Ave., Tampa, Florida 33602
        (sound effects)

For further information check:

Simon's Directory of Theatrical Materials, Services and Information published by Package Publicity Service, 1564 Broadway, New York, New York 10036 (approx. $5.00).

Yellow pages of local telephone directory: see Music; Musical Instruments; Sound Equipment; Recorders—Sound and Video; Recording Service.

Advertisements in theatrical journals, dance magazines, and professional periodicals.

Also, contact the staff of local community centers, schools, theaters.


## SOURCES FOR BUSINESS AND PUBLICITY NEEDS

Check the following for publicity packages, printers, postcards, banners, posters, tickets, crowd-control equipment, theater and auditorium chairs.

Arcus-Simplex-Brown Inc.
    15 Laight St., New York, New York 10013
        (tickets—in Chicago, Arcus Ticket Co., 348 North Ashland, Chicago, Illinois 60607)

Globe Ticket Company
    112 North 12th St., Philadelphia, Pennsylvania 19107
        (racks, machines, nation-wide service)

Linopress Company
    P.O. Box 337, Costa Mesa, California 92627

National Ticket Co.
    1564 Broadway, New York, New York 10036
        (branches in Detroit, Cleveland, Philadelphia, Puerto Rico)

Package Publicity Service
    1564 Broadway, New York, New York 10036
        (directory of sources throughout the U.S. and Canada: schedules,
        press releases, posters, displays, postcards, mats, publicity materials,
        sign-making and letter sets, etc.)

Queen Feature Service, Inc.
    2409 First Ave. No., Birmingham, Alabama 35202
        (equipment, supplies, seats, tickets)

United Seating Co.
    94-98 Lexington Ave., Brooklyn, New York 11238

    For further information check:
Simon's Directory of Theatrical Materials, Services and Information,
published by Package Publicity Service, 1564 Broadway, New York, New
    York 10036 (approx. $5.00).

Yellow pages of local telephone directory: see Printers, Accounting Materials,
    Advertising, Ticket Printers, Art Goods, Bleacher Seats, Business Forms,
    Copying and Duplicating Service, Display Lithographers, Photographers,
    Stationers.


## SOURCES FOR COSTUMES

    See the following for fabrics, ready-made costumes, accessories, trimmings,
    hats, shoes, designing.

Associated Fabrics
    10 East 39th St., New York, New York 10016
        (fluorescent fabrics, glitter products)

Baum's Inc.
    106-114 South 11th St., Philadelphia, Pennsylvania 19107
        (plus audio equipment)

Capezio
    1612 Broadway, New York, New York 10019
        (shoes, leotards, tights, accessories—branches in Los Angeles, Holly-
        wood, Boston, Chicago, San Francisco, San Mateo)

Dance Fashions
6 East Lake St., 3rd Floor, Chicago, Illinois 60601

Dazians
30 East 29th St., New York, New York 10016
(curtains, settings, costumes, auditorium decoration, tights and leotards—also in Dallas, Chicago, Boston, Los Angeles)

Eaves Costume Company, Inc.
151 West 46th St., New York, New York 10036
(costume rental)

Far Eastern Fabrics, Inc.
171 Madison Ave., New York, New York 10016
(Asian silks and cottons)

Herbert Dancewear
1657 Broadway, New York, New York 10019

Hollywood Dancewear
6512 Van Nuys Blvd., Van Nuys, California 91401
(plus records, books)

Hyman Hendler and Sons, Inc.
763 South Los Angeles St., Los Angeles, California 90014
(fabrics, trimmings, and accessories)

Leo Advance Theatrical Co.
125 North Wabash Ave., Chicago, Illinois 60602

Loshin's Costume Center
215 East Eighth St., Cincinnati, Ohio 45202
(plus records and books)

Maurice Danswear, Inc.
33 John R, Detroit, Michigan 48226

Northwestern Costume House (Norcostco)
3203 North Highway 100, Minneapolis, Minnesota 55422
(theatrical costume rental, costumes made to order; make-up; lighting materials, hardware, scenery materials, stage draperies; a complete theatrical service center)

Pacific Dance Supplies
P.O. Box 16038, San Francisco, California 94116 (1724 Taraval St.)
(plus records and audio equipment)

Selva and Sons
1607 Broadway, New York, New York 10019

Herbert L. Toffler and Sons, Inc.
902 Broadway, New York, New York 10023
(metallic and novelty elastic fabrics)

## SOURCES FOR THEATRICAL MAKE-UP

Advance Theatrical Co.
 125 N. Wabash, Chicago, Illinois 60603

Associated Theatrical Contractors
 310 W. 80th St., Kansas City, Missouri 64114

Max Factor
 1655 N. McCadden Pl., Hollywood, California 90028

Paramount Theatrical Supplies
 32A W. 20th St., New York, New York 10011

Stagecraft Industries
 615 Bradford, P.O. Box 686, Redwood City, California 95863

Wolff-Fording Company
 88 Kingston St., Boston, Massachusetts 02111

Zauder Bros., Inc.
 75 W. 45th St., New York, New York 10036

 For further information check:

Simon's Directory of Theatrical Materials, Services and Information, published by Package Publicity Service, 1564 Broadway, New York, New York 10036 (approx. $5.00).

Yellow pages of local telephone directory: see Dressmakers' Supplies, Fabric Shops, Textile Manufacturers and Representatives, Textile Printers, Textile Finishers, Theatrical Supplies, Costumers, Theatrical Make-Up, etc.

## SOURCES FOR SPECIAL FABRICS

Alda Plastics Inc.
 442 Broadway, New York, New York 10013

Degussa, Chemicals Division
 2 Penn Plaza, New York, New York 10001

King's Theatrical Shoe Co.
 218 So. Wabash Ave., Chicago, Illinois 60604
 (stretch sequin leotards)

Maharam Fabric Corporation
 1113 So. Los Angeles St., Los Angeles, California 90015
 (Celastic, a plastic molding material for sets, props; lace wire, Plastex—agents in New York City and Chicago)

Teener's Theatrical Department Store
 729 Hennepin Ave., Minneapolis, Minnesota 55403
 (designers and creators of costumes, Celastic props, fabrics, accessories, make-up, lighting equipment, special fabrics)

SOURCES FOR LIGHTING APPARATUS

The following carry equipment, rigging, hardware, boards, and motors.

American Stage Lighting Co., Inc.
1331c North Ave., New Rochelle, New York 10804
(regular and package deals; agents for Hunt 21-pound portable dimmer board)

Ariel Davis Manufacturing Company
2975 South Second West, Salt Lake City, Utah 84115

Associated Theatrical Co.
32 West Randolph St., Chicago, Illinois 60601
(branches in all major cities)

Bash Stage Lighting Co.
407 South Washington Ave., Bergenfield, New Jersey 07621
(repairs, rentals, sales, remodeling)

Capitol Stage Lighting Co., Inc.
509 West 56 St., New York, New York 10019
(branch agent: L.A. Stage Lighting Co., Ltd., 1451 Venice Blvd. Los Angeles, California)

Century Strand, Inc.
3411 W. El Segundo Blvd., Hawthorne, California 90250
(branches in all major cities)

Duwico
250 West 54 St., New York, New York 10019

Hub Electric Co., Inc.
940 Industrial Dr., Elmhurst, Illinois 60126
(resident engineers in principal cities)

Kliegl Brothers
2333 North Valley, Burbank, California 91504
(branches in all major cities)

Lighting Services, Inc.
77 Park Ave., New York, New York 10016
(regular and special equipment; projection kaleidoscopes, color strobe)

Little Stage Lighting Company
P.O. Box 20211, 10507 Hines Blvd., Dallas, Texas 75220

Naren Industries, Inc.
1214-22 West Madison St., Chicago, Illinois 60607

Northwestern Costume House (Norcostco)
3203 North Highway 100, Minneapolis, Minnesota 55422
(lighting instruments and control systems)

eson Company
    1535 Ivar St., Hollywood, California 90028

ckaged Lighting Services, Inc.
    P.O. Box 104—Main Station, Yonkers, New York 10702

>sco Laboratories, Inc.
    214 Harrison Ave., Harrison, New York 10528
        (theatrical color media, gels, plastics)

•radlin Brothers
    Mallory Road, Red Oak, Georgia 30272
        (rental, sales, service)

agecraft Industries, Inc.
    P.O. Box 686, Redwood City, California 94064
        (agents in Portland, Oregon, and Bellevue, Washington)

rand Century
    6334 Viscount Road, Malton, Ontario

    For further information check:
mon's Directory of Theatrical Materials, Services and Information,
    blished by Package Publicity Service, 1564 Broadway, New York, New
    York 10036 (approx. $5.00).

llow pages of local telephone directory: see Theatrical Equipment and
    Supplies, Lighting Systems and Equipment, Lighting, Lighting Fixtures

dvertisements in theatrical journals, professional periodicals.

so, contact the staff of local community centers, schools, theaters.


OURCES FOR STAGECRAFT MATERIALS AND EQUIPMENT

ssociated Theatrical Contractors
    308 W. 80th St., Kansas City, Missouri 64114
        (scenic materials, stage curtains, rigging, lighting equipment,
        make-up)

allet Barres
    P.O. Box 717, Sarasota, Florida 33578
        (portable barres)

TPS Inc. (Theatre Production Service)
    52 W. 46th St., New York, New York 10036

noxville Scenic Studios, Inc.
    P.O. Box 1029, Knoxville, Tennessee 37901
        (sales, rentals of complete theatrical supplies)

National Theatre Equipment Co., Ltd.
    1434 Ste. Catherine W., Montreal, Quebec
        (complete theatrical materials and equipment)

Oleson Company
    1535 Ivar St., Hollywood, California 90028
        (stage hardware and tools, scenery paints and brushes, scenery fab
        rics, materials and precut scenery and drops; color media for light
        stage lights, and control equipment; make-up; audio-visual material
        and equipment; books; films; records; theater crafts; filmstrips)

Paramount Theatrical Supplies
    32A W. 20th St., New York, New York, 10011

Richker & Co.
    312 Fannin St., Houston, Texas 77002

Stagecraft Industries, Inc.
    P.O. Box 686, Redwood City, California 94064
        (scenery materials, hardware, rigging, drapery, paint, portabl
        stages, lighting equipment, make-up—branches in Portland, Oregon
        and Bellevue, Washington)

Stagecraft Studios
    1854 Alcatraz Ave., Berkeley, California 94703
        (scenic supplies, stage lights, costumes, and make-up)

Stage Decoration & Supplies Inc.
    1204 Oakland Ave., P.O. Box 5007, Greensboro, North Carolina 2740.

Stage Engineering and Supply, Inc.
    P.O. Box 2002, Colorado Springs, Colorado 80901
        (architectural consultants and suppliers)

Texas Scenic Company, Inc.
    1419 Mulberry Ave., P.O. Box 5116, San Antonio, Texas 78201

Tobin's Lake Studios
    2650 Seven Mile Road, South Lyon, Michigan 48178
        (complete theatrical supplies, sales, and rentals)

For further information check:
Simon's Directory of Theatrical Materials, Services and Information,
published by Package Publicity Service, 1564 Broadway, New York, New
    York 10036 (approx. $5.00).

Yellow pages of local telephone directory: see Theatrical Equipment and
    Supplies, Scenery, Studios.

Advertisements in theatrical and professional journals.

Also, contact local centers, schools, theaters.

# Glossary

Apron    That part of the stage in front of the main curtain.

Backdrop    1. Curtain, screen, or drapery that can be lowered in back of a stage area. 2. A flat cloth painted to represent a scene or design.

Batten    1. Permanent or temporary pipes or lengths of lumber tied to cables from grid above and used for flying scenery. 2. A piece of wood used to fasten two or more flats together.

Borders (valence, teaser)    Draperies that mask upper part of the stage from audience view.

Box (plugging box)    A portable box for electrical hook-ups.

Cyc (cyclorama)    Permanent or temporary backdrop, used to simulate a sky.

C-clamp    1. C-shaped clamp with a single bolt to tighten. Used for fastening platforms together, holding lumber for gluing, and for attaching equipment to battens or standards. 2. The clamp part of a spotlight or floodlight. Used to fasten the light to a pipe.

Duvetyn    Twill-weave fabric with a lustrous, velvet-like surface.

First pipe    The usual name given to the batten used for hanging lights just behind the main curtain. It may be called the "first electric." The next pipe upstage for lights is called the second pipe, the next after that, the third pipe.

Gel (gelatine)    Thin, transparent sheets of dyed gelatine or plastic used for the color medium for stage lights. Standard 20 X 24-inch sheets come in some 80 to 90 colors and shades.

Ground row    Painted silhouette or design that stands independently in the background. It is usually two-dimensional and ordinarily is made of plywood, cardboard, or canvas stretched on a frame.

Legs    1. Wing-draperies to mask off-stage area. 2. Supports for platforms, steps, etc.

Leko (Lekolite)    Common name for an ellipsoidal reflector spotlight equipped with shutters for shaping the sides of the light beam it produces.

Lightboard    Board or panel with switches or dimmers for controlling stage lights.

Lobsterscope    An attachment disc that fits onto a spotlight for producing a flickering light.

**Patch panel**   Panel board for interconnecting dimmers and outlets. Sometimes also called a plug board.

**Pipe**   Common name for the pipes used above the stage to hold lights or scenery.

**Proscenium (arch)**   The frame that defines the audience's view of the stage.

**Receptacle**   An electric outlet. Stage receptacles may be the same as those used at home to plug in a radio or toaster, or they may come in different shapes.

**Scoop**   A round floodlight, usually with a 1000-watt bulb.

**Scrim**   Material of loose and wide weave used for special-effects drop on stage. It is transparent if lit from behind.

**Spill**   In stage lighting, illumination that extends beyond the area that should be lit.

**Stage directions**   Directions according to dancer's right or left, as he faces the audience. Upstage is at back of the stage; downstage is at the front, nearest the audience.
Common abbreviations:

| | |
|---|---|
| DR—downstage right | UR—upstage right |
| DL—downstage left | UL—upstage left |
| DCL—downstage center left | UCR—upstage center right |
| DCR—downstage center right | UCL—upstage center left |

**Stobe (stroboscopic) light**   A light that produces an intense, repeated flash.

**Switchboard**   The board housing switches, dimmers, and fuses necessary to control stage lights.

**Terminal**   End of electrical circuit where conductor attaches.

**Traveller curtain**   Draw curtain, mounted on a special track, that parts in the center and opens to each side of the stage.

**Velour (plush)**   One of the napped fabrics used for draperies or flat cover.

**Wings**   Draperies or flats on each side of stage to mask off-stage area from audience view.

# Selected References

BOOKS AND ARTICLES

Apel, Willie, and Ralph T. Daniel. THE HARVARD BRIEF DICTIONARY OF MUSIC. New York: Washington Square Paperback W589, 1960.

Clear and concise manual of terms, styles, forms; not too technical.

Barton, Lucy. HISTORIC COSTUME FOR THE STAGE. Boston: Walter H. Baker, 1935.

Scholarly survey of costume, and the "why" of period style from Egyptian to New Century (1900-1914). Some notes on costume construction.

Bascom, F., and C. Irey. COSTUME CUES. Washington, D.C.: National Section on Dance, American Association for Health, Physical Education, and Recreation, 1952.

Thirty pages of cues, some sketches, patterns, and general suggestions. Hard to find this—out of print; see library.

Beitler, E.J., and B.C. Lockhart. DESIGN FOR YOU. New York: John Wiley & Sons, 1965.

Interesting discussion of proportion, shape, scale, division of space, creation of optical illusions, balance gradation, form—all valuable to designer of costume and set.

Boucher, Francois. TWENTY THOUSAND YEARS OF FASHION. New York: Harry N. Abrams, 1966.

Costumes from prehistory to fashions of late 1940's; color illustrations and clear descriptions according to cultural/ethnic groups.

Boyle, Walden P. CENTRAL AND FLEXIBLE STAGING. Berkeley and Los Angeles: University of California Press, 1956.

One of the few sources on the subject. This book can suggest ideas for studio productions, if you can find it.

Dlugoszewski, Lucia, "Notes on New Music for the Dance." DANCE OBSERVER, vol. 24, no. 9, Nov. 1957.

FOCUS ON DANCE V. Washington, D.C.: American Association for Health, Physical Education, and Recreation, 1969.

A symposium on composition with two short articles on scene design and lighting for dance.

215

Gilbert, Pia, and Aileene Lockhart. MUSIC FOR THE MODERN DANCE. Dubuque, Iowa: W.C. Brown, 1961.
> One of the few sources for relating music and contemporary dance; principles, suggestions, resources.

Gorsline, Douglas W. WHAT PEOPLE WORE. New York: Viking Press, 1952.
> Visual history of dress from ancient times to twentieth century America.

Gruver, Elbert. THE STAGE MANAGER'S HANDBOOK. New York: Harper & Row, 1953.
> Gruver tells you more than you want to know, but his book reminds you that theatrical production is not something to be thrown together at the last minute.

Haire, F.H. THE FOLK COSTUME BOOK. New York: Barnes, 1934.
> One of the classics of folk costume sources; illustrations, some discussion.

Hayes, Elizabeth. DANCE COMPOSITION AND PRODUCTION FOR HIGH SCHOOL AND COLLEGE. New York: Barnes, 1955 (currently published and distributed by Ronald Press, New York City).
> The last two chapters are particularly helpful for someone attempting a dance production.

Joiner, Betty. COSTUMES FOR THE DANCE. New York: Barnes, 1937.
> One of the best books on costumes for dance. Out of print and hard to get; search libraries.

Klapper, Marvin. FABRIC ALMANAC. New York: Fairchild, 1966.
> Excellent glossary of old and new terms; clear and concise information on fabrics from natural and man-made fibers.

Köhler, Carl. A HISTORY OF COSTUME. New York: Dover Paperback T1030, 1963.
> A phenomenal range of authentic illustrations and reliable patterns of costume from antiquity to 1870. Every costume designer should be familiar with this for period reference.

Laver, James. COSTUME THROUGH THE AGES. New York: Simon and Schuster, 1963.
> Picture book of black-and-white illustrations from the first century to 1930.

_____. COSTUME IN ANTIQUITY. New York: Potter, 1964.
> Documented reproductions of authentic costumes, detail, accessory, and design from 3000 B.C. Mesopotamia to fifth to sixth century A.D. Byzantium.

Lippincott, Gertrude, and Robert Moulton. "Case History of a Costume." DANCE OBSERVER, vol. 19, no. 9, Nov. 1952, pp. 132-34.

   The process of making a costume.

Lippincott, Gertrude (ed.). DANCE PRODUCTION. Washington, D.C.: National Section on Dance, A.A.H.P.E.R., 1956.

   A compilation of material dealing with dance production.

Lloyd, Norman. "American Composers Write for the Dance." DANCE OBSERVER, vol. 18, no. 9, Nov. 1951.

_____. "Composing for the Dance." DANCE OBSERVER, vol. 28, no. 8, Oct. 1961.

_____. THE GOLDEN ENCYCLOPEDIA OF MUSIC. New York: Golden Press, 1968.

Long, Ralph Gerry. "Introduction to Music for the Choreographer." DANCE MAGAZINE, vol. 43, no. 2, Feb. 1969, pp. 63-65.

Lounsbury, Warren C. THEATRE BACKSTAGE FROM A TO Z. Seattle, Wash.: University of Washington Press, 1967.

   A concise encyclopedia of stagecraft from the A of alternating current to the Z of zoom lens. The historical introduction on scenery and lighting is short but sufficient.

McCandless, Stanley. A METHOD OF LIGHTING THE STAGE. 4th ed. New York: Theatre Arts, 1958.

   For many years this has been an influential book. It is well worth study.

Melcer, Fannie H. STAGING THE DANCE. Dubuque, Iowa: W.C. Brown, 1955.

   One of the few sources specifically for dance. This is a series of outlines for teachers with no previous experience in production.

Miller, Hugh M. HISTORY OF MUSIC. College Outline Series 55. New York: Barnes and Noble, 1947.

   A condensed history from antiquity to the twentieth century; includes composers and something of their style.

_____. INTRODUCTION TO MUSIC. College Outline Series 109. New York: Barnes and Noble, 1958.

   Basic elements of form and style; condensed and comprehensive.

Parker, W. Oren, and Harvey K. Smith. SCENE DESIGN AND STAGE LIGHTING. 2nd ed. New York: Holt, Rinehart and Winston, 1968.

   A standard textbook, illustrated with drawings. It includes sections on design, construction, painting, scenery handling, props, and lighting. The book can carry an amateur through difficult times.

Pischl, A.J., and S.J. Cohen, (eds.). "Composer/Choreographer." DANCE PER-
SPECTIVES 16, 1963.

> Includes Horst, Fine, Starer, Dello Joio, Dlugoszewski, Surinach,
> Nikolais, Schuller, Cage, El-Dabh, Lloyd.

Plummer, Gail. THE BUSINESS OF SHOW BUSINESS. New York: Harper &
Row, 1961.

> Tickets, publicity, and the troublesome details of management are
> the subject of this book.

Prisk, Bernice. STAGE COSTUME BOOK. New York: Harper & Row, 1966.

> Details of costuming for the stage; parts are relevant to dance.

Randolf, David. THIS IS MUSIC. New York: Mentor Paperback MP647,
1964.

> Popular, oriented to music appreciation—a guide to good listening.
> This is basic, nontechnical, and will aid in recognizing the styles of
> composers.

Selden, Samuel, and Hunton D. Sellman. STAGE SCENERY AND LIGHT-
ING. 3rd ed. New York: Appleton-Century-Crofts, 1959.

> This has long been a standard text for college and community
> theater technical crews.

SIMON'S DIRECTORY. 4th ed. N.Y.: Package Publicity Service, Inc., 1969.

> Complete guide to theatrical materials, services, and information in
> the United States and Canada. This includes where to buy, rent,
> lease, and find out almost anything needed for the production of
> theatricals; also theater management.

> The publisher also has books, schedules, publicity materials, and
> packets.

Southern, Richard. STAGE SETTING. 2nd ed. New York: Theatre Arts,
1962.

> Curtain sets, screens, and other portable settings are the subject of
> this valuable book.

Tovey, Sir Donald. THE FORMS OF MUSIC. New York: Meridian Paperback
M36, 1957.

> Comprehensive survey of musical forms with reference to musical
> works; scholarly and consistent.

Walberg, Betty. "Music and Dance." IMPULSE, 1968, pp. 39-50.

White, Ruth. "Compose Concrete Music for your Compositions." DANCE
MAGAZINE, Sept. 1967, pp. 59-61.

Wilcox, R. Turner. FIVE CENTURIES OF AMERICAN COSTUME. New York: Scribners, 1963.

> From the early Viking settlers, Maya, Inca, and North American Indians to twentieth century children. Excellent black and white line drawings.

_____. FOLK AND FESTIVAL COSTUMES OF THE WORLD. New York: Scribners, 1965.

> Characteristic national and ethnic costumes; delightfully illustrated.


PERIODICALS AND CATALOGS

DANCE INDEX, out-of-print periodical but available in most libraries.

> Scholarly materials usually devoted to one or two special topics; some volumes from 1944-46 include such classics as stage designs of Picasso, Chagall, and Junyer.

DANCE MAGAZINE, 268 West 47 St., N.Y., N.Y. 10036

> Monthly; general overview of dance world; reviews; some special articles and pictures of production details.

DANCE NEWS, 119 West 57 St., N.Y., N.Y. 10036

> Reviews ballet, modern, and theatrical dance; occasional discussions of production techniques.

DANCE PERSPECTIVES, 29 East 9 St., N.Y., N.Y.: 10003

> Scholarly quarterly that selects some special topic for each issue.

DANCE SCOPE, published semi-annually by National Dance Teachers Guild, Inc., 124-16 84th Road, Kew Gardens, N.Y. 11415

> Articles on all aspects of dance in education and theater.

EDUCATIONAL THEATRE JOURNAL, American Educational Theatre Association, 1701 Pennsylvania Ave., N.W., Washington, D.C. 20006

> Materials relevant to theater in schools; teaching, techniques, special articles, resources.

FOCUS ON DANCE (Vols. I, II, III, IV, V), National Section on Dance, American Association for Health, Physical Education, and Recreation, 1201 16 St., N. W., Washington, D.C. 20036

> Issued irregularly. Vol. I appeared in 1960, II in 1962, III in 1965, IV in 1967, and V in 1970.

HIGH FIDELITY, Billboard Publications, 2160 Patterson St., Cincinnati, Ohio 45214

> Source for records, tapes, sound equipment; reviews and articles.

IMPULSE, ANNUAL OF CONTEMPORARY DANCE, 160 Palo Alto Ave. San Francisco, California 94114

> Excellent source for information about dance production. Author itative articles.

SCHWANN LONG PLAYING RECORD CATALOG, W. Schwann Inc. Boston, Mass., 02116

> Complete monthly listing of all currently available L.P. records

SCHWANN SUPPLEMENTARY CATALOG, W. Schwann Inc., Boston, Mass 02116

> Includes imports, religious, spoken, Latin-American, international pop and folk, children's and noncurrent pop.

STEREO REVIEW, Ziff-Davis Publishing Co., Portland Place, Boulder Colorado 80302

> Complete musical monthly; editorials, news, reviews, articles record lists, tapes, sound equipment.

THEATRE CRAFTS, Rodale Press, Emmaus, Pennsylvania 18049

> Bimonthly; featuring production techniques, charts, record reviews

WORLD THEATRE, Editions Michel Brient, 64 rue de Saintouge, Paris France

> Includes three sections: national, international, and technical data In English and French.


OTHER PLACES TO LOOK FOR IDEAS

Advertising books: posters and layouts you can adapt for your own purposes
Art books: pictures for all occasions.
Art magazines: articles and pictures.
Dance books: pictures and ideas.
Magic books (late nineteenth and early twentieth century): stage illusions.
Opera books: scene and costume designs.
Scene design books: illustrations and ideas.

---

This book was set in Journal Roman by the S. P. Miller Company at Oakland, California